ADIRONDACK COMMUNITY COLLEGE
LIBRARY
BAY ROAD
QUEENSBURY, NY 12804

DISCARDED

W9-COP-738

THE AGE OF MIGRATION

THE AGE OF MIGRATION

International Population Movements
in the Modern World

Stephen Castles
Mark J. Miller

THE GUILFORD PRESS
New York

© Stephen Castles and Mark J. Miller 1993

Published by The Guilford Press
A Division of Guilford Publications, Inc.
72 Spring Street, New York, NY 10012

All rights reserved

No part of this book may be reproduced, stored in a retrieval system, or transmitted, in any form or by any means, electronic, mechanical, photocopying, microfilming, recording, or otherwise, without written permission from the Publisher.

Printed in Hong Kong

This book is printed on acid-free paper.

Last digit is print number: 9 8 7 6 5 4 3 2

Library of Congress Cataloging-in-Publication Data

Castles, Stephen.
  The age of migration : international population movements in the modern world / Stephen Castles, Mark J. Miller.
    p. cm.
  Includes bibliographical references and index.
  ISBN 0–89862–249–2.   ISBN 0–89862–248–4 (pbk.)
  1. Emigration and immigration.   I. Miller, Mark J.   II. Title.
JV6032.C37   1993
325'.09'04—dc20   93–15342
                                                      CIP

Contents

List of Maps, Tables and Exhibits

Maps

Tables

Exhibits

Acknowledgements

The idea for this book took shape at a conference on Minority Language Rights and Minority Education sponsored by the Western Societies Program of Cornell University in 1988. A conference on East–West migration sponsored by the European Culture Research Centre of the European University Institute in Florence in 1991 again enabled the authors to meet to discuss the project. We would like to thank our publisher, Steven Kennedy, for his advice and encouragement, as well as his patience throughout the project and John Solomos and Fred Halliday for their constructive and helpful comments.

Stephen Castles wishes to thank Ellie Vasta of the Department of Sociology, University of Wollongong, for reading the whole manuscript and providing many useful suggestions, as well as giving a great deal of support and encouragement. Jock Collins of the University of Technology, Sydney, also read parts of the work and made valuable comments. Colleen Mitchell of the Centre for Multicultural Studies (CMS), University of Wollongong, edited the manuscript and helped prepare the bibliography. Kim McCall of CMS worked on the tables, prepared the final manuscript and gave administrative support throughout. Thanks also to my colleagues at CMS who put up with my preoccupation with this task and provided useful ideas.

Mark Miller wishes to thank Gloria Parisi and Debjani Bagchi, in particular, for the assistance they provided during the preparation of the manuscript. He also wishes to thank the clerical staff of the Department of Political Science and International Relations at the University of Delaware and that of the Center for Migration Studies in Staten Island, New York, for their unflagging assistance. A leave of absence granted by the University of Delaware in Autumn 1991 greatly facilitated completion of this book. The maps were drawn by David Martin of Cadmart Drafting, Wollongong.

A final word of thanks to the inventors and developers of electronic mail, who provided the means of communication which enabled two authors in different continents to co-operate closely.

STEPHEN CASTLES
MARK J. MILLER

1

Introduction

The year 1992 had more than its fair share of dramatic events. In May, the Los Angeles riots shocked the American nation. At first they were widely portrayed as black–white race riots – a rerun of the ghetto insurrections of the mid-1960s, which helped to bring about civil rights laws and President Johnson's 'Great Society' programme. But a closer look showed that the 1992 riots had a new character. Few of the businesses destroyed by arson and looting were white-owned: about half belonged to Koreans, and around a third to Latinos – mainly Mexican Americans and Cubans. Most of the looters were black, but there was a sizable share of whites. Moreover one-third of those killed were Latinos, and so were about one-third of the 13 000 people arrested in the week of mayhem. About 1200 of those arrested were illegal immigrants, who were turned over to the Immigration and Naturalisation Service for deportation. The white against black violence of the Rodney King (a black motorist beaten up by the police) case may have precipitated the disturbances, but other ethnic and social divisions played a major part. An article in New York's radical *Voice* spoke of 'the first multicultural riots' (Kwong, 1992), while another writer referred to 'the nation's first multi-ethnic riot' (Rutten, 1992).

In August and September, Europe was alarmed by an almost daily series of neo-Nazi onslaughts on refugee hostels in Germany. The attacks were marked by extreme violence, the apparent inability of the police to prevent them, and by the incapacity of the political parties to get a grip on the root causes. Most of the attacks were in the area of the former German Democratic Republic, where the collapse of the communist regime had left a legacy of unemployment, poor

1

environmental conditions and a disintegration of social institutions. Young Germans seemed to be flocking to extreme-right organisations as the only groups able to fill the void in their lives. But there were disturbing reminders of the past: the neo-Nazis used the symbols and methods of the 1930s, while the main target among the refugees – Eastern European gypsies – were one of the groups to which Hitler had applied his 'final solution'. Many Europeans feared the beginning of a new period of political conflict and instability in Germany.

Throughout 1992, the world watched helplessly while Yugoslavia disintegrated into warring fragments. Shelling of civilians, concentration camps and 'ethnic cleansing' became instruments of politics, as elites claiming to represent distinct historical peoples struggled to create new states. Millions of people sought refuge from the war in nearby countries, which were reluctant to receive them, because they added to the already insoluble problems of the European refugee crisis.

All of these happenings were linked to mass international population movements and to the problems of living together in one society for ethnic groups with diverse cultures and social conditions. The list could easily be extended. The year also witnessed mass refugee movements in Africa, arising from wars and political upheavals but also from environmental catastrophes; movements of Jews from the former Soviet Union to Israel, which added to political tensions in the region; a refugee outflow from Burma to Bangladesh, which put a great strain on the resources of one of the world's poorest countries; the turning back by the US Coastguard of desperate attempts of Haitian boat-people to reach Florida; and, in every continent, large-scale movements of labour migrants and their families.

The events of 1992 were symptomatic of major changes in international relations and in the societies of both highly-developed and less developed countries. New forms of global migration and growing ethnic diversity are related to fundamental transformations in economic, social and political structures in this post-modern and post-Cold War epoch. These changes took on momentum at the end of the 1980s and the beginning of the 1990s. Developments included the upheavals in the former Soviet Bloc; the Gulf War; the Intifada in occupied Palestine; the crumbling of apartheid in South Africa; wars, famines and crises throughout Africa; rapid growth and development in Asia; a shift from dictatorships to unstable and debt-plagued democracies in Latin America; and growing economic and political integration in Western Europe. All these developments have one thing in common: they have been linked in various ways with mass population movements. It therefore seems fitting to predict that the last decade of the twentieth century and the first of the twenty-first will be the age of migration.

Millions of people are seeking work, a new home or simply a safe place to live outside their countries of birth. In many underdeveloped countries of origin, emigration is one aspect of the social crisis which accompanies integration into the world market and modernisation. Population growth and the 'green revolution' in rural areas lead to massive surplus populations. Large-scale rural–urban migration is the result: people move to burgeoning cities, where employment opportunities are inadequate and social conditions miserable. Massive urbanisation outstrips the creation of jobs in the early stages of industrialisation. Some of the previous rural–urban migrants embark on a second migration, seeking to improve their lives by moving to highly-developed countries.

Only a minority of the inhabitants of less-developed countries take this step, but their numbers still total millions. The movements take many forms: people migrate as manual workers, highly-qualified specialists, entrepreneurs, refugees or as family members of previous migrants. Whether the initial intention is temporary or permanent movement, many migrants become settlers. Migratory networks develop, linking areas of origin and destination, and helping to bring about major changes in both. Migrations can change demographic, economic and social structures, and bring a new cultural diversity, which often brings into question national identity.

This book is about contemporary international migrations, and the way they are changing societies. The perspective is international: large-scale movements of people arise from the accelerating process of global integration. Migrations are not an isolated phenomenon: movements of commodities and capital almost always give rise to movements of people. Global cultural interchange, facilitated by improved transport and the proliferation of print and electronic media, also leads to migration. International migration is not an invention of the late twentieth century, nor even of modernity in its twin guises of capitalism and colonialism. Migrations have been part of human history from the earliest times. However international migration has grown in volume and significance since 1945 and most particularly since the mid-1980s. The perspective for the 1990s and the early part of the next century is that migration will continue to grow, and that it is likely to be one of the most important factors in global change.

There are several reasons for this assumption: growing inequalities in wealth between the North and South are likely to impel increasing numbers of people to move in search of better living standards; political, ecological and demographic pressures may force many people to seek refuge outside their own countries; the end of the Cold War, which led to massive population movements in Europe, could in the future do the same in Asia; increasing ethnic strife in a number of regions could lead to future mass flights, as has already happened, for instance, in Palestine and Yugoslavia; and the creation of new free trade areas will cause movements of labour – whether or not this is intended by the governments concerned. One corollary is the virtual certainty that states around the world will be increasingly affected by international migration, either as receiving societies, lands of emigration, or both.

No one knows exactly how many international migrants there are worldwide. In 1990, the International Organisation for Migration (IOM) ventured an estimate of over 80 million persons, including all types of migrants whether documented or not (IOM, 1990). Out of this total 15 million were refugees and asylum seekers. By 1992, some estimates put the total of number of migrants at over 100 million, of whom 20 million were refugees and asylum seekers. The 1990 figure was about equal to the population of united Germany, and suggests that about 1.7 per cent of the world's population lives abroad, which approximates the annual increase in the world's population. This indicates that the vast majority of human beings reside in their countries of birth and citizenship, and that taking up residence abroad is the exception, not the rule.

Yet the impact of migration is much greater than the small percentage suggests. People tend to move not individually but in groups. Their departure may have considerable consequences for social and economic relationships in the area of origin. In the country of immigration, settlement is closely linked to employment opportunities, and is almost always concentrated in industrial and urban areas, where the impact on receiving communities is considerable. Migration thus affects not only the migrants themselves but the sending and receiving societies as a whole. There can be few people in either industrial countries or underdeveloped countries today who do not have personal experience of migration and its effects. For example, some 25–30 million of the estimated 80 million recent immigrants are thought to be foreign workers. They are believed to remit over $67 billion annually to their homelands. If accurate, this figure would place labour second only to oil in world trade (Martin, 1992).

Contemporary migrations: an overview

International migration is part of a transnational revolution that is reshaping societies and politics around the globe. It has affected the world's regions in different ways. Some areas, like the United States, Canada, Australia, New Zealand or Argentina, are classical countries of immigration. Their populations consist mainly of European immigrants and their descendants. The aboriginal populations of these countries have been partially destroyed and dispossessed; today the survivors have a marginal and discriminated existence. In the last 20 years the USA, Canada and Australia have experienced large-scale immigration from new source countries, particularly from Asia. The USA also has large influxes of migrant workers from Mexico and other countries of Latin America and the Caribbean.

Another striking development of recent years has been the growing number of countries that have experienced immigration in addition to the classical cases. Virtually all of Northern and Western Europe was affected by labour migration between 1945 and the early 1970s, and must now be considered an immigration area. Even Southern European states like Greece, Italy and Spain, which long were zones of emigration, have become immigration areas. Several Central and Eastern European states, particularly Hungary, Poland and Czechoslovakia, are becoming immigration lands.

The Middle East is affected by complex population movements. Turkey is both a country of emigration and of immigration. In the 1960s and 1970s millions of Turks went to work in Germany and other Western European countries. When labour recruitment stopped, family reunion and refugee movements took over, while workers started to go to the oil states of the Persian Gulf. Turkey has also been a haven for ethnic Turks and Muslims encountering

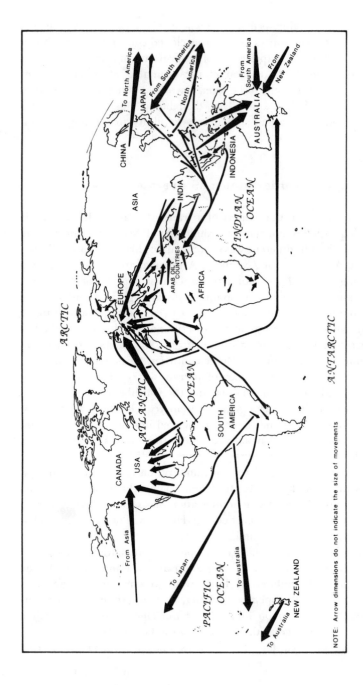

MAP 1.1
Global migratory movements from 1973

NOTE: Arrow dimensions do not indicate the size of movements

persecution in Eastern Europe, as witnessed by the influx of some 370 000 Bulgarian Turks in 1989. In addition, Turkey has received large numbers of Iranian and Kurdish refugees. To its south, Syria has been a major recipient of Palestinian refugees, as has Lebanon. Israel is a state whose raison d'être is the gathering in of Jews from around the world. Jordan serves as a refuge for hundreds of thousands of Palestinian refugees and hosts many other immigrants as well. The oil-rich Gulf Arab states, particularly Saudi Arabia and Kuwait, became major magnets to immigrants from the Arab world and Asia following the oil-price explosion of the 1970s.

Migration plays an important role in Africa too. In the past, colonialism and white settlement led to the establishment of migrant labour systems for plantations and mines. The largest international recruitment system was set up by South Africa, and continues to function in a modified form. West Africans from former French colonies still go in search of work to the former colonial power. Algeria had mass emigration to France until recently, but also has a significant refugee population from the Western Sahara. The Sudan, which is one of the world's poorest nations despite its enormous resources, houses a huge population of refugees. Indeed throughout Africa there were an estimated five million refugees in 1989. Many African states, such as Nigeria and the Ivory Coast, also receive foreign workers, both legal and illegal.

In Asia, large-scale international migrations have also become frequent. Iran houses millions of Afghan refugees, as does Pakistan. Several Indian states have received inflows of immigrants from Bangladesh, Sri Lanka and Nepal. To the north, in the area of the ex-Soviet Union, the potential for migration unleashed by the momentous changes of recent years seems enormous. In East and Southeast Asia, the emerging industrial and economic powers, Japan, Hong Kong, Taiwan and Singapore, have all joined the ranks of immigration lands. Malaysia also receives hundreds of thousands of foreign workers, many of whom arrive illegally. Outflows of refugees from Indo-China have greatly affected Thailand, Malaysia, Hong Kong and other states. Large proportions of the population of some of the smaller Pacific Islands have migrated to New Zealand or the USA.

Virtually all Latin American countries experience movements of refugees or foreign workers. Venezuela, Brazil, the Dominican Republic and Argentina are major poles of immigration. Many countries are simultaneously countries of emigration and immigration. Dominican emigrants journey northward to the East Coast of the United States while Haitian cane-cutters traditionally are employed during the Dominican Republic's sugar cane harvest. Large-scale labour migration (often illegal) across the long border between Mexico and the USA is of great economic and political significance. There have been mass labour migrations from Jamaica and other Caribbean countries to the USA, while refugees from Cuba and Haiti continue to arrive and settle in the USA.

Comparing migration movements around the world, it is possible to identify certain general tendencies, which are likely to pay a major role in the next 20 years.

● The first might be referred to as the *globalisation of migration*, the tendency for more and more countries to be affected by migratory movements at the same time. Moreover, the diversity of the areas of origin is also increasing, so that most immigration countries have entrants from a broad spectrum of economic, social and cultural backgrounds.

● The second tendency is the *acceleration of migration*, the fact that migrations are growing in volume in all major regions at the present time. Clearly this quantitative growth increases both the urgency and the difficulties of government policies.

● The third tendency is the *differentiation of migration*: most countries do not simply have one type of immigration, such as labour migration, refugee or permanent settlement, but a whole range of types at once. Typically, migratory chains which start with one type of movement often continue with other forms, despite (or often just because of) government efforts to stop or control the movement. This differentiation presents a major obstacle to national and international policy measures.

● The fourth tendency is the *feminisation of migration*: women play an increasing role in all regions and all types of migration. In the past most labour migrations and many refugee movements were male-dominated, and women were often dealt with under the category of family reunion. Since the 1960s, women have played a major role in labour migration: for instance, Turkish women often preceded their men to Germany. Today women workers form the majority in movements as diverse as those of Cape Verdians to Italy, Filipinos to the Middle East and Thais to Japan. Some refugee movements, including those from the former Yugoslavia, are marked by a majority of women. The feminisation of migration raises new issues both for policy-makers and for those who study the migratory process.

Migration and international politics

Issues linked to international migration play a surprisingly large part in the problems confronting the world today. In 1992, for instance, direct links could be seen in several of the major conflicts which hit the headlines: recent Hispanic and Asian immigrants were involved both as looters and as victims in the Los Angeles riots; the war in the remnants of Yugoslavia led to a new refugee emergency in Europe; migration to Israel continued to exacerbate the political conflict over the future of Palestine; in Germany neo-Nazi violence against foreigners (especially gypsies from Romania) caused a major political crisis, leading to calls for changes in the Constitution. Two examples of recent political upheavals are discussed in Exhibits 1.1 and 1.2, to give an idea of the complex ramifications of migratory movements.

Until recently, international migration was generally not seen by governments as a central political issue. Rather migrants were divided up into categories, such as permanent settlers, foreign workers or refugees, and dealt with by a variety of special agencies, such as immigration departments, labour offices, aliens police, welfare authorities and education ministries. It was only in the late 1980s that international migration began to be accorded high-level and systematic attention. For example, as the European Community countries removed their internal boundaries, they became increasingly concerned about strengthening external boundaries, to prevent an influx from the South and the East. It became clear that the old distinctions between types of migration were losing their validity: a migratory chain that started with workers could continue with family reunion or refugees. By the 1990s, the successful mobilisation of extreme-right groups over immigration and supposed threats to national identity helped bring these issues to the centre of the political stage. States found it increasingly difficult to find satisfactory solutions.

Starting with the 1985 Schengen Agreement between Germany, France and the Benelux countries, there was a series of conferences

---

EXHIBIT 1.1

The Gulf War

After the oil-price leap of 1973, the oil-rich states of the Persian Gulf recruited masses of foreign workers from both Arab and Asian countries for construction and industrialisation. At first most were men; later many female domestic servants were recruited from the Philippines and Sri Lanka. Resentments over the status accorded to various categories of aliens in Kuwait became a major factor in Iraq–Kuwait tensions. At the beginning of the Gulf Crisis in 1990 there were 1.1 million foreigners in Iraq, of whom 900 000 were Egyptians and 100 000 Sudanese. Kuwait had 1.5 million foreigners – two thirds of the total population. The main countries of origin were Jordan/Palestine (510 000 people), Egypt (215 000), India (172 000), Sri Lanka (100 000), Pakistan (90 000) and Bangladesh (75 000).

The Iraqi occupation of Kuwait and the subsequent war led to mass departures of foreign workers. Most Egyptians left Iraq, hundreds of thousands of Palestinians and other migrants fled Kuwait, and perhaps a million Yemenis were forced out of Saudi Arabia when their government sided with Iraq. An estimated five million persons were displaced, resulting in enormous losses in remittances and income for states from Southeast Asia to North Africa.

The Gulf War suggested, as perhaps never before, the centrality of migration in contemporary international relations. Migrants were viewed as potentially subversive – a fifth column – by the major Arab protagonists, and became scapegoats for domestic and international tensions. Hundreds of migrants were killed in the outbreaks of violence. The political realignments occasioned by the conflict had major repercussions upon society and politics in the Arab region and beyond. For example, emigration had long served as a safety-valve for Palestinian Arabs in the Israeli-occupied West Bank and Gaza Strip. The War foreclosed the possibility of emigration to the Gulf, further exacerbating tensions in the Gaza Strip. Hundreds of thousands of Palestinians forced out of Kuwait found refuge in the Kingdom of Jordan. The new influx of Palestinian refugees threatened to compound Jordan's severe economic and political difficulties.

---

and treaties between Western European countries designed to improve control of migration. This took on new momentum after 1989, as both South–North and East–West movements escalated. In North America and Australia, public debates took place on the volume of immigration and its changing character. Government commissions of inquiry were set up, and new legislation was enacted. In 1991, the so-called G-7 Group, the leaders of the seven major industrial democracies, declared that '[international] migration has made and can make a valuable contribution to economic and social development [and that] . . . there is a growing concern about worldwide migratory pressures, which are due to a variety of political, social and economic factors'. This declaration constituted

---

EXHIBIT 1.2

Eastern Europe and the collapse of the Berlin Wall

Migration played an important part in the political transformation of Central and Eastern Europe. The Hungarian government, under the pressure of a wave of would-be emigrants to the West, dismantled the border barriers with Austria in late 1989. This destroyed a major symbol of the Cold War and created the first opportunity for emigration for East Germans since the construction of the Berlin Wall in 1961. Tens of thousands rushed to depart. The steady haemorrhage to the West helped create a political crisis in the German Democratic Republic, forcing a change in leadership. In a final gambit to maintain control, the new government opened the Wall, enabling East Germans to travel freely to West Germany. The communist regime quickly collapsed and Germany was reunited in 1990. Large-scale migration continued: at least one million East Germans moved West from the opening of the Wall to the end of 1991.

The collapse of East Germany had a 'domino effect' upon other communist regimes. The political transformation of the region enabled hundreds of thousands to emigrate. During 1989 alone, some 1.2 million people left the former Warsaw Pact area. Most were ethnic minorities welcomed as citizens elsewhere: ethnic Germans who had the right to enter the Federal Republic, ethnic Greeks going to Greece, or Jews who automatically become citizens according to the Israeli Law of Return. The mass arrival of Soviet Jews in Israel was viewed with alarm by Arabs who feared that one result would be further dispossession of the Palestinians.

The spectre of uncontrolled mass emigration from Eastern Europe became a public issue in the West. Before long, Italy deployed troops to prevent an influx of Albanian asylum-seekers, while Austria used its army to keep out Romanian gypsies. For Western European leaders, the initial euphoria prompted by the destruction of the barriers to movement was quickly succeeded by a nostalgia for the ease of migration control of an earlier epoch.

The disintegration of the USSR led to the creation of a plethora of successor states. Some of the 25 million or so ethnic Russians living outside the Russian Republic suddenly confronted the possibility of losing their citizenship. The crisis in the new Republic of Moldova in April 1992, where Russians fought the desire of the ethnic Romanian majority for unification with Romania, was indicative of things to come. Economic crisis and the potential for inter-ethnic violence attendant on the reshaping of the former Warsaw Bloc area made emigration a preferred option for many. But the great mass of Eastern Europeans did not see the welcome mat rolled out for them. Even in Germany, Greece and Israel, there was resentment over the massive arrival of newcomers from the ex-USSR and Warsaw Bloc states.

---

a watershed (Martin, 1992: 171). Against the backdrop of the enormous changes associated with the end of the Cold War period, and the groping efforts to inaugurate a 'New World Order', the significance of international migration as a major determinant of global politics was finally coming into focus.

Ethnic diversity, racism and multiculturalism

Regulation of international migration is one of the two central issues arising from the mass population movements of the current epoch. The other is the effects of growing ethnic diversity on the societies of immigration countries. Settlers are often distinct from the receiving populations in various ways: they may come from different types of societies (for example, agrarian–rural rather than urban–industrial) with different traditions, religions and political institutions. They often speak a different language and follow different cultural practices. They may be visibly different, through physical appearance (skin colour, features, hair type and so on) or style of dress. The distinction is often a socioeconomic one: some migrant groups become concentrated in certain types of work (generally of low social status) and live segregated in low-income residential areas. The position of immigrants is sometimes marked by a specific legal status: that of the foreigner or non-citizen. The differences are often summed up in the concepts of 'ethnicity' or 'race', which will be discussed in Chapter 2. Immigration societies are frequently seen as being made up of distinct ethnic groups. In many cases, immigration complicates existing conflicts or divisions in societies with long-standing ethnic minorities.

The social meaning of ethnic diversity depends to a large extent on the significance attached to it by the populations and states of the receiving countries. The classical immigration countries have generally seen immigrants as permanent settlers who were to be assimilated or integrated. However not all potential immigrants have been seen as suitable for assimilation: the USA, Canada and Australia all had policies to keep out non-Europeans and even some categories of Europeans until the 1960s. Countries which emphasised temporary labour recruitment – Western European countries in the 1960s and early 1970s, more recently the Gulf oil states and some of the fast-growing Asian economies – have tried to prevent family reunion and permanent settlement. Despite the emergence of permanent settler populations, such countries have declared themselves not to be countries of immigration, and have denied citizenship and other rights to settlers. Between these two extremes are a wealth of variations, which will be discussed in later chapters.

Culturally distinct settler groups almost always maintain their languages and some elements of their homeland cultures, at least for a few generations. Where governments have wanted or recognised permanent settlement, there has been a tendency to move from policies of individual assimilation to acceptance of some degree of long-term cultural difference. The result has been granting of minority cultural and political rights, as embodied in the policies of multiculturalism introduced in Canada, Australia and Sweden since the 1970s. Governments which reject the idea of permanent settlement also oppose pluralism, which they see as a threat to national unity and identity. In such cases, immigrants tend to turn into marginalised and discriminated ethnic minorities. In other cases (France, for example), governments may accept the reality of settlement, but demand individual cultural assimilation as the price for granting of rights and citizenship. This can lead to serious contradictions.

Whatever the policies of the governments, the cultural and social changes resulting from immigration may lead to strong reactions from some sections of the population. Immigration has often taken place at the same time as economic restructuring and major changes in political and social structures. Immigration and growing ethnic diversity can appear threatening: people whose conditions of life are already changing in an unpredictable way often see the new-comers as the cause of insecurity. They fear that they are being 'swamped' by forces beyond their control. One of the dominant images in the highly-developed countries today is that of masses of people flowing in from the poor South and the turbulent East, taking away jobs, pushing up housing prices and overloading social services. Migrations and minorities are seen as a danger to living standards, life styles and social cohesion. Extreme-right parties have grown and flourished through anti-immigrant campaigns. Hostility to immigrants and ethnic minorities – whether labelled racism, xenophobia or ethnocentrism – has become a major political issue in most countries of immigration. Racism is a threat, not only to immigrants themselves, but also to democratic institutions and social order. Analysis of the causes and effects of racism must therefore take a central place in any discussion of international migration and its effects on society.

International migration does not always create diversity. Some migrants, such as Britons in Australia or Austrians in Germany, are virtually indistinguishable from the general population. Other groups, like western Europeans in North America, are quickly assimilated. 'Professional transients', that is highly-skilled personnel who move temporarily within specialised international labour markets, are rarely seen as presenting an integration problem. But these are the exceptions; in most instances, international migration increases diversity within a society. This presents a number of problems for the state. The most obvious is that of shaping social policies so that they meet the needs of the various groups. Social services may have to be planned and delivered in new ways to correspond to different life situations and cultural practices.

More serious is the challenge to national identity presented by growing diversity. The nation-state, as it has developed since the eighteenth century, is premised on the idea of cultural as well as political unity. In many countries, ethnic homogeneity, defined in terms of common language, culture, traditions and history, has been seen as the basis of the nation-state. This unity has often been fictitious – a construction of the ruling elite which claimed to express it – but it has provided powerful national myths. Immigration and ethnic diversity threaten such ideas of the nation, because they create a people without common ethnic origins. The classical countries of immigration have been able to cope with this situation most easily, since absorption of immigrants has been part of their myth of nation building. But countries which place common culture at the heart of their nation-building process (Germany is the most obvious case) have found it very difficult to resolve the contradiction.

One of the central ways in which the link between the people and the state is expressed is through the rules governing citizenship and naturalisation. States which readily grant citizenship to immigrants, without requiring common ethnicity or cultural assimilation, seem most able to cope with ethnic diversity. On the other hand, states which link citizenship to cultural homogeneity tend to have exclusionary policies which marginalise and disadvantage immigrants. This distinction is related to, but not identical with, that between classical immigration countries and labour migration countries, to be discussed in more detail in Chapter 8.

It is one of the central themes of this book that continuing international population movements will increase the ethnic diversity of more and more countries. This has already called into question prevailing notions of the nation-state and citizenship. New approaches are being sought. They seem most likely to develop out of the multicultural models which are currently evolving in certain countries of immigration. But countries must adapt foreign models to meet their own circumstances and needs. Debates over how best to do so will shape the politics of many countries in coming decades.

Aims and structure of the book

The first goal of this book is to describe and explain contemporary international migration. We set out to show the enormous complexity of the phenomenon, and to communicate both the variations and the common factors in international population movements as they affect more and more parts of the world.

The second goal is to explain how migrant settlement is bringing about increased ethnic diversity in many societies, and how this is related to broader social, cultural and political developments. Understanding these changes is the precondition for political action to deal with problems and conflicts linked to migration and ethnic diversity.

The third goal is to link the two discourses, by showing the complex interaction between migration and growing ethnic diversity. There are large bodies of empirical and theoretical work on both international migration and on ethnic diversity. However the two are often inadequately linked. There is a tendency towards specialisation both in academic circles and among policy-makers. Many of the research institutes which deal with migration are distinct from those concerned with ethnic relations. For instance, the International Sociological Association has separate research committees for 'ethnic, race and minority relations' and for 'sociology of migration'. Similarly many governments have one ministry or agency to deal with immigration, and another to deal with ethnic or race relations.

Immigration and ethnic relations are closely interrelated in a variety of ways. The linkages can best be understood by analysing the migratory process in its totality. It is an ambitious (some would say elusive) undertaking to try to do this on a global level in one short book. Hence accounts of the various migratory movements must inevitably be concise, but a global view of international migration is the precondition for understanding each specific flow. The central aim of this book is therefore to provide an introduction to the subject of international migration and the emergence of multicultural societies, which will help readers to put more detailed accounts of specific migratory processes in context.

The book is structured as follows: Chapter 2 examines some of the theories and concepts used to explain migration and formation of ethnic minorities, and emphasises the need to study the migratory process as a whole. Chapter 3 describes the history of international migration up to 1945. There is some discussion of the role of migration in the period leading up to the emergence of European nation-states, but the main focus is the migrations brought about by capitalism and colonialism, in the process of creating a world market.

Chapter 4 is concerned with migration to industrial countries since 1945. It shows the patterns of labour migration which developed during the post-war boom and discusses the differences and similarities between permanent, post-colonial and guestworker migration systems. The major changes in migratory patterns after the oil shock of 1973 are examined. Finally the increasing volume and complexity of migrations in the late 1980s and early 1990s are discussed. (Japan, although an industrial country of immigration, is not discussed here because the migratory movement is too new to permit adequate comparison. Instead Japan is discussed in the context of Asian regional migration in Chapter 6.)

Chapter 5 presents studies of the migratory process in two countries which appear at first sight to have had almost diametrically opposed experiences of immigration: Australia and Germany. The aim is to show both parallels and differences, and to discuss the factors which determine them.

Chapter 6 shows how major political, social and economic changes are leading to mass movements from and within specific regions: the Middle East, Eastern Europe, Africa, Latin America and Asia. These areas are major sources of migrants to highly-developed countries, and it is from here that the 'next waves' are likely to come. But, as the chapter shows, movements within these regions are of growing importance, particularly where the emergence of new industrial countries is leading to growing economic and demographic imbalances.

Chapter 7 considers the economic position of immigrants in highly-developed countries, looking at labour market segmentation, the role played by immigrants in economic crisis and why employment of migrants can continue despite high unemployment. The recent history of foreign worker employment in the French motor construction and building industries is used as an example. Chapter 8 looks at the position of immigrants within the societies of some of the main countries of immigration, examining factors such as legal status, social policy, formation of ethnic communities, racism, citizenship and national identity. It discusses the reasons for the different policies and attitudes in the various countries, as well as their possible consequences.

Chapter 9 examines some of the key political effects of increasing ethnic diversity, looking both at the involvement of minorities in politics and at the way mainstream politics are changing in reaction to migrant settlement. Perspectives for the emergence of multicultural societies are discussed. Chapter 10 sums up the arguments of the book and presents some conclusions on the future of international migration, and what it is likely to mean for individual societies and for the global community as a whole.

2

The Migratory Process and the Formation of Ethnic Minorities

International migration is hardly ever a simple individual action, in which a person decides to move in search of better life-chances, pulls up his or her roots in the place of origin and quickly becomes assimilated in the new country. Much more often migration and settlement is a long-drawn-out process, which will be played out for the rest of the migrant's life, and affect subsequent generations too.[1] It is a collective action, arising out of social change and affecting the whole society in both sending and receiving areas. Moreover the experience of migration and of living in another country often leads to modification of the original plans, so that migrants' intentions at the time of departure are poor predictors of actual behaviour. Similarly no government has ever set out to build an ethnically diverse society through immigration, yet labour recruitment policies often lead to the formation of ethnic minorities, with far-reaching consequences for social relations, public policies, national identity and international relations.

The aim of the chapter is to link two bodies of theory which are often dealt with separately: theories on migration and settlement, and theories on ethnic minorities and their position in society. It will start by looking at the concept of the migratory process, and then go on to examine theories of ethnicity and racism. These will be related to the process of ethnic minority formation, which in turn will be discussed in relation to concepts of nation, state and citizenship. In this chapter, the theories will be discussed mainly in abstract terms (though with some examples). The discourse provides a framework for understanding the more descriptive accounts of migration, settlement and minority formation in later chapters. However the reader may prefer to read those first and come back to the theory later.

Explaining migration and settlement

There are a variety of theoretical approaches to explaining international migration. One reason for this is that the study of migration cannot be confined to a single social-scientific domain: the explanations offered by geographers, demographers, economists, sociologists and political scientists often derive from different premises and methodologies. Beyond this, though, is a fundamental difference of paradigms between approaches which aim at generalisations based on quantitative analysis from large numbers of individual cases, and more collectivist and institutional approaches, which seek to examine migrations within the historical context of an emerging global economy.

The earliest systematic approaches to migration derive from the nineteenth-century work of the geographer Ravenstein, who advocated the formulation of statistical laws of migration (Ravenstein, 1885 and 1889). These took the form of general statements unconnected with any actual migratory movement and were generally quite ahistorical (Cohen, 1987: 34–5; Zolberg, 1989: 403–5). This tradition remains alive in the work of many demographers, geographers and economists (for example, Jackson, 1969). The 'general theories' advocated in such work emphasise tendencies of people to move from densely to sparsely populated areas, or from low- to high-income areas, or link migrations to fluctuations in the business cycle. Such approaches are often known as 'push–pull' theories, because they perceive the causes of migration in a combination of 'push factors', impelling people to leave the areas of origin, and 'pull factors', attracting them to certain receiving countries. 'Push factors' include demographic growth, low living standards, lack of economic opportunities and political repression, while 'pull factors' are demand for labour, availability of land, good economic opportunities and political freedoms.

This type of model is essentially individualistic and ahistorical. It emphasises the individual decision to migrate, based on rational comparison of the relative costs and benefits of remaining in the area of origin or moving to various alternative destinations. Constraining factors, such as government restrictions on emigration or immigration, are either ignored or dealt with as distortions of the rational market, which should be removed. Clearly the model has much in common with neo-classical theories of the labour market, and indeed this approach is currently mainly found in the work of neo-classical economists. For example Borjas (1989 and 1990) puts forward the · model of an immigration market:

> Neoclassical theory assumes that individuals maximise utility: individuals 'search' for the country of residence that maximises their well-being . . . The search is constrained by the individual's financial resources, by the immigration regulations imposed by competing host countries and by the emigration regulations of the source country. In the immigration market the various pieces of information are exchanged and the various options are compared. In a sense, competing host countries make 'migration offers' from which individuals compare and choose. The information gathered in this marketplace leads many individuals to conclude that it is 'profitable' to remain in their birthplace . . . Conversely, other individuals conclude that they are better off in some other country. The immigration market nonrandomly sorts these individuals across host countries. (Borjas, 1989: 461)

Borjas claims that 'this approach leads to a very clear – and empirically testable – categorisation of the types of immigrant flows that arise in a world where individuals search for the "best" country' (Borjas, 1989: 461). On the basis of this theory, one would expect the most disadavantaged people to move from the poor countries to richer areas. Moreover it would appear that the mere existence of economic disparities between various areas would be sufficient to generate migrant flows. In the long run, such flows should help to equalise wages and conditions in underdeveloped and developed regions, leading towards economic equilibrium.

However, in recent literature, such theories have been criticised as simplistic and incapable of explaining actual movements or predicting future ones (see Sassen, 1988; Portes and Rumbaut, 1990; Boyd, 1989). For instance, empirical study shows that it is rarely the poorest people from the least-developed countries who move to the richest countries. More frequently the migrants are people of intermediate social status from areas which are undergoing economic and social change. Similarly a push–pull model would predict movements from densely populated areas to more sparsely peopled regions, yet in fact countries of immigration like the Netherlands and Germany are amongst the world's more densely populated. Finally a push–pull model cannot explain why a certain group of migrants goes to one country rather than another, for example, why have most Algerians migrated to France and not Germany, while the opposite applies to Turks?

Many researchers therefore suggest that migratory movements generally arise from the existence of prior links between sending and receiving countries based on colonisation, political influence, trade, investment or cultural ties. Thus migration from Mexico to the USA originated in the southwestward expansion of the USA in the nineteenth century and the deliberate recruitment of Mexican workers by US employers in the twentieth century (Portes and Rumbaut, 1990: 224–30). The migration from the Dominican Republic to the USA was initiated by the US military occupation in the 1960s. Similarly both the Korean and the Vietnamese migrations were the long-term consequence of US military adventures in the countries of origin (Sassen, 1988: 6–9). The migrations from India, Pakistan and Bangladesh to Britain are clearly linked to the British colonial presence on the Indian sub-continent. Similarly Caribbean migrants have tended to move to their respective former colonial power: for example, from Jamaica to Britain, Martinique to France and Surinam to the Netherlands. The Algerian migration to France (and not to Germany) is explained by the French colonial presence in Algeria, while the Turkish presence in Germany is the result of direct labour recruitment by Germany in the 1960s and early 1970s.

This discussion indicates a further problem of 'push–pull' and neo-classical models: they tend to treat the role of the state as an aberration which disrupts the 'normal' functioning of the market (Borjas, for instance, suggests that the US government should 'deregulate the immigration market' by selling visas to the highest bidder: 1990: 225–8). But examination of most historical and contemporary migrations (see Chapters 3, 4, 5 and 6 below) shows that the state almost invariably plays a major role in initiating, shaping and controlling movements. Although governments of countries of origin play a part in encouraging or restricting migration, it is particularly the governments of potential immigration areas which permit, restrict or prohibit movements. The most common reason to permit entry is the need for workers – with states sometimes taking on the role of labour recruiter on behalf of employers – but demographic or humanitarian considerations may also be important. Immigration as part of nation building has played a major role in new world countries such as the USA, Canada, Argentina, Brazil and Australia. State policies on refugees and asylum-seekers are major determinants of contemporary population movements.

Thus the idea of individual migrants who make free choices which not only 'maximise their well-being' but also 'lead to an equilibrium in the marketplace' (Borjas, 1989: 482) is so far from historical reality that it has little explanatory value. It seems better, as Zolberg suggests, to analyse labour migration 'as a movement of workers propelled by the dynamics of the transnational capitalist economy, which simultaneously determines both the "push" and the "pull"' (Zolberg, 1989: 407). This implies that migrations are collective phenomena, which should be examined as sub-systems of an increasingly global economic and political system.

Fawcett and Arnold argue that migrations can best be understood by using the conceptual framework of a 'migration system', which refers to a set of places linked by flows and counterflows of people. The migration systems approach means examining both ends of the flow, putting a specific flow or destination in the context of other possible flows or destinations, and studying all the linkages between the places concerned: not just movements of people, but also of information, goods, services and ideas. These linkages can be categorised as 'state-to-state relations and comparisons, mass culture connections and family and social networks' (Fawcett and Arnold, 1987: 456–7).

Another way of stating the migrations systems approach is to say that each specific migratory movement can be seen as the result of interacting macro- and micro-structures. Macro-structures refer to large-scale institutional factors, while micro-structures embrace the networks, practices and beliefs of the migrants themselves. This type of analysis presupposes an historical approach based on a concept of global interdependence: 'Immigration, like other international processes, does not so much take place between compartmentalised nation units as within an overarching system, itself a product of past historical development' (Portes and Böröcz, 1989: 626).

The macro-structures include the political economy of the world market, inter-state relationships, and the laws, structures and practices established by the states of sending and receiving countries to facilitate or to prevent migration and to control settlement. The evolution of production, distribution and exchange over the last five centuries – with a tendency towards ever-greater integration of the world economy – has clearly been a major determinant of migrations (and not merely of labour migration but also of nation-building migrations and refugee flows). The role of international relations and of the states of both sending and receiving areas in organizing or facilitating movements is also significant (Dohse, 1981; Böhning, 1984; Cohen, 1987; Fawcett, 1989; Mitchell, 1989; Manfrass, 1992). Industrial states guard their borders and admit workers or refugees as exceptions, rather than the rule, so 'it is necessary to account for the wall they have erected as well as for the small doors they have provided in it' (Zolberg, 1989: 408).

The micro-structures are the informal networks developed by the migrants themselves, in order to cope with migration and settlement. Earlier literature used the concept of 'chain migration' to refer to such networks (for example, Price, 1963: 108–10). Today many authors emphasise the role of information and 'cultural capital' (knowledge of other countries, capabilities for organising travel, finding work and adapting to a new environment) in starting and sustaining migratory movements. Informal networks include psychological adaptations, personal relationships, family and household patterns, friendship and community ties, and mutual help in economic and social matters. Informal networks bind 'migrants and nonmigrants together in a complex web of social roles and interpersonal relationships' (Boyd, 1989: 639). These bonds are double-sided: they link migrants with non-migrants in their areas of origin, but also connect settlers with the receiving populations in relationships of co-operation, competition and conflict. Such networks can be understood as dynamic cultural responses, which are at the basis of ethnic community formation and the maintenance of family and group ties which transcend national boundaries.

Macro- and micro-structures are linked at all levels with each other. Together they can be examined as facets of an overarching *migratory process*. This concept sums up the complex sets of factors and interactions which lead to international migration and influence its course. No single cause is ever sufficient to explain why people decide to leave their country and settle in another. When examining a migratory movement, it is essential to try to understand all aspects of the process, by asking questions like:

● what economic, social, demographic, environmental or political factors have changed so much that people feel a need to leave their area of origin?
● what factors provide opportunities for migrants in the destination area?
● how do links develop between the two areas, providing information, means of travel and the possibility of entry to prospective migrants?
● what legal, political, economic and social structures and practices exist or emerge to regulate migration and settlement?
● how do migrants turn into settlers, and why does this lead to discrimination, conflict and racism in some cases, but to pluralist or multicultural societies in others?
● what is the effect of settlement on the social structure, culture and national identity of the receiving societies?
● how does emigration change the sending area?
● to what extent do migrations lead to new linkages between sending and receiving societies?

Although each migratory movement has its specific historical patterns, it is possible to generalise on the way migrations evolve, and to find certain internal dynamics in the process. For example, it may be observed that most migrations have started with young, economically active people (often mainly men). They are 'target-earners', who want to save enough in a higher-wage economy to improve conditions at home, by buying land, building a house, setting up a business, or paying for education or dowries. After some period in the receiving country, a proportion of these 'primary migrants' return home, but others prolong their stay, or return and then remigrate. This may be because of relative success: they find living and working conditions in the new country better than in the homeland. But it may also be because of relative failure: migrants find it impossible to save enough to achieve the aims they have for their return, necessitating a longer sojourn. As time goes on, many erstwhile temporary migrants send for spouses, or find partners in the new country. With the birth of children, settlement takes on a more permanent character, whatever the original intentions. Sometimes settlers are quickly absorbed into the majority population, but often processes of economic, social and cultural exclusion lead to the emergence of distinct ethnic minorities. These patterns can be summarised in a four-stage model:

● Stage 1: temporary labour migration of young workers, remittance of earnings and continued orientation to the homeland;
● Stage 2: prolonging of stay and the development of social networks based on kinship or common area of origin and the need for mutual help in the new environment;
● Stage 3: family reunion, growing consciousness of long-term settlement, increasing orientation towards the receiving country, and emergence of ethnic communities with their own institutions (associations, shops, cafes, agencies, professions);
● Stage 4: permanent settlement which, depending on the policies of the government and the behaviour of the population of the receiving country, leads either to secure legal status and eventual citizenship, or to political exclusion, socioeconomic marginalisation and the formation of permanent ethnic minorities.

In the post-1945 period this model of the migratory process applies most obviously to the large-scale migrations from the Mediterranean basin to Western Europe and Australia, and from Latin America and Asia to North America. A high proportion of these movements was labour migration, followed by family reunion, settlement and community formation. The model also fits the migrations from former colonies to the colonial powers fairly well. It is less appropriate to refugee movement or to temporary migrations of highly-skilled personnel. Nonetheless the model has analytical value for these groups too, since both refugee movement and highly-skilled migration are often at the beginning of migratory chains which lead to family reunion and community formation.

In any case it is important to realise that the distinctions between the various types of migrations, however important for the people concerned, are only relative. Labour migrants, permanent settlers and refugees have varying motivations and move under different conditions. Yet all these types of population movement are symptomatic of modernisation and globalisation. Colonialism, industrialisation and integration into the world economy destroy traditional forms of production and social relations, and lead to reshaping of nations and states. Such fundamental societal changes lead both to economically motivated migration and to politically motivated flight. Sometimes it is difficult to distinguish between the two, as the current European asylum-seeker crisis demonstrates.

The formation of ethnic minorities

Discussion of the long-term effects of immigration on society concentrates on the fourth stage of the migratory process: that of permanent settlement. This stage can have significantly different outcomes, depending on the actions of the state and population of the receiving society. At one extreme, openness to settlement, granting of citizenship and gradual acceptance of cultural diversity may allow the formation of ethnic communities, which can be seen as part of a multicultural society. At the other extreme, denial of the reality of settlement, refusal of citizenship and rights to settlers, and rejection of cultural diversity may lead to formation of ethnic minorities, whose presence is widely regarded as undesirable and divisive. In the first case, the immigrants and their descendants are seen as an integral part of a society which is willing to reshape its culture and identity. In the second, immigrants are excluded and marginalised, so that they live on the fringes of a society which is determined to preserve myths of a static culture and a homogeneous identity. Most of the countries of immigration discussed in this book fit somewhere between these two extremes.

Critics of immigration portray ethnic minorities as a threat to economic well-being, public order and national identity. Yet these ethnic minorities may in fact be the creation of the very people who fear them. An ethnic minority can be defined as a group having some of the following characteristics:

● subordinate groups in complex societies;
● special physical or cultural characteristics which are held in low esteem by dominant groups in the society;

● self-conscious groups, bound together on the one hand by language, culture and feelings of shared history, tradition and destiny, on the other hand by a common position within the society concerned;

● membership in the ethnic minority is to some extent transmitted to subsequent generations by descent.[2]

An ethnic minority is therefore a product of both 'other-definition' and of self-definition. Other-definition means ascription of undesirable characteristics and assignment to inferior social positions by dominant groups. Self-definition refers to the consciousness of group members of belonging together on the basis of shared cultural and social characteristics. The relative strength of other- and self-definition can vary. Some minorities are mainly constructed through processes of exclusion (which may be referred to as *racism*) by the majority. Others are mainly constituted on the basis of cultural and historical consciousness (or *ethnic identity*) among their members. The concept of the ethnic minority always implies some degree of marginalisation or exclusion, leading to situations of actual or potential conflict. Ethnicity is rarely a theme of political significance when it is simply a matter of different group cultural practices.

Ethnicity

In popular usage, ethnicity is usually seen as an attribute of minority groups, but most social scientists argue that everybody has ethnicity, which may be understood as a sense of group belonging, based on ideas of common origins, history, culture, experience and values (see Fishman, 1985: 4; A. D. Smith, 1986: 27). These ideas change only slowly, which gives ethnicity durability over generations and even centuries. But that does not mean that ethnic consciousness and culture within a group are homogeneous and static. Cohen and Bains refer to ethnicity as 'a myth of origins which does not imply a congenital destiny; unlike race, it refers to a real process of historical individuation – namely the linguistic and cultural practices through which a sense of collective identity or "roots" is produced and transmitted from generation to generation, *and is changed in the process*' (Cohen and Bains, 1988: 24–5, emphasis in original).

The origins of ethnicity may be explained in various ways. In the work of Geertz, for example, ethnicity is a 'primordial attachment', which results: 'from being born into a particular religious community, speaking a particular language, or even a dialect of a language and following particular social practices. These congruities of blood, speech, custom and so on, are seen to have an ineffable, and at times, overpowering coerciveness in and of themselves' (Geertz, 1963, quoted here from Rex, 1986: 26–7).

In this approach, ethnicity is not a matter of choice – it is presocial, almost instinctual, something one is born into. On the other hand, many anthropologists use a concept of 'situational' ethnicity. Members of a specific group decide to 'invoke' ethnicity, as a criterion for self-identification, in a situation where such identification is necessary or useful. This explains the variability of ethnic boundaries and changes in salience at different times. The markers chosen for the boundaries are also variable, generally emphasising cultural characteristics, such as language, shared history, customs, religion, and so on, but sometimes including physical characteristics: 'Once it is clear that ethnic relations follow on the social construction of difference, phenotype falls into place as one element in the repertoire of ethnic boundary markers' (Wallman, 1986: 229). In this view there is no essential difference between the drawing of boundaries on the basis of cultural difference or of phenotypical difference (popularly referred to as 'race').[3]

This approach comes close to sociological theories which perceive ethnic identification or mobilisation as rational behaviour, designed to maximise the power of a group in a situation of market competition. Such theories have their roots in Max Weber's concept of 'social closure', whereby a status group establishes rules and practices to exclude others, in order to gain a competitive advantage. For Weber (as for Marx), organisation according to 'affective criteria' (such as religion, ethnic identification or communal consciousness) was in the long run likely to be superseded by organisation according to economic interests (class) or bureaucratic rationality. Nonetheless the instrumental use of these affiliations could be rational if it led to successful mobilisation and development of social power.

On the other hand, many sociologists reject the concept of ethnicity altogether, seeing it as 'myth' or 'nostalgia', which cannot survive against the rational forces of economic and social integration in large-scale industrial societies (Steinberg, 1981). But it is hard to ignore the growing significance of ethnic identification and mobilisation in most highly-developed countries, so that many attempts have been made to show the links between ethnicity and power. For instance, the studies of the 'ethnic revival' by the US sociologists Glazer and Moynihan (1975) and Bell (1975) emphasise the political role of ethnic identification: phenotypical and cultural characteristics are used to strengthen group solidarity, in order to struggle more effectively for market advantages, or for increased allocation of resources by the state. Bell sees ethnic mobilisation as a substitute for the declining power of class identification in advanced industrial societies. For Bell, the decision to organise on ethnic lines and as to what markers to use for the ethnic group appear to be almost arbitrary – an instrumental decision or, as he says, 'a strategic choice'. This does not imply that markers, such as skin colour, language, religion, shared history and customs, are not real, but rather that the decision to use them to define an ethnic group is not predetermined.

Whether ethnicity is 'primordial', 'situational' or 'instrumental' need not concern us further here. The point is that ethnicity leads to identification with a specific group, but its visible markers – phenotype, language, culture, customs, religion, behaviour – may also be used as criteria for exclusion by other groups. Ethnicity only takes on social and political meaning when it is linked to processes of boundary drawing between dominant groups and minorities. Becoming an ethnic minority is not an automatic result of immigration, but rather the consequence of specific mechanisms of marginalisation, which affect different groups in different ways.

Racism

As will be shown in later chapters, hostility towards certain immigrant groups is to be found in all the countries examined. We refer to exclusionary practices against ethnic minorities as racism, which may be defined as the process whereby social groups categorise other groups as different or inferior, on the basis of phenotypical or cultural markers. This process involves the use of economic, social or political power, and generally has the purpose of legitimating exploitation or exclusion of the group so defined.

Racism means making (and acting upon) predictions about people's character, abilities or behaviour on the basis of socially constructed markers of difference. The power of the dominant group is sustained by developing structures (such as laws, policies and administrative practices) that exclude or discriminate against the dominated group. This aspect of racism is generally known as institutional or structural racism. Racist attitudes and discriminatory behaviour on the part of members of the dominant group are referred to as informal racism. In some countries, notably Germany and France, there is reluctance to speak of racism. Euphemisms such as 'hostility to foreigners', 'ethnocentrism' or 'xenophobia' are used. But the debate over the label seems sterile: it is more important to understand the phenomenon and its causes. Racism operates in different ways according to the specific history of the society and the interests of the dominant group. In many cases, supposed biological differences are not the only markers: culture, religion, language or other factors are taken as indicative of phenotypical differences. For instance, anti-Muslim racism in Europe is based on cultural symbols, which, however, are clearly linked to phenotypical markers (such as Arab or African features).

The historical explanation for racism in western Europe and in post-colonial settler societies lies in traditions, ideologies and cultural practices, which have developed through ethnic conflicts associated with nation building, as well as through centuries of European colonial expansion (compare Miles, 1989). The reasons for the recent increase in racism must be sought in fundamental economic and social changes which have questioned the prevailing optimistic view of progress embodied in Western modernism. Since the early 1970s, world economic restructuring and increasing international cultural interchange have been experienced by many sections of the populations of developed countries as a direct threat to their livelihood, social conditions, life style and national identity. Since these changes have coincided with the implantation of new ethnic minorities in their midst, the tendency has been to perceive the newcomers as the cause of the threatening changes – an interpretation eagerly encouraged by the extreme right, but also by many mainstream politicians. Moreover the very changes which have affected the life situation of the more disadvantaged sections of the populations have also weakened the labour movement and working class cultures, which might otherwise have provided some measure of protection. The decline of working class parties and trade unions, and the erosion of local communicative networks have created the social space for racism to become more virulent (Wieviorka, 1991).[4]

Ethnicity, class, gender and life-cycle

It is important to realise that racial and ethnic divisions are only one aspect of social differentiation. Other important categories include social class, gender and position in the life-cycle. None of these distinctions are reducible to each other, yet they constantly cross-cut and interact, affecting life chances, life styles, culture and social consciousness. Immigrant groups and ethnic minorities are just as heterogeneous in this respect as the rest of the population. Indeed the migrant experience and the links to both sending and receiving societies make their situation even more complex. It must therefore always be remembered that the migrant is also a gendered subject, embedded in a whole set of social relationships.

A crucial linkage is that between ethnicity, class and gender. For example, a woman who lacks power compared with men of her own group may be a member of a white majority which dominates a black minority. Black entrepreneurs may enjoy economic privileges and yet suffer racial vilification. Men who are racially oppressed may still benefit from and contribute to a patriarchal system of discrimination against women. Racism has the ideological effect of increasing the salience of ethnic identification and minimising the importance of class and gender. Racism has often been important in the process of nation building: people feel common interests as members of an ethnic group, the significance of divisions between men and women, or between workers and employers is minimised. Women are often the symbolic representations of ethnic and national groups, and the nation is portrayed as a loved woman in danger (Anthias and Yuval-Davis, 1989: 8–9).

In the early stages of post-1945 migrations in Europe, the vital nexus of the migrant labour system appeared to be that between racism and class, and considerations of gender and ethnic consciousness were often neglected. However the role of women in maintaining families and reproducing workers in the country of origin was one of the main reasons for the economic benefits of labour migration for the employers. Moreover a large proportion of migrant workers were women. As Phizacklea (1983: 5) points out, it was particularly easy to ascribe inferiority to women migrant workers, just because their primary roles in patriarchal societies were defined as wife and mother, dependent on a male breadwinner. They could therefore be paid lower wages and controlled more easily than men.

Developments since the 1970s have made one-sided emphasis on the link between racism and class all the more inadequate. Restructuring and unemployment often mean that normal employment situations have become more the exception than the rule for ethnic minorities. Workforce participation rates – very high in the period of primary migration – are now generally below average. The work experience of immigrants is heteregeneous, including low-skilled jobs, informal sector work, small business and white-collar work. Very high rates of unemployment among ethnic minority youth may mean that 'they are not the unemployed, but the never employed' (Sivanandan, 1982: 49). Many members of ethnic minorities have experienced racism from some white workers and therefore find it hard to define their political consciousness in class terms. Minority groups may form ethnic associations or networks, which mobilise not only around cultural symbols, but also in defence of material interests and civil rights.

Migrant women's experience often remains distinct from that of men. They continue to form the lowest segment in a labour market divided according to ethnicity and gender. Immigrant women often provide unpaid labour in ethnic small businesses, giving a competitive edge that makes survival possible. In some sectors, most notably the garment industry, complex patterns of division of labour on ethnic and gender lines have developed. Male ethnic entrepreneurs use female labour from their own groups, but are themselves dependent on large retail corporations (Waldinger *et al.*, 1990). The significance of women's family and educational roles in reproducing and maintaining ethnic languages and cultures and resisting racism has been emphasised in many studies (see, for instance, Vasta, 1990). In ideological terms, threats of being 'swamped' by ethnic minorities have centred around supposed high birth rates of immigrant women.

The stages of the life-cycle – childhood, youth, maturity, middle age, old age – are also important determinants of economic and social positions, culture and consciousness. There is often a gulf between the experiences of the migrant generation and those of their children, who have grown up and gone to school in the new country. Ethnic minority youth become aware of the contradiction between the prevailing ideologies of equal opportunity and the reality of discrimination and racism in their daily lives. This can lead to emergence of countercultures and political radicalisation. In turn, ethnic minority youth are perceived by those in power as a 'social time-bomb' or a threat to public order, which has to be contained through social control institutions such as the police, schools and welfare bureaucracies. The disturbances which took place in many European cities in the 1980s (see Chapter 8) epitomise such conflicts.

Culture, identity and community

Culture has become a central theme in debates on the new ethnic minorities for several reasons. Firstly, as already outlined, cultural difference serves as a marker for ethnic boundaries: alleged cultural inferiority or difference is a justification for discrimination or subordination. Secondly, ethnic cultures play a central role in community formation: when ethnic groups cluster in specific areas, they establish their own spaces, marked by distinctive use of housing and public areas. Thirdly, such areas are perceived by some members of the majority group as confirmation of their fears of 'swamping' or a 'foreign take-over'. The emergence of ethnic communities is thus seen as a threat to the dominant culture and national identity. Fourthly, retention of language and culture by ethnic minorities is taken as proof of inability to come to terms with an advanced industrial society. Dominant groups tend to see migrant cultures as primordial, static and regressive. Cultural assimilation and abandonment of the language of origin is seen as the precondition for integration and upward mobility. Those who do not assimilate 'have only themselves to blame' for their marginalised position.

For members of ethnic minorities, culture plays a key role as a source of identity and as a way of organising resistance to exclusion and discrimination. Reference to the culture of origin helps people maintain self-esteem and personal identity in a situation where their capabilities and experience are undermined. But a static, primordial culture cannot fulfil this task, for it does not provide orientation or protection in a hostile environment. The dynamic nature of culture lies in its capacity to link a group's history and traditions with the actual situation in the migratory process. Migrant or minority cultures are constantly recreated on the basis of the needs and experience of the group and its interaction with the actual social environment (Schierup and Alund, 1987; Vasta *et al.*, 1992). An apparent regression, for instance to religious fundamentalism, may be precisely the result of a form of modernisation which has been experienced as discriminatory, exploitative and destructive of identity.

It is therefore necessary to understand the development of ethnic cultures, the stabilisation of personal and group identities, and the formation of ethnic communities as facets of a single process. Moreover this process is not closed off and self-contained. It depends on constant interaction with the state, the civil society and other groups in the country of immigration, as well as with groups and institutions in the country of origin. In addition, ethnic culture and identity is only one aspect of social being for members of ethnic minorities. Gender, class and age group culture and identities are also ever-present. Thus immigrants and their descendants do not have a static, closed and homogeneous ethnic identity, but rather dynamic multiple identities, influenced by a variety of cultural, social and other factors.

Indeed the whole concept of national culture and identity has become highly questionable. Increasing global economic and cultural integration is leading to a simultaneous homogenisation and fragmentation of culture. As multinational companies take over and repackage the artifacts of local cultures it becomes possible to consume all types of cultural products everywhere, but at the same time they lose their meaning as symbols of group identity. National or ethnic cultures shed their distinctiveness and become just another celebration of the cultural dominance of the international industrial apparatus. Hence the constant search for new sub-cultures, styles and sources of identity, particularly on the part of youth (compare Castles *et al.*, 1990: 139–41). The recreation of ethnic identities is part of this process. As Fishman points out:

> Characteristic of postmodern ethnicity is the stance of simulta- neously transcending ethnicity as a complete self-contained system, but of retaining it as a selectively preferred, evolving, participatory system. This leads to a kind of self-correction from within and from

without, which extreme nationalism and racism do not permit. (Fishman, 1985: 11)

Fishman uses the term 'mainstream ethnicity' to refer to the dominant ethnic consciousness in a society (for example, American ethnicity in the USA) and 'sidestream ethnicities' to refer to the consciousness of minority groups. He emphasises that the two are not mutually exclusive, are constantly changing and are linked in complex and contradictory ways (Fishman, 1985: 490–517).

Gilroy sees the focus of this recreation of culture in the social movements of local communities, as well as in youth sub-cultures. He argues that legacies of anti-colonial struggles have been reshaped in Britain in the reproduction of classes and 'races' which become youth culture:

> The institutions they create: temples, churches, clubs, cafés and blues dances confound any Eurocentric idea of where the line dividing politics and culture should fall. The distinction between public and private spheres cuts across the life of their households and communities in a similar manner. Traditional solidarity mediates and adapts the institutions of the British political system against which it is defined. (Gilroy, 1987: 37)

Culture is becoming increasingly politicised in all countries of immigration. As ideas of racial superiority lose their ideological strength, exclusionary practices against minorities increasingly focus on issues of cultural difference. At the same time, the politics of minority resistance crystallise more and more around cultural symbols. Yet these symbols are only partially based on imported forms of ethnicity. Their main power as definers of community and identity comes from the incorporation of new experiences of ethnic minority groups in the immigration country.

State, nation and citizenship

One of the central issues which arises from large-scale migrations is the effect of growing ethnic diversity on state and nation. A state, according to Seton-Watson (1977: 1), 'is a legal and political organisation, with the power to require obedience and loyalty from its citizens'. Strictly speaking, this definition only applies to the modern nation-state, as first established by the American and French revolutions. Older state forms based their authority on the absolute power of a monarch over a specific territory. Within this area, all people were subjects of the monarch (rather than citizens). The modern nation-state is formally defined by a constitution and laws, according to which all power derives from the people (or nation). It is therefore vital to define who belongs to the people. Membership is marked by the status of citizenship, which lays down rights and duties. Non-citizens are excluded from at least some of these. Citizenship is therefore the essential link between state and nation, and obtaining citizenship is of central importance for newcomers to a country.

A nation is harder to define, because it is not institutionalised in the same way as a state. Seton-Watson describes a nation as 'a community of people, whose members are bound together by a sense of solidarity, a common culture, a national consciousness' (Seton-Watson, 1977: 1). In the light of recent world history, the strength of such feelings of nationhood cannot be denied, yet we are still left with the question of how to observe or measure such essentially subjective phenomena. Anderson provides an answer with his definition of the nation: 'it is an imagined political community – and imagined as both inherently limited and sovereign' (Anderson, 1983: 15). This concept points to the political character of the nation, in particular its links with a specific territory and state.

Anderson regards the nation-state as a modern phenomenon, whose birthdate is that of the US Constitution of 1787. Gellner (1983) argues that nations could not exist in pre-modern societies, owing to the cultural gap between elites and peasants, while modern industrial societies require cultural homogeneity to function, and therefore generate the ideologies needed to create nations. However both Seton-Watson (1977) and A. D. Smith (1986) argue that the nation is of much greater antiquity, going back to the ancient civilizations of East Asia, the Middle East and Europe. What all these authors seem to agree on is that the nation is essentially a belief system, based on collective cultural ties and sentiments. These convey a sense of identity and belonging, which may be referred to as national consciousness.

Attempts to establish state territories controlled by specific nations can mean subjugation, exclusion or even genocide of other nations.

The nationalist ideologies of the last two centuries have postulated that ethnic group, nation and state should be facets of the same community and have the same boundaries. In other words, every ethnic group should constitute itself as a nation and should have its own state, with all the appropriate trappings: flag, army, Olympic team and postage stamps. In fact such congruence has rarely been achieved: nationalism has always been an ideology, trying to achieve such a condition, rather than an actual state of affairs. The history of all existing states has been marked by the presence on their territory of a variety of ethnic groups, which over time may or may not coalesce into a single nation.

Although the concept of ethnicity is fairly new (Glazer and Moynihan, 1975: 1–3), the existence of ethnic groups has been significant throughout history (A. D. Smith, 1986). The construction of nation-states has involved the extension of state power over ever-larger areas, and the incorporation of hitherto distinct ethnic groups or nations. It is possible to keep relatively small groups in situations of permanent subjugation and exclusion from the 'imagined community'. This has applied for instance, to Jews and gypsies in various European countries, to indigenous peoples in settler colonies and to the descendants of slaves and contract workers in some areas of European colonisation. It is much harder to maintain this situation if the subjugated nation retains a territorial base, as do the Scots, Welsh and Irish in the United Kingdom, the Bretons in France or the Basques in Spain.

Such 'historical minorities' are not our central concern here. But it is important to realise that the existence of the older minorities has helped to mould social structures and attitudes, which help determine the conditions for the implantation of new immigrant groups. These differ from 'historical' minorities in that they lack their own territory in the immigration country and are relatively dispersed. The pervasive fear of 'ghettoes' or 'ethnic enclaves' indicates that minorities appear most threatening when they appear to be occupying distinct areas. For nationalists, an ethnic group is a potential nation which does not (yet) control any territory, or have its own state. Most modern states have made conscious efforts to achieve cultural and political integration of minorities. Mechanisms include citizenship itself, centralised political institutions, the propagation of national languages, emphasis on a unitary culture, universal education systems and creation of national institutions like the army and/or an established church. The problem is similar in character everywhere, whether the minorities are 'old' or 'new': how can a nation be defined, if not in terms of a shared (and single) ethnic identity? How are core values and acceptable behavioural forms to be laid down, if there is a plurality of cultures and traditions?

The states of immigration countries have had to devise a wide range of policies and institutions to respond to the social and political problems which arise through settlement and increased ethnic diversity. These policies and institutions will be examined in later chapters. However it is important to realise that they all relate to certain central issues: defining who is a citizen, how newcomers can become citizens and what citizenship means. In principle the nation-state only permits a single membership, but immigrants or their decendants have a relationship to more than one state. They may be citizens of two states, or they may be a citizen of one state but live in another. Sometimes special forms of residence permits for immigrants may be seen as constituting forms of quasi-citizenship, which confers some but not all rights. All of these situations appear to pose problems. They lead to 'divided loyalties' and undermine the cultural homogeny which is the nationalist ideal. Thus large-scale settlement inevitably leads to a debate on citizenship. Bauböck suggests the following definition of citizenship:

> Citizenship designates a political status of individuals as well as a particular quality of a political system. As a normative concept citizenship is a set of rights, exercised by the individuals who hold the rights, equal for all citizens, and universally distributed within a political community, as well as a corresponding set of institutions guaranteeing these rights. (1991: 28)

However the formal equality of rights of all citizens is rarely accomplished in practice. For instance, citizenship has always meant something different for men than for women, because the concept of the citizen has been premised on the male family-father, who represents his woman and children (Anthias and Yuval-Davis, 1989). The citizen has also generally been defined in terms of the cultures, values and interests of the majority ethnic group. Finally, the citizen has usually been explicitly or implicitly conceived in class terms, so that gaining real participatory rights for members of the working class has been one of the central historical tasks of the labour movement. The history of citizenship has therefore been one of conflicts over the real content of the category in terms of civil, political and social rights (Marshall, 1964).

However the primary issue for immigrants is not the exact content of citizenship, but how they can obtain it, in order to achieve a legal status formally equal to that of other residents of a country. The answers have varied considerably in different countries, depending on the prevailing concepts of the nation itself. We can distinguish the following ideal-types of citizenship:

● The imperial model: definition of belonging to the nation in terms of being a subject of the same power or ruler. This is a notion which predates the French and American revolutions. It allowed the integration of the various peoples of multi-ethnic empires (the British, the Austro-Hungarian, the Ottoman). This model remained formally in operation in Britain until the Nationality Act of 1981, which created a modern type of citizenship for the first time. It also had some validity for the former Soviet Union. The concept almost always has an ideological character, in that it helps to veil the actual dominance of a particular ethnic group or nationality over the other subject peoples.

● The folk or ethnic model: definition of belonging to the nation in terms of ethnicity (common descent, language and culture), which means exclusion of minorities from citizenship and from the community of the nation. (Germany has come close to this model in both the past and the present.)

● The republican model: definition of the nation as a political community, based on a constitution, laws and citizenship, with the possibility of admitting newcomers to the community, providing they adhere to the political rules and are willing to adopt the national culture. This assimilationist approach dates back to the French and American revolutions. France is the most obvious current example.

● The multicultural model: definition of the nation as a political community, based on a constitution, laws and citizenship, with the possibility of admitting newcomers to the community, providing they adhere to the political rules, while at the same time accepting cultural difference and the formation of ethnic communities. This pluralist or multicultural approach is relatively new. It has gained most ground in Australia, Canada and Sweden, although it is also influential in the the Netherlands, USA, Britain and other countries.

The applicability of these models to specific countries will be discussed in more detail in Chapter 8. In fact, the models are neither universally accepted nor static even within a single country. For example, Gordon has argued that three main variants can be found in approaches to ethnic diversity in the USA: 'Anglo-conformity', that is the attempt to assimilate minorities completely so that they conformed with existing institutions and values; the 'melting pot', in which the folkways of various groups were mixed and fused together into a new American type; and 'cultural pluralism', in which ethnic groups maintained their own cultures and languages as distinct communities within an embracing commonwealth (Gordon, 1978: 181–208).

The European Community provides another example for transition and differentiation in citizenship. People who move from one community country to another enjoy important rights (concerning work, residence, legal status, and so on) which give them an intermediate status: they are not full citizens, since they lack voting rights, but they are considerably privileged compared with people from 'third countries' (non-EC countries). However the various EC countries also differentiate among 'third country' nationals. Some have granted special residence permits to some long-term immigrants, which confer considerable advantages concerning security of residence and the right to work compared with other immigrants. Thus there are various forms of 'quasi-citizenship'. Hammar (1990: 12) has coined the phrase 'denizenship' to refer to such intermediate forms.

The question is whether democratic states can in the long run successfully operate with a population differentiated into full citizens, quasi-citizens and foreigners. The central principle of the democratic state is that all members of civil society should be incorporated into the political community. That means granting full citizenship to all permanent residents. But in the post-modern world, migrations are likely to continue and there will be increasing numbers of people with affiliations to more than one society. That means that dual or multiple citizenship will become increasingly common. It corresponds with the multiple identities which are becoming the rule for most people, but particularly for migrants. The consequence is that the meaning of citizenship itself is likely to change, and that the exclusive link to one nation-state will become more tenuous. This could lead to some form of 'transnational citizenship', as Bauböck

(1991: 46) suggests. But that in turn raises the question of how states will regulate immigration if citizenship becomes more universal.

Conclusion

This chapter has been concerned with some of the theoretical explanations of migration and formation of ethnic minorities. One central argument is that migration and settlement are closely related to other economic, political and cultural linkages being formed between different countries in an accelerating process of globalisation. International migration – in all its different forms – must be seen as an integral part of contemporary world developments. It is likely to grow in volume in the years ahead, because of the strong pressures for continuing global integration. This means that national and international governmental measures are unlikely to significantly reduce migration. At best they can hope to regulate movements, and ensure that these take place under more humane conditions.

A second argument is that the migratory process has certain internal dynamics based on the social networks which are at its core. These internal dynamics can lead to developments not initially intended either by the migrants themselves or by the states concerned. The most common outcome of a migratory movement, whatever its initial character, is settlement of a large proportion of the migrants, and formation of ethnic communities or minorities in the new country. Thus the emergence of societies which are more ethnically and culturally diverse must be seen as an inevitable result of initial decisions to recruit foreign workers, or to permit migratory movements.

The third theoretical argument concerned the nature of ethnic minorities and the process by which they are formed. Most minorities are formed by a combination of other-definition and self-definition. Other-definition refers to various forms of exclusion and discrimination which can be designated as racism. Self-definition has a dual character. It includes assertion and recreation of ethnic identity, centred upon premigration cultural symbols and practices. It also includes political mobilisation against exclusion and discrimination, using cultural symbols and practices in an instrumental way. Since settlement and ethnic minority formation often intersect with times of economic and social crisis, they can become highly politicised. The issues of culture, identity and community can thereby take on great significance, not only for immigrants, but also for the receiving populations and for society as a whole.

The fourth argument focuses on the significance of post-1945 immigration for the nation-state. It seems likely that increasing ethnic diversity will contribute to changes in central political institutions, such as citizenship, and may affect the very nature of the nation-state. Such effects will be even more profound if mass migration continues, as seems likely.

These theoretical conclusions help to explain the growing political salience of issues connected with migration and ethnic minorities in virtually all developed countries. The migratory movements of the last 50 years have led to irreversible changes in most highly-developed countries. Continuing migrations will cause new transformations, both in the societies already affected and in further countries now entering the international migration arena. Migration and ethnic diversity are powerful factors for social and cultural change, and must be taken account of in future political strategies.

The more descriptive accounts which follow will present some evidence to permit further discussion of these ideas. Chapters 3, 4 and 6 are mainly concerned with the early stages of the migratory process: they show how migrations have developed in both highly-developed and less-developed regions, and how initial movements lead to migratory chains and long-term settlement. Chapter 5 presents case studies of the whole migratory process for two countries, demonstrating the way in which initial migratory movements lead on to formation of ethnic communities or minorities, whatever the original intentions of both policy-makers and migrants. Chapters 7, 8 and 9 are concerned mainly with the later stages of the migratory process. They discuss the way in which settlement and minority formation affect the economies, societies and political systems of immigration countries.

3

International Migration before 1945

The post-1945 migrations may be new in scale and in the number of countries affected, but population movements in response to demographic growth, climatic change and the development of production and trade have always been part of human history. Warfare, conquest, formation of nations and the emergence of states and empires have all led to migrations, whether voluntary or forced. The enslavement and deportation of conquered people was a frequent early form of labour migration. From the end of the Middle Ages, the development of European states and their colonisation of the rest of the world gave a new impetus to international migrations of many different kinds, foreshadowing the mass movements of the contemporary period.

The centrality of migration is not adequately reflected in prevailing academic views on the past: as Gérard Noiriel (1988: 15–67) has pointed out, the history of immigration has been a 'blind spot' of historical research in France. This applies equally to other European countries, though less to the USA and Australia. Perhaps denial of the role of immigrants in nation building has been part of the process of creation of myths of national homogeneity in European countries, which obviously was impossible in the 'classical countries of immigration'. It is only in very recent times that French, German and British historians have started serious investigation of the significance of immigration. Exhibit 3.1 provides an illustration of the significance of migration in early processes of nation building.

EXHIBIT 3.1

Migration and nation in French history

Ancient Gaul encompassed much of the area of modern-day France. It was in this area that one of the mediaeval world's most significant political entities came into being. At the collapse of the Western Roman Empire in the fifth century AD, Gaul was inhabited by a crazy-quilt of culturally and politically diverse peoples, including Roman citizens and soldiers, slaves, settled Germanic tribes and more recent arrivals. There were multiple centres of political power. In the area of present-day Brittany, the population had been decimated by Hun cavalry under Roman command following a peasant revolt. Celts from the West of Britain moved in across the English Channel, to escape the invading Saxons. These Celts, the ancestors of today's Bretons, fought with the embryonic Frankish state, from which the mediaeval French kingdom would emerge.

Norse raiders wreaked havoc upon the Frankish territory and, from 900 AD on, they settled to the north-west of Paris, in the area now called Normandy. It took centuries before the Normans and Celts ceased to be regarded as aliens by the Franks. The expansion of the Frankish state and its steady incorporation of adjacent lands and peoples was a long process, and French identity and consciousness emerged slowly. Life for most inhabitants of mediaeval France was encapsulated by the village and its environs, but there was awareness of the exterior world. To the inhabitants of the Frankish state, the people of Avignon, Aix-en-Provence or Arles to the south were foreigners.

But there were also newcomers – traders and artists from Italy, mercenaries, itinerant clergy, scholars and musicians, Muslim slaves from North Africa, the Eastern Mediterranean and Spain, as well as Jews and gypsies. The first Jewish colonies appeared in Gaul in the fourth century AD. Jews lived interspersed with the rest of the population and most appear to have spoken the local language. During the Crusades, Jews became scapegoats and victims of violence and persecution. Enforced residential segregation – ghettoes – became commonplace. In 1306, the French king, Philip the Fair, ordered the expulsion of the Jews, who by that time numbered about 100 000, allowing him to seize Jewish possessions. But in 1715 economic and financial considerations led King Louis X to reopen the doors of the French kingdom to Jews. Throughout mediaeval Christian Europe, Jews were regarded as outsiders and were periodically subject to persecution. It was only with the French Revolution of 1789 that Jews gained legal equality with the Christian population as citizens. However, some people continued to regard Jews as foreigners to the French nation. Even today, anti-immigrant sentiment as expressed by the *Front National* has marked anti-semitic overtones.

The gypsies, also called the Rom or the Tzigane, are the descendants of a people who emigrated from the area of present-day India. Gypsies were first recorded in France in 1419. Travelling in groups of 50 to 100, they spread throughout the kingdom, hawking their wares. There were soon manifestations of hostility towards them. French cities such as Angers banned them in 1498, followed soon after by King François I's edict prohibiting them from entering his kingdom. Like the Jews, the gypsies returned and became part of French society, but they were never fully accepted by some elements of French and other European populations. Together with the Jews, they were singled out for extermination by the Nazis during the Second World War. The roots of twentieth century genocide were deeply etched in the history of immigration to

European countries. Jews and gypsies have been perhaps the most enduring targets of European racism. The neo-Nazi riots in Rostock and other towns of the former East Germany in August September 1992 were mainly directed against Romanian gypsies who had sought refuge in Germany.

The fifteenth century was a turning point at which early modern states emerged, distinguished by growing economic, military and diplomatic power. This is the dawn of the Age of Discovery in which Europeans circumnavigated the globe, beginning a long process which eventually brought the world under European domination. The French monarchy's rule was legitimated by the doctrine of the 'divine right of kings'. However by the eighteenth century, the legitimacy of royal authority was increasingly questioned. The ideas that helped give rise to the French revolution in 1789 included the belief that sovereignty was vested in the people, as well as the concept of the nation-state and the idea that every human being belongs to a state. These ideas are particularly significant for our theme: international migration would be meaningless in a world not organised into nation-states. One of the key legal attributes of sovereignty is the idea, now universally accepted, that states have the authority to regulate movement into and out of the territory of the state. Illegal immigration has become such a politically volatile issue today partly because it is seen as violating one of the main perogatives of sovereign states.

Source: Lequin, 1988.

Individual liberty is generally portrayed as one of the great moral achievements of capitalism, in comparison with earlier societies, where liberty was restricted by traditional bondage and servitude. Neo-classical theorists portray the capitalist economic system as being based on free markets. One of these is the labour market, where employers and workers encounter each other as free legal subjects, with equal rights to make contracts. International migration is portrayed as a market in which workers make the free choice to move to the area where they will receive the 'best return on their human capital', that is the highest wages (compare Borjas, 1990: 9–18). But, this harmonious picture of free choice often fails to match reality. As Cohen (1987) has shown, capitalism has made use of both free and 'unfree' workers in every phase of its development. Labour migrants have frequently been unfree workers, either because they are taken by force to the place where their labour is needed, or because they are denied some of the rights enjoyed by other workers, and cannot therefore compete under equal conditions. Even where migration is voluntary and unregulated (such as migration to the USA up to the 1880s, or Commonwealth migration to Britain from 1945 to 1962) institutional and informal discrimination may limit the real freedom and equality of the workers concerned.

Migratory movements nearly always have both political and economic causes, and clear distinctions between the two are impossible. Because economic power is usually linked to political power, mobilisation of labour often has an element of coercion, sometimes involving violence, military force and bureaucratic control. Labour migration has gone hand-in-hand with limitation of individual liberty and denial of equality in many cases, such as the slave economy of the Americas; indentured colonial labour in Asia, Africa and the Americas; mineworkers in southern Africa in the nineteenth and twentieth centuries; foreign workers in German and French agriculture and industry before the Second World War; forced labourers in the Nazi war economy; 'guestworkers' in post-1945 Europe; and 'illegals' denied the protection of law in many countries today.

We should point to one theme that is not dealt with here – not because it is unimportant, but because it requires more intensive treatment than is possible in the present context. International migration, because of its links with colonialism and industrialisation, has had devastating effects on the indigenous peoples of colonised countries. European conquest of Africa, Asia, America and Oceania led either to the domination and exploitation of native peoples or to genocide – both physical and cultural. Nation building – particularly in the Americas and Oceania – was based on the importation of new populations. Thus immigration contributed to the exclusion and marginalisation of aboriginal peoples. One starting-point for the construction of new national identities was the idealisation of the destruction of indigenous societies: images such as 'how the West was won' or the struggle of Australian pioneers against the Aborigines became powerful myths. The roots of racist stereotypes – today directed against new immigrant groups – often lie in historical treatment of colonised peoples.

Colonialism

The great European expansion, which led to the colonisation of most of the rest of the world, gave rise to various types of migration. One was the outward movement of thousands of people from Europe, first to Africa and Asia, then to the Americas, and later to Oceania. In addition to the settlement of colonists in the conquered areas,

47

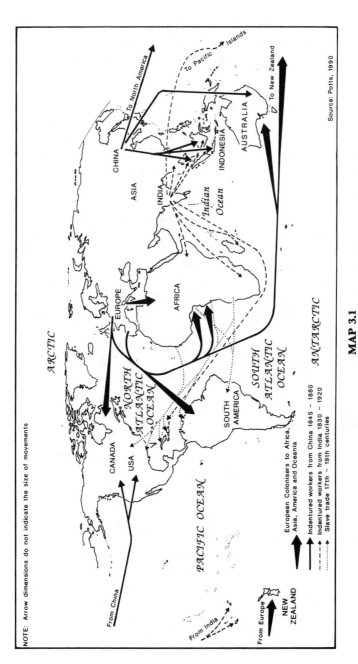

NOTE: Arrow dimensions do not indicate the size of movements

European Colonisers to Africa, Asia, America and Oceania

Indentured workers from China 1845 – 1880

Indentured workers from India 1830 – 1920

Slave trade 17th – 19th centuries

Source: Potts, 1990

MAP 3.1

Colonial migrations from the seventeenth to the nineteenth centuries

Europeans migrated, either permanently or temporarily, as sailors, soldiers, traders, priests and administrators. These migrations helped to bring about major changes in the economic structures and the cultures of both the European sending countries and the colonies.

An important antecedent of modern labour migration is the system of chattel slavery, which formed the basis of commodity production in the plantations and mines of the New World from the late seventeeth century to the mid-nineteenth century. The production of sugar, tobacco, coffee, cotton and gold by slave labour was crucial to the economic strength and political power of Britain and France – the dominant states of the eighteenth century – and played a major role for Spain, Portugal and the Netherlands as well. By 1770 there were nearly two and a half million slaves in the Americas, producing a third of the total value of European commerce (Blackburn, 1988: 5). The slave system was organised in the famous 'triangular trade': ships laden with manufactured goods, such as guns or household implements, sailed from ports like Bristol and Liverpool, Bordeaux and Le Havre, to the coasts of West Africa. There Africans were either forcibly abducted by the ship's crews or were purchased from local chiefs or traders in return for the goods. Then the ships sailed to the Caribbean or the coasts of North or South America, where the slaves were sold for cash. This in turn was used to purchase the products of the plantations, which were then brought back for sale in Europe.

An estimated 15 million slaves – both men and women – were transported from Africa to the Americas before 1850 (Appleyard, 1991: 11). For the women, hard labour in the mines, plantations and households was frequently accompanied by sexual exploitation. The children of slaves remained the chattels of the owners. Slavery was not abolished until 1834 in British colonies, 1863 in Dutch colonies and 1865 in the southern states of the USA (Cohen, 1991: 9). Despite slave rebellions and the abolition of the Atlantic traffic by the great powers in 1815, slavery continued to grow in economic significance. The number of slaves in the Americas doubled from three million in 1800 to six million in 1860, with corresponding growth in the area of plantation agriculture in the south-western United States, Cuba and Brazil (Blackburn, 1988: 544). Slavery had existed in many pre-capitalist societies, but the colonial system was new in character. Its motive force was the emergence of global empires, which began to construct a world market, dominated by merchant capital. Slaves were transported great distances by specialised traders, and bought and sold as commodities. Slaves were economic property and were subjected to harsh forms of control to maximise their output. The great majority were exploited in plantations using new production techniques based on gang labour. The plantations produced commodities for export, as part of an internationally integrated agricultural and manufacturing system (Blackburn, 1988; Fox-Genovese and Genovese, 1983).

In the latter half of the nineteenth century, slaves were replaced by indentured workers as the main source of plantation labour. Indenture (or the 'coolie system') involved recruitment of large groups of workers, sometimes by force, and their transportation to another area for work. British colonial authorities recruited over 30 million people from the Indian sub-continent (Appleyard, 1991: 11). Some were taken to Trinidad, Guyana and other Caribbean countries to replace the labour of emancipated slaves in the sugar plantations. Others were employed in plantations, mines and railway construction in Malaya and East Africa. Dutch colonial authorities used Chinese labour on construction projects in the Dutch East Indies. According to Potts (1990: 63–103) indentured workers were used in 40 countries by all the major colonial powers. She estimates that the system involved from 12 to 37 million workers between 1834 and 1941, when indentureship was finally abolished in the Dutch colonies. Indentured workers were bound by strict labour contracts for a period of several years. Wages and conditions were generally very poor, workers were subject to rigid discipline and breaches of contract were severely punished. Indentured workers were often cheaper for their employers than slaves (Cohen, 1991: 9–11).

Indenture epitomised the principle of divide and rule, pitting one colonised people against another. Indentured workers were used to undercut the wages of free workers (sometimes former slaves). Most of the indentured workers were men, but there were some women, both as workers and as dependants. Family formation and permanent settlement took place in many areas. A number of post-colonial interethnic conflicts (for example, hostility against Asians in Africa, against Chinese in Southeast Asia, against Indians in Fiji) have their roots in the divisions brought about by indenture. The Caribbean experience shows the effect of changing colonial labour practices on dominated peoples: the original inhabitants, the Caribs and Arawaks, were wiped out completely by European diseases and violence. With the development of the sugar industry in the eighteenth century, Africans were brought in as slaves. Upon emancipation in the nineteenth century, these generally became small-scale subsistence farmers, and were replaced with indentured workers from India. Upon completion of their indentures, many settled, bringing in dependants. Some remained labourers on large estates, while others became established as a trading class, mediating between the white ruling class and the black majority.

Industrialisation and migration to North America and Australia before 1914

The wealth accumulated in Western Europe through colonial exploitation provided much of the capital which was to unleash the industrial revolutions of the eighteenth and nineteenth centuries. In Britain, profits from the colonies was invested directly in new forms of manufacture, as well as encouraging commercial farming and speeding up the process of enclosure of arable land for pasture. The tenant farmers displaced in this way swelled the impoverished urban masses and became available as labour for the new manufactures and factories. This emerging class of wage labourers was soon joined by destitute artisans, such as hand-loom weavers, who had lost their livelihood through competition from the new manufactures. Herein lay the basis of the new class which was crucial for the growth for the British industrial economy: the 'free proletariat' which was free of traditional bonds, but also of ownership of the means of production.

However, from the outset, various types of unfree labour played an important part in the emergence of the industrial working class. Throughout Europe, draconian poor laws were introduced to control the displaced farmers and artisans, the 'hordes of beggars' who threatened public order. Workhouses and poorhouses were often the first form of manufacture, where the disciplinary instruments of the future factory system were developed and tested. In Britain, 'parish apprentices', orphan children under the care of local authorities, were hired out to factories as cheap unskilled labour. This was a form of forced labour, with severe punishments for insubordination or refusal to work, and not even a hint of free choice.

The first half of the nineteenth century – the peak of the industrial revolution – was also the main period of British migration to

America. Between 1800 and 1860, 66 per cent of migrants to the USA were from Britain, and a further 22 per cent were from Germany. Between 1800 and 1930, 40 million Europeans migrated permanently overseas, mainly to North and South America and Australia (Decloîtres, 1967: 22). From the mid-nineteenth century until 1914 most migrants came from Ireland, Italy, Spain and Eastern Europe, areas in which industrialisation came somewhat later. One of the main motivations for overseas migration was the desire to avoid having to become an industrial worker. America offered the dream of becoming an independent farmer or trader in new lands of opportunity. Often this dream was disappointed: the migrants became wage-labourers building roads and railways across the vast expanses of the New World, 'cowboys', gauchos or stockmen on large pastoral estates, or factory workers in the emerging industries of the north-eastern United States. However a considerable proportion of the settlers did eventually succeed in their dream, becoming farmers, white-collar workers or business people, while others were at least able to see their children achieve education and upward social mobility.

The USA is generally seen as the most important of all immigration countries. It is estimated that 54 million people migrated to the USA between 1820 and 1987 (Borjas, 1990: 3). The peak period was 1861 to 1920, during which 30 million people came. Until the 1880s, this migration was unregulated: anyone who could afford the ocean passage could come to seek a new life in America. However American employers did organise campaigns to encourage potential workers to come, and a multitude of agencies and shipping companies helped organise the movement. Many of the migrants were young single men, hoping to save enough to return home and start a family. But there were also single women, couples and families. Racist campaigns led to exclusionary laws to keep out Chinese and other Asians from the 1880s. For Europeans and Latin Americans, entry remained free until 1920 (Borjas, 1990: 27). The census of that year showed that there were 13.9 million foreign born people in the USA, making up 13.2 per cent of the total population (Briggs, 1984: 77).

Immigration played a key role in the development of the US population and economy. Slavery had been a major source of capital accumulation in the early USA. The industrial take-off after the Civil War (1861–65) was fuelled by mass immigration from Europe. At the

the same time the racist 'Jim Crow' system was used to keep the now nominally free Afro-Americans in the southern states to provide labour power for the plantations, since cheap cotton and other agricultural products were central to the success of industrialisation. The largest immigrant groups from 1860 to 1920 were Irish, Italians and Jews from Eastern Europe, but there were also people from just about every other European country, as well as from Mexico. Their patterns of settlement were closely linked to the labour needs of the emerging industrial economy. Labour recruitment by canal and railway companies led to settlements by Irish and Italians along the construction routes. Some groups of Irish, Italians and Jews settled in the east coast ports of arrival, where work was available in construction, transport and factories. The same was true of the Chinese on the west coast. Some central and eastern European peoples became concentrated in the Midwest, where the development of heavy industry at the turn of the century provided work opportunities (Portes and Rumbaut, 1990: 29–32). The American working class thus developed along patterns of ethnic segmentation, linked to processes of chain migration.

Canada was also an important destination for migrants from Europe. After the American Revolution, many loyalists of British origin went north to Canada. From the late eighteenth century there was immigration from Britain, France, Germany and other Northern European countries. Many Afro-Americans came across the long frontier from the USA to escape slavery: by 1860, there were 40 000 black people in Canada. In the nineteenth century, immigration from Europe was stimulated by the gold rushes, while rural immigrants were encouraged to settle the vast prairie areas. Between 1871 and 1931, Canada's total population increased from 3.6 million to 10.3 million. Immigration from China, Japan and India also began in the late nineteenth century, though on a fairly small scale. Most of the Chinese came to the west coast, particularly to British Columbia, where they helped build the Canadian Pacific Railway. Starting in 1886, a series of restrictive measures was introduced to stop Asian immigration (Kubat, 1987: 229–35). Canada received a large influx from Southern and Eastern Europe over the 1895 to 1914 period. But Canada began to encourage British immigration: in 1931, four preferred classes of immigrants were designated: British subjects with adequate financial means from the United Kingdom, Ireland and four other domains of the crown; US citizens; dependants of permanent residents of Canada, and agriculturists. Canada thereby discouraged further 'unwanted' migration from Southern and Eastern Europe. Asian immigration was prohibited from 1923 to 1947.

In Australia, immigration has been a crucial factor in economic development and nation building ever since British colonisation started in 1788. The Australian colonies were integrated into the British Empire as suppliers of raw materials such as wool, wheat and gold. The imperial state took an active role in providing workers for expansion through convict transportation (another form of unfree labour!) and the encouragement of free settlement. Initially there were large male surpluses, especially in the frontier areas, which were often societies of 'men without women'. But female migration did play a part from the outset: many female convicts were transported, and there were special schemes to bring out single women as domestic servants and as wives for settlers.

When the surplus population of Britain was inadequate for labour needs from the mid-nineteenth century, Britain supported Australian employers in their demand for cheap labour from elsewhere in the Empire: China, India and the South Pacific Islands. At this point the economic interests of Britain came into conflict with the demands of the nascent Australian labour movement. The call for decent wages came to be formulated in racist (and sexist) terms, as the demand for wages 'fit for white men'. Hostility towards Chinese and other Asian workers took on a violent character. The exclusionary boundaries of the emerging Australian nation were drawn on racial lines, and one of the first Acts of the new Federal Parliament in 1901 was the introduction of the White Australia Policy (see de Lepervanche, 1975).

Labour migration within Europe

In Europe, overseas migration and intra-European migration existed side-by-side throughout the nineteenth century. Of the 15 million Italians who emigrated from their country between 1876 and 1920, nearly half (6.8 million) went to other European countries (mainly France, Switzerland and Germany) (Cinanni, 1968: 29). As western Europeans went overseas in the (often vain) attempt to escape proletarianisation, workers from peripheral areas, like Poland,

54

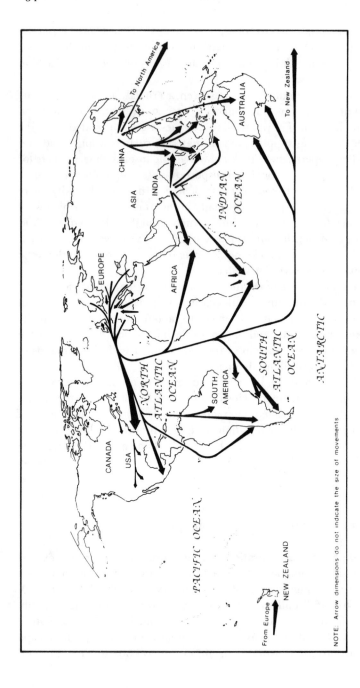

MAP 3.2

Labour migrations connected with industrialisation, 1850–1920

NOTE: Arrow dimensions do not indicate the size of movements

Ireland and Italy, were drawn in as replacement labour for large-scale agriculture and for industry.

As the earliest industrial country, Britain was the first to experience large-scale labour immigration. The new factory towns quickly absorbed labour surpluses from the countryside. Atrocious working and living conditions led to poor health, high infant mortality and short life expectancy in industrial areas. Low wage levels often forced both women and children to work, with disastrous results for the family. Natural increase was inadequate to meet the labour needs of rapidly growing industries and Britain's closest colony, Ireland, became a labour reserve. The devastation of Irish peasant agriculture through absentee landlords and enclosures, combined with the ruin of domestic industry through British competition, had led to widespread poverty. The famines of 1822 and 1846–7 triggered off massive migrations to Britain, the USA and Australia. By 1851 there were over 700 000 Irish in Britain, making up 3 per cent of the population of England and Wales and 7 per cent of the population of Scotland (Jackson, 1963). They were concentrated in the industrial cities, where they formed a high proportion of the workforce of the textile factories and the building trades. Irish 'navvies' (a slang term derived from 'navigators') dug Britain's canals and built her railways. Engels (1962) described the appalling situation of Irish workers, arguing that Irish immigration was a threat to the wages and living conditions of English workers (see also Castles and Kosack, 1973: 16–17). Certainly there was considerable conflict between the two groups, sometimes exploding in violence. Hostility and discrimination against the Irish was marked right into the twentieth century, and this was true of Australia too, where Irish immigration accompanied British settlement from the very outset. In both countries it was the active role played by Irish workers in the labour movement which was to finally overcome this split in the working class – just in time for its replacement by new divisions after 1945, when black workers came to Britain and Southern Europeans to Australia.

The next major migration to Britain was that of the 120 000 Jews, who came as refugees from the pogroms of Russia between 1875 and 1914. Most settled initially in the impoverished East End of London, where a large proportion became workers in the clothing industry. Jewish settlement became the focus of racist campaigns and demonstrations, leading to the first restrictionary legislation on immigration: the Aliens Act of 1905 and the Aliens Restriction Act of 1914 (Foot, 1965; Garrard, 1971). The Jewish experience of social mobility is often given as an example for the possibility of migrant success. Many of the first generation managed to shift out of wage employment to become small entrepreneurs in the rag trade or in the retail sector. They placed strong emphasis on good education for their children. The second generation was able, to a considerable extent, to move into business or white-collar employment, often paving the way for professional careers by the third generation. Interestingly one of Britain's newer immigrant groups – Bengalis from Bangladesh – now live in the same areas of the East End, often working in the same sweatshops, and worshipping in the same buildings – synogogues converted to mosques. However they are isolated by racism and violence, and show little sign at present of repeating the Jewish trajectory. It seems that British racism today is more rigid than a century ago.

Irish and Jewish migrant workers cannot be categorised as 'unfree workers'. The Irish were British subjects, with the same formal rights as other workers, while the Jews rapidly became British subjects. The constraints on their labour market freedom were not legal but economic – poverty and lack of resources made them accept inferior jobs and conditions – and social – discrimination and racism restricted their freedom of movement. It is in Germany and France that one finds the first large-scale use of the status of 'foreigner' to restrict workers' rights.

The heavy industries of the Ruhr, which emerged in the mid-nineteenth century, attracted agricultural workers away from the large agricultural estates of Eastern Prussia. Conditions in the mines were hard, but still preferable to low wages and semi-feudal oppression under the Junkers (large landowners). The workers who moved West were of Polish ethnic background, but had Prussian (and later German) citizenship, since Poland was at that time divided up between Prussia, the Austro-Hungarian Empire and Russia. By 1913, it was estimated that 164 000 of the 410 000 Ruhr miners were of Polish background (Stirn, 1964: 27). The Junkers tried to make up for the resulting labour shortages by recruiting 'foreign Poles' and Ukrainians as agricultural workers. Often workers were recruited in pairs – a man as cutter and a woman as binder – leading to what were known as 'harvest marriages'. However there was fear that settlement of Poles might weaken German control of the Eastern provinces. In

1885, the Prussian government deported some 40 000 Poles and closed the frontier. The landowners protested at the loss of up to two-thirds of their labour force (Dohse, 1981: 29–32), arguing that it threatened their economic survival.

By 1890, a compromise between political and economic interests emerged in the shape of a system of rigid control of foreign workers. 'Foreign Poles' were recruited as temporary seasonal workers only, were not allowed to bring dependants and were forced to leave German territory for several months each year. At first they were restricted to agricultural work, but later were permitted to take industrial jobs in Silesia and Thuringia (but not in Western areas such as the Ruhr). They were forced to accept work contracts giving rates of pay and conditions inferior to those of German workers. Special police sections were established to deal with 'violation of contracts' (that is, workers leaving for better-paid jobs) through forcible return of workers to their employers, imprisonment or deportation. Thus police measures against foreigners were deliberately used as a method to keep wages low and to create a split labour market (Dohse, 1981: 33-83).

Foreign labour played a major role in German industrialisation. Apart from the Poles in the East, there were large numbers of Italian workers in Southern Germany, and some Belgians and Dutch. In 1907, there were 950 000 foreign workers in the German Reich, of whom nearly 300 000 were in agriculture, 500 000 in industry and 86 000 in trade and transport (Dohse, 1981: 50). No figures are available on the total foreign population. The authorities did their best to prevent family reunion and permanent settlement. Both in fact took place, but the exact extent is unclear. The system developed to control and exploit foreign labour was a precursor both of the system of forced labour in the Nazi war economy, and of the 'guestworker system' in the German Federal Republic after the Second World War.

In France, too, the role of foreign labour was important, though different in character. The number of foreigners in France increased rapidly from 381 000 in 1851 (1.1 per cent of total population) to 1 million (2.7 per cent) in 1881, and then more slowly to 1.2 million (3 per cent) in 1911 (Weil, 1991: Appendix, Table 4). The majority came from neighbouring countries: Italy, Belgium, Germany and Switzerland, and later from Spain and Portugal. It was a relatively spontaneous movement, though some recruitment was carried out by farmers' associations and mines (Cross, 1983: Chapter 2). The foreign workers were mainly men and carried out unskilled manual work in agriculture, mines and steelworks – the heavy, unpleasant jobs that French workers were unwilling to take.

The peculiarity of the French case lies in the reasons for the shortage of labour during industrialisation. Birth rates fell sharply after 1860. The excess of births over deaths dropped from 5.8 per thousand of population in the period 1821–30, to 0.7 per thousand in the period 1891–1900. Peasants, shopkeepers and artisans followed 'Malthusian' birth control practices, which led to small families earlier than anywhere else (Cross, 1983: 5–7). According to Noiriel (1988: 297–312) the motives for this *grève des ventres* (belly strike) were bound up with resistance to proletarianisation on the part of petty proprietors. Keeping the family small meant that property could be passed on intact from generation to generation, and that there would be sufficient resources to permit a decent education for the children. Unlike Britain and Germany, France therefore saw relatively little overseas emigration during industrialisation. The only important exception was the movement of settlers to Algeria, which France invaded in 1830. Rural–urban migration was also fairly limited. The 'peasant worker' developed: the small farmer, who supplemented subsistence agriculture through sporadic work in local industries. Where people did leave the countryside it was often to move straight into the new government jobs that were proliferating in the latter part of the nineteenth century: straight from the primary to the tertiary sector.

In these circumstances, the shift from small to large-scale enterprises, made necessary by international competition from about the 1880s, could only be made through the employment of foreign workers, whose lack of resources compelled them to take unskilled factory and construction jobs. Thus labour immigration played a particularly important role both in the emergence of modern industry and in the constitution of the working class in France. Noiriel states that, from the mid-nineteenth century to the present, the labour market has been regularly fed by foreign immigration, making up, on average, 10–15 per cent of the working class. He estimates that without immigration the French population today would be only 35 million (instead of over 50 million) (Noiriel, 1988: 308–18).

The inter-war period

At the onset of the First World War, many migrants returned home to do military service or to participate in munitions production. In several countries, legislation was introduced to allow tight control of immigration and of foreign residents. However labour shortages soon developed in the combatant countries, leading to efforts to recruit foreign workers. The main demand was for male workers, to replace nationals sent to the front. The German authorities prevented 'foreign Polish' workers from leaving the country, and recruited additional workers by force in occupied areas of Russia and Belgium (Dohse, 1981: 77–81), foreshadowing the practices of the Nazis 25 years later. The French government set up recruitment systems for three separate categories. The first were workers from the North African and Indo-Chinese colonies, and from China (about 225 000 in all), who were recruited and controlled by a paramilitary organisation. They were housed in barracks, paid minimal wages and supervised by former colonial overseers. The second group were about 160 000 Iberian and Italian farmworkers, recruited by a body controlled by French farming employers. The third group consisted of about 81 000 workers recruited in Portugal, Spain, Italy and Greece to work in French factories (Cross, 1983: 34–42). Britain too recruited colonial workers during the conflict, although in smaller numbers. All the warring countries also made use of the forced labour of prisoners of war.

The period from 1918 to 1945 was one of reduced international labour migrations. This was partly because of economic stagnation and crisis, and partly because of increased hostility towards immigrants in many receiving areas. Migration to Australia, for example, fell to low levels as early as 1891, and did not grow substantially until after 1945. Southern Europeans who came to Australia in the 1920s were treated with suspicion. Immigrant ships were refused permission to land and there were 'anti-Dago' riots in the 1930s. Queensland passed special laws, prohibiting foreigners from owning land, and restricting them to certain industries (de Lepervanche, 1975).

Organised labour campaigned against immigration, fearing the effects on wages and conditions. Anti-immigration movements often took on a racist character. In the USA, for instance, it was alleged that Southern and Eastern Europeans were 'unassimilable' and that they presented threats to public order and American values. Congress enacted a series of laws in the 1920s designed to drastically limit entries from any area except Northwest Europe (Borjas, 1990: 28–9). The resulting national-origins quota system stopped large-scale immigration to the USA until the 1960s. But the new mass production industries of the Fordist era had a substitute labour force at hand: black workers from the Deep South. The period from about 1914 to the 1950s was that of the 'Great Migration' in which Afro-Americans fled segregation and exploitation in the southern states for better wages and – they hoped – equal rights in the Northeast, Midwest and West. Often they simply encountered new forms of segregation in the ghettoes of New York or Chicago, and new forms of discrimination, such as exclusion from the unions of the American Federation of Labor.

France was the only Western European country to experience substantial immigration in the inter-war years. Indeed, France briefly became the world's premier immigration land during this period. The 'demographic deficit' had been exacerbated by the war losses: 1.4 million men had been killed and 1.5 million permanently handicapped (Prost, 1966: 538). Workers were needed for reconstruction as well as for the industrial expansion of the 1920s. There was no return to the prewar free movement policy; instead the government and employers refined the foreign labour systems established during the war. Recruitment agreements were concluded with Poland, Italy and Czechoslovakia. Much of the recruitment was organised by the *Société générale d'immigration* (SGI), a private body set up by farm and mining interests. Foreign workers were to be controlled through a system of identity cards and work contracts, and were channelled into manual jobs in farming, construction and heavy industry, but most foreign workers probably arrived spontaneously outside of the recruiting system. The non-communist trade union movement co-operated with immigration, in return for measures designed to protect French workers from displacement and wage cutting, such as the law of 1926 which restricted foreign workers' rights to change jobs (Cross, 1983: 51–63; Weil, 1991a: 24–7).

Just under two million foreign workers entered France from 1920 to 1930 – about 567 000 of them recruited by the SGI (Cross, 1983:

60). Some 75 per cent of French population growth between 1921 and 1931 is estimated to have been the result of immigration (Decloîtres, 1967: 23). In view of the large female surplus in the French population, mainly men were recruited, and a fair degree of intermarriage took place. By 1931, there were 2.7 million foreigners in France (6.6 per cent of the total population). The largest group were Italians (808 000), followed by Poles (508 000), Spaniards (352 000) and Belgians (254 000) (Weil, 1991a: Appendix, Table 4). North African migration to France was also developing. Large colonies of Italians and Poles sprang up in the mining and heavy industrial towns of the North and East of France: in some towns the foreign population was a third or more of the total. There were Spanish and Italian agricultural settlements in the South-west.

During the depression of the 1930s, hostility towards foreigners increased, and a policy of discrimination in favour of French workers was followed. In 1932 a law fixed maximum quotas for foreign workers in firms, and this was followed by laws permitting dismissal of foreign workers in sectors where there was unemployment. Migrants were sacked and deported in large numbers (Weil, 1991a: 27–30). The foreign population dropped by half a million by 1936. Cross concludes that in the 1920s foreign workers 'provided a cheap and flexible workforce necessary for capital accumulation and economic growth; at the same time, aliens allowed the French worker a degree of economic mobility'. In the 1930s, on the other hand, immigration 'attenuated and provided a scapegoat for the economic crisis' (Cross, 1983: 218).

In Germany, the crisis-ridden Weimar Republic had little need of foreign workers: by 1932 their number was down to about 100 000, compared with nearly a million in 1907 (Dohse, 1981: 112). Nonetheless a new system of regulation of foreign labour developed in this period. Its principles were: strict state control of labour recruitment, employment preference for nationals, sanctions against employers of illegal migrants and unrestricted police power to deport unwanted foreigners (Dohse, 1981: 114–7). This system was partly attributable to the influence of the strong labour movement, which wanted measures to protect German workers, but it confirmed the weak legal position of migrant workers. Exhibit 3.2 describes the use of forced foreign labour during the Second World War.

EXHIBIT 3.2

Forced foreign labour in the Nazi war economy

The Nazi regime recruited enormous numbers of foreign workers – mainly by force – to replace the 11 million German workers conscripted for military service. The occupation of Poland, Germany's traditional labour reserve, was partly motivated by the need for labour. Labour recruitment offices were set up within weeks of the invasion, and the police and army rounded up thousands of young men and women (Dohse, 1981: 121). Forcible recruitment took place in all the countries invaded by Germany, while some voluntary labour was obtained from Italy, Croatia, Spain and other 'friendly or neutral countries'. By the end of the war, there were 7.5 million foreign workers in the Reich, of whom 1.8 million were prisoners of war. It is estimated that a quarter of industrial production was carried out by foreign workers in 1944 (Pfahlmann, 1968: 232). The Nazi war machine would have collapsed far earlier without foreign labour.

The basic principle for treating foreign workers declared by Sauckel, the Plenipotentiary for Labour, was that: 'All the men must be fed, sheltered and treated in such a way as to exploit them to the highest possible extent at the lowest conceivable degree of expenditure' (Homze, 1967: 113). This meant housing workers in barracks under military control, the lowest possible wages (or none at all), appalling social and health conditions, and complete deprivation of civil rights. Poles and Russians were compelled, like the Jews, to wear special badges showing their origin. Many foreign workers died through harsh treatment and cruel punishments. These were systematic; in a speech to employers, Sauckel emphasised the need for strict discipline: 'I don't care about them [the foreign workers] one bit. If they commit the most minor offence at work, report them to the police at once, hang them, shoot them. I don't care. If they are dangerous, they must be liquidated' (Dohse, 1981: 127).

The Nazis took exploitation of rightless migrants to an extreme which can only be compared with slavery, yet its legal core – the sharp division between the status of national and foreigner – was to be found both in earlier and later of foreign labour systems.

Conclusion

This historical account has given some examples of migratory movements before 1945. Contemporary migratory movements and policies are often profoundly influenced by such historical precedents. The chapter has shown how migratory movements arose out of European expansion into the New World, as well as through the industrial revolutions of the nineteenth century. It has described the key role of labour migration in colonial economies and in the process of industrialisation. Clearly labour migration has always been a major factor in the emergence of a capitalist world market. In the

USA, Canada, Australia, Britain, Germany and France (as well as in other countries not discussed here) migrant workers have played a role which varies in character, according to economic and social conditions and the role of the state. But in every case the contribution of migration to industrialisation and population building was important – sometimes even decisive.

To what extent does the four-stage model of the migratory process suggested in Chapter 2 apply to the historical examples given? Involuntary movements of slaves and indentured workers do not easily fit the model, for the intentions of the participants played little part. Nonetheless some aspects apply: labour recruitment as the initial impetus, predominance of young males in the early stages, family formation, long-term settlement and emergence of ethnic minorities. Worker migrations to England, Germany and France in the nineteenth and twentieth centuries fit the model well. Their original intention was temporary, but they led to family reunion and settlement. With regard to the migrations to North America and Australasia in the nineteenth and early twentieth centuries, there is a widespread belief that most migrants went with the intention of permanent settlement. This is true of many people, but not all. Many young men and women went in order to work for a few years and then return home. Many did return, while others stayed and settled. In the long run, the majority remained in the New World, forming new ethnic groups which were to remain visible for generations. Here too, the model seems to fit.

Our account cannot be comprehensive, in view of the large variety of migratory movements in the last few hundred years. Clearly the study of migrant labour is not the only way of looking at the history of migration. Movements caused by political or religious persecution have always been important. Refugee settlement has played a major part in the development of countries as diverse as the USA and Germany. It is often impossible to draw strict lines between the various types of migration. Migrant labour systems have always led to some degree of settlement, just as settler and refugee movement have always been bound up with the political economy of capitalist development.

The period from about 1850 to 1914 was an era of mass migration. It was also a time of industrialisation and economic growth in Western Europe and the USA. Industrialisation was a cause of both emigration and immigration (sometimes in the same country, as the

British case shows). After 1914, war, xenophobia and economic stagnation caused a considerable decline in migration, and the large-scale movements of the preceding period seemed to be the results of a unique and unrepeatable constellation. When rapid and sustained economic growth got under way after the Second World War, the new age of migration was to take the world by surprise.

4

Migration to Highly-developed Countries since 1945

Since the end of the Second World War, international migrations have grown in volume and changed in character. There have been two main phases. In the first, from 1945 to the early 1970s, the main economic strategy of large-scale capital was concentration of investment and expansion of production in the existing highly-developed countries. As a result, large numbers of migrant workers were drawn from less-developed countries or from the European periphery into the fast-expanding industrial areas of Western Europe, North America and Australia. The end of this phase was marked by the 'oil crisis' of 1973–4. The ensuing recession gave impetus to a restructuring of the world economy, involving capital investment in new industrial areas, altered patterns of world trade, and introduction of new technologies. The result was a second phase in international migration, starting in the mid-1970s and gaining momentum in the late 1980s and early 1990s. This phase involved complex new patterns of migration, affecting both old and new receiving countries. This chapter will discuss post-1945 migratory movements to highly-developed countries, including Western Europe, North America and Australia. Labour migration to Japan, which is a phenomenon of the last ten years, will be discussed in Chapter 6, in the context of Asian regional migration.

Migration in the long boom[1]

Between 1945 and the early 1970s, three main types of migration led to the formation of new, ethnically distinct populations in advanced industrial countries:

● migration of workers from the European periphery to western Europe, often through 'guestworker systems';
● migration of 'colonial workers' to the former colonial powers;
● permanent migration to North America and Australia, at first from Europe and later from Asia and Latin America.

The precise timing of these movements varied somewhat. For instance they started later in Germany and ended earlier in Britain. Migration to USA grew rapidly after the new Immigration Act of 1965 and, unlike the case of Western Europe and Australia, did not decline at all in the mid-1970s. These three types, which all engendered processes of family reunion and other kinds of chain migration, will be examined here. There were also other types of migration which will not be examined in detail here, since they did not contribute decisively to the formation of ethnic minorities:

● mass movements of European refugees at the end of the Second World War;[2]
● return migrations of former colonists to their countries of origin as colonies gained their independence.
● mobility of highly-qualified personnel, often within trans-national corporations and intergovernmental organisations.

Foreign workers and 'guestworker' systems

All the highly-industrialised countries of Western Europe used temporary labour recruitment at some stage between 1945 and 1973, although in certain cases this played a smaller role than spontaneous entries of foreign workers. The rapidly expanding economies were able to utilise the labour reserves of the poorer and less industrialised European periphery: the Mediterranean countries, Ireland and Finland. The reasons for underdevelopment in these countries varies. In some cases it was the result of former colonisation

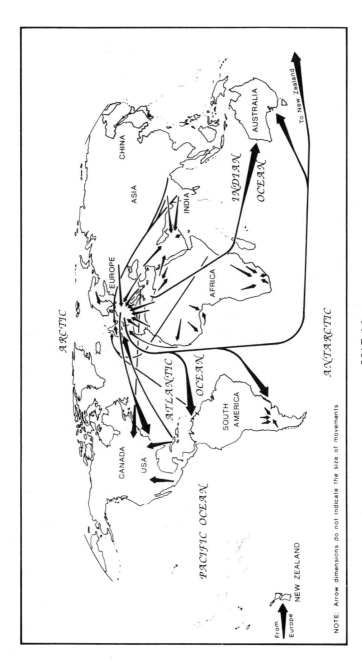

MAP 4.1
Global migrations, 1945–73

NOTE: Arrow dimensions do not indicate the size of movements

(Ireland, Finland, Algeria). The backwardness of Southern European countries was partly the result of domination by more powerful neighbours, partly the result of wartime devastation.

Immediately after the Second World War, the British government brought in 90 000 mainly male workers from refugee camps and from Italy through the European Voluntary Worker (EVW) scheme. EVWs were tied to designated jobs, had no right to family reunion, and could be deported for indiscipline. The scheme was fairly small and only operated until 1951, because it was easier to make use of colonial workers (see below). A further 100 000 Europeans entered Britain on work permits between 1946 and 1951, and some European migration continued subsequently, though it was not a major flow.

Belgium also started recruiting foreign workers immediately after the war. They were mainly Italian men, and were employed in the coal mines and the iron and steel industry. The system operated until 1963, after which foreign work-seekers were allowed to come of their own accord. Many brought in dependants and settled permanently, changing the ethnic composition of Belgium's industrial areas.

France established an Office National d'Immigration (ONI) in 1945 to organise recruitment of foreign workers from Southern Europe. Migration was seen as a solution to post-war labour shortages, particularly of male workers, and was expected to be mainly temporary. However, in view of continuing low birth rates, some family settlement was envisaged. Employers had to apply to ONI for foreign labour, and to pay a per capita fee. ONI also co-ordinated the employment of up to 150 000 seasonal agricultural workers per year, mainly from Spain. By 1970, two million foreign workers and 690 000 dependants had entered France. Many found it easier to come as 'tourists', get a job and then regularise their situation. This applied particularly to Portuguese and Spanish workers escaping their respective dictatorships, who generally lacked passports. By 1968, ONI statistics revealed that 82 per cent of the aliens admitted by the ONI came illegally as 'clandestines'. In any case, ONI had no jurisdiction over French citizens from overseas departments and territories and immigrants from former colonies, who could enter freely or under special arrangements.

Switzerland pursued a policy of large-scale labour import from 1945 to 1974. Foreign workers were recruited abroad by employers, while admission and residence were controlled by the government.

Conditions were restrictive, with prohibitions on job changing, permanent settlement and family reunion. Considerable use was also made of seasonal workers (in agriculture and the tourism industry) and of cross-frontier commuters. Both these groups were seen as part of the labour force but not of the population – 'guestworkers' par excellence. Swiss industry became highly dependent on foreign workers, who made up nearly a third of the labour force by the early 1970s. The need to attract and retain workers, in a situation of international competition for labour, coupled with diplomatic pressure from Italy, led to relaxations on family reunion and permanent stay, so that Switzerland too experienced the formation of migrant communities and increasing cultural diversity.

The examples could be continued: the Netherlands brought in 'guestworkers' in the 1960s and early 1970s, Luxembourg's industries were highly dependent on foreign labour, and Sweden employed workers from Finland and from southern European countries.[3] The key case for understanding the 'guestworker system' was the Federal Republic of Germany (FRG) which set up a highly organised state recruitment apparatus (see Exhibit 4.1)

In the FRG we see in the most developed form all the principles – but also the contradictions – of temporary foreign labour recruitment systems. These include the belief in temporary sojourn, the restriction of labour market and civil rights, the recruitment of single workers (men at first, but with increasing numbers of women as time went on), the inability completely to prevent family reunion, the gradual move towards longer stay, the inexorable pressures for settlement and community formation. The FRG took the system furthest, but its central element – the legal distinction between the status of citizen and of foreigner as a criterion for determining rights of work, social security and residence – was to be found throughout Europe (see Hammar, 1985a, for an overview).

Multinational and bilateral agreements were also used to facilitate labour migration. Free movement of workers within the European Community, which came into force in 1968, was relevant mainly for Italian workers going to Germany, while the Nordic Labour Market affected Finns going to Sweden. The European Community arrangements were the first step towards creating a 'European labour market', which becomes a reality from 1993. However, in the 1960s and early 1970s, labour movement within the Community was

---

EXHIBIT 4.1

The German 'guestworker' system

The German Government started recruiting foreign workers in the late 1950s. The Federal Labour Office (*Bundesanstalt für Arbeit* – BfA) set up recruitment offices in the Mediterranean countries. Employers requiring foreign labour paid a fee to the BfA, which selected workers, testing occupational skills, providing medical examinations and screening police records. The workers were brought in groups to Germany, where employers had to provide initial accommodation. Recruitment, working conditions and social security were regulated by bilateral agreements between the FRG and the sending countries: first Italy, then Greece, Turkey, Morocco, Portugal, Tunisia and Yugoslavia.

The number of foreign workers in the FRG rose from 95 000 in 1956 to 1.3 million in 1966 and 2.6 million in 1973. This massive migration was the result of rapid industrial expansion and the shift to new methods of mass production, which required large numbers of low-skilled workers. Foreign women workers played a major part, especially in the later years: their labour was in high demand in textiles and clothing, electrical goods and other manufacturing sectors.

German policies conceived migrant workers as temporary labour units, which could be recruited, utilised and sent away again as employers required. To enter and remain in the FRG, a migrant needed a residence permit and a labour permit. These were granted for restricted periods, and were often valid only for specific jobs and areas. Entry of dependants was discouraged. A worker could be deprived of his or her permit for a variety of reasons, leading to deportation.

But it was impossible to prevent family reunion and settlement. Often officially recruited migrants were able to get employers to request their wives or husbands as workers. Competition with other labour-importing countries for labour led to relaxation of restrictions on entry of dependants in the 1960s. Families became established and children were born. Foreign labour was beginning to lose its mobility and social costs (for housing, education and health care) could no longer be avoided. When the Federal government stopped labour recruitment in November 1973, the motivation was not only the looming 'oil crisis', but also the belated realisation that permanent immigration was taking place.

---

actually declining, owing to gradual equalisation of wages and living standards within the EC, while migration from outside the community was increasing. Table 4.1 shows the development of minority populations arising from migration in selected Western European countries.

TABLE 4.1

Minority population in the main Western European countries of immigration, 1950–75 (thousands)

Country	1950	1960	1970	1975	Per cent of total population 1975
Belgium	354	444	716	835	8.5
France	2 128	2 663	3 339	4 196	7.9
West Germany	548	686	2 977	4 090	6.6
Great Britain	1 573	2 205	3 968	4 153	7.8
Netherlands	77	101	236	370	2.6
Sweden	124	191	411	410	5.0
Switzerland	279	585	983	1 012	16.0

Notes: Figures for all countries except Great Britain are for foreign residents. They exclude naturalised persons and immigrants from the Dutch and French colonies. Great Britain data are Census figures for 1951, 1961 and 1971 and estimates for 1975. The 1951 and 1961 data are for overseas-born persons, and exclude children born to immigrants in Great Britain. The 1971 and 1975 figures include children born in Great Britain, with both parents born abroad.

Source: Castles *et al.*, 1984: 87–8 (where detailed sources are given).

Colonial workers

Migration from former colonies was significant for Britain, France and the Netherlands. Britain had a net inflow of about 350 000 from Ireland, its traditional labour reserve, between 1946 and 1959. Irish workers provided a source of manual labour for industry and construction. Many brought in their families and settled permanently. Irish residents in Britain enjoyed all civil rights, including the right to vote. Immigration of workers – both male and female – from the New Commonwealth (former British colonies in the Caribbean, the Indian sub-continent and Africa) started after 1945 and grew during the 1950s. Some workers came as a result of direct recruitment by London Transport, but most came spontaneously in response to labour demand. By 1951, there were 218 000 people of New Commonwealth origin,[4] a figure which increased to 541 000 in 1961. Entry of workers from the New Commonwealth almost stopped after 1962, partly owing to the introduction of severe restrictions through the Commonwealth Immigrants Act of 1962, and partly as the result of the early onset of economic stagnation in Britain.

However most of the Commonwealth immigrants had come to stay, and family reunion continued, until it in turn was restricted by the 1971 Immigration Act. The population of New Commonwealth origin increased to 1.2 million in 1971 and 1.5 million in 1981. Most Afro-Caribbean and Asian immigrants and their children in Britain enjoyed formal citizenship (although this no longer applies to the small number admitted since the 1981 Nationality Act). Their minority status was not defined by their being foreign, but by widespread institutional and informal discrimination. Most black and Asian workers found unskilled manual jobs in industry and the services, and a high degree of residential segregation emerged in the inner cities. Educational and social disadvantage of black and Asian settlers became marked – a further obstacle to social mobility out of initial low-status positions. By the 1970s, the emergence of ethnic minorities was inescapable.

France experienced large-scale spontaneous immigration from its former colonies, as well as from Southern Europe. By 1970 there were over 600 000 Algerians, 140 000 Moroccans and 90 000 Tunisians. Increasing numbers of black workers were also coming in from the former West African colonies of Senegal, Mali and Mauritania. Some of these migrants came before independence, for example before 1962 in the case of Algeria, when they were still French citizens. Others came later through preferential migration arrangements, or simply came illegally. Many people also came from the 'Overseas Departments' of Guadeloupe and Martinique in the Caribbean, and Réunion in the Indian Ocean. These migrants were French citizens, so there were no figures, though estimates put their number at 250 000 to 300 000 in 1972. All these migrations were initially male-dominated, but with increasing proportions of women as the movement matured. The situation of non-European immigrants in France was very like that of New Commonwealth immigrants in Britain: they were relegated to the bottom of the labour market, often working in highly exploitative conditions. Housing was frequently segregated, and very poor in quality – indeed shanty towns (known as 'bidonvilles') appeared in France in the 1960s. Extreme-right groups began to subject non-European immigrants to a campaign of racial violence: 32 Algerians were murdered in 1973.

The Netherlands had two main inflows from former colonies. Between 1945 and the early 1960s up to 300 000 'repatriates' from the former Dutch East Indies (now Indonesia) entered the Netherlands.

Although most had been born overseas and many were of mixed Dutch and Indonesian parentage, they were Dutch citizens. The official policy of assimilation appears to have worked well in this case, and there is little evidence of racism or discrimination against this group.[5] After 1965, increasing numbers of black workers came to the Netherlands from the Caribbean territory of Surinam. A peak was reached in the two years leading up to independence in 1975, at which time Surinamese (except those already living in the Netherlands) lost their Dutch citizenship. By the late 1970s there were estimated to be 160 000 Surinamese in the Netherlands.

Permanent migration to North America and Australia

Large-scale migration to the USA developed later than in Western Europe, owing to the restrictive legislation enacted in the 1920s. Intakes averaged 250 000 persons annually in the 1951–60 period, and 330 000 annually during 1961–70 – a far cry from the average of 880 000 immigrants per year during 1901–10. The 1970 Census showed that the number of overseas-born people had declined to 9.6 million, only 4.7 per cent of the population (Briggs, 1984: 7). The 1965 amendments to the Immigration and Nationality Act were seen as part of the civil rights legislation of the period, designed to remove the discriminatory national-origins quota system. They were not expected or intended to lead to large-scale non-European immigration (Borjas, 1990: 29–33). In fact the amendments created a system of worldwide immigration, in which the most important criterion for admission was kinship with US citizens or residents. The result was a dramatic upsurge in migration from Asia and Latin America.

US employers, particularly in agriculture, also recruited temporary migrant workers, mainly men, in Mexico and the Caribbean. Organised labour was highly critical, arguing that domestic workers would be displaced and wages held down. Government policies varied: at times, systems of temporary labour recruitment, such as the Mexican *Bracero* Programme of the 1940s, were introduced. In other periods recruitment was formally prohibited, but tacitly tolerated, leading to the presence of a large number of illegal workers. These temporary contract workers, whether legal or illegal, have had a role similar to that of seasonal workers from Southern Europe in French and Swiss agriculture.

Canada followed policies of mass immigration after 1945. At first only Europeans were admitted. The Immigration Act of 1952 permitted the refusal of immigrants on the basis of nationality, citizenship, ethnic group, occupation, class or geographical area. In the early years most entrants were British, but Eastern and Southern Europeans soon played an increasing role. The largest immigrant streams in the 1950s and 1960s were of Germans, Italians and Dutch. The introduction of a non-discriminatory 'points system' for screening potential migrants after the 1966 White Paper opened the door for non-European migrants. The main source countries in the 1970s were Jamaica, India, Portugal, the Philippines, Greece, Italy and Trinidad (Breton *et al.*, 1990: 14–16). Throughout the period, family entry was encouraged, and immigrants were seen as settlers and future citizens.

Australia initiated a programme of large-scale immigration after 1945, because policy-makers believed that the population of 7.5 million needed to be increased for both economic and strategic reasons.[6] The policy, summed up in the popular slogan 'populate or perish', was one of population expansion through permanent, family immigration. The initial target was 70 000 migrants per year and a ratio of ten British migrants to every 'foreigner'. However it proved impossible to attract enough British migrants. The Department of Immigration began recruiting in European Displaced Persons Camps, giving preference to refugees from the Baltic and Slavic countries, who were perceived as both 'racially acceptable' and anti-communist. Gradually the concept of 'acceptable European races' widened to included Northern Europeans and then Southern Europeans. By the 1950s, the largest sources of migrants were Italy, Greece and Malta. Non-Europeans were not admitted at all, as the White Australia Policy remained in force until the late 1960s. Despite the policy of family migration, there was a male surplus among entrants, leading to schemes to encourage single women to come from Britain and elsewhere. It was not until 1975 that women were allowed to migrate as heads of families.

Immigration was high throughout the 1950s and 1960s and was widely regarded as the motor of post-war growth: from 1947 to 1973 it provided 50 per cent of labour force growth, giving Australia the highest rate of increase of any OECD country. By the late 1960s, it was becoming hard to attract Southern European migrants, and many were returning to their homelands, in response to economic developments there. The result was a series of measures to attract and retain migrants: further liberalisation of family reunions, recruitment in Yugoslavia and Latin America, and some relaxations of the White Australia Policy. By the 1970s Australian manufacturing industry relied heavily on migrant labour and factory jobs were popularly known as 'migrant work'.

Comparative perspectives

One common feature in the migratory movements of the 1945–73 period is the predominance of economic motivations. Foreign worker movements to Western Europe were caused primarily by economic considerations on the part of migrants, employers and governments. The same is true of temporary worker recruitment for US agriculture. Economic motives played a major part in Australia's post-war migration programme, although population building was also a consideration. The colonial workers who migrated to Britain, France and the Netherlands generally had economic reasons, although for the governments political considerations (such as the desire to maintain links with former colonies) also played a part. Permanent migration to the USA was probably the movement in which economic factors were least dominant – at least for policy-makers. The post-1965 admission criteria were based mainly on family links. Yet the migrants themselves often had economic motivations, and their labour played a major role in the growth of the US economy. Of course there were also refugee migrations, in which economic motivations were secondary. The overwhelmingly economic motivation for migration was to become less clear-cut in the post-1973 period.

How important was labour migration for the economies of the receiving countries? Some economists have argued that availability of large supplies of additional labour was crucial to expansion. Moreover the migrants provided replacements for local workers, who were able to obtain more highly-skilled jobs during the boom. Without the flexibility provided by immigration, bottlenecks in production and inflationary tendencies would have developed, leading to restraints on growth. However other economists have argued that immigration reduced the incentive for rationalisation, keeping low-productivity firms viable and holding back the shift to more capital-intensive forms of production. This school of thought also claims that social capital expenditure on housing and social services for immigrants reduced the capital available for productive investment. Without going into a detailed analysis, it may be said that there is strong evidence that it was the high net immigration countries, like the FRG, Switzerland, France and Australia, which had the highest economic growth rates in the 1945–73 period. Countries with relatively low net immigration (like Britain and the USA at this time) had much lower growth rates.[7] Thus the argument that immigration was economically beneficial in this period is convincing.

Another general feature of the 1945–73 period was growing diversity of areas of origin, and increasing cultural difference between migrants and receiving populations. At the beginning of the period, most migrants to all main receiving countries came from various parts of Europe. As time went on, increasing proportions came from Asia, Africa and Latin America. This trend was to become even more marked in the following period.

A comparison of the situation of colonial workers with that of guestworkers is instructive. The differences are obvious: colonial workers were citizens of the former colonial power, or had some preferential entitlement to enter and live there. They usually came spontaneously, often following lines of communication built up in the colonial period. Once they came in, they generally had civil and political rights; most (though by no means all) intended to stay permanently. On the other hand, guestworkers and other foreign workers were non-citizens. They had no right to enter or work in the receiving country. Most came because they were recruited; some came spontaneously and were able to regularise their situation; others came illegally and worked without documentation. In each case, their rights were severely restricted. Generally they were seen as temporary workers who were expected to leave after a few years. Permanent settlement and family reunion was not envisaged.

But there are also similarities, especially in the economic and social situations of the two categories. Both became overwhelmingly concentrated in low-skilled manual work, mainly in industry and construction. Both tended to suffer sub-standard housing, poor social conditions and educational disadvantage. Over time, there was a convergence of legal situations, with family reunion and social rights of foreign workers improving, while the colonial migrants lost many of their privileges with regard to entry, family reunion and citizenship. Finally, as will be shown below, both groups were affected by similar processes of marginalisation, leading to a degree of separation from the rest of the population and an emerging ethnic minority position.

Migrations in the period of global economic restructuring

The ending of organised recruitment of manual workers by industrialised countries in the early 1970s was not a mere conjunctural phenomenon, but rather a reaction to a fundamental restructuring of the labour process and of the world economy. The subsequent period has been marked by:

● changes in global investment patterns, with increased capital export from developed countries and establishment of manufacturing industries in some previously underdeveloped areas;

● the micro-electronic revolution, which has reduced the need for manual workers in manufacturing;

● erosion of traditional skilled manual occupations in highly-developed countries;

● expansion in the services sector, with demand for both highly-skilled and low-skilled workers;

● growing informal sectors in the economies of developed countries;

● casualisation of employment, growth in part-time work, increasingly insecure conditions of employment;

● increased differentiation of labour forces on the basis of gender, age and ethnicity, through mechanisms which push many women, young people and members of minorities into casual or informal-sector work.

These rapid changes in global economic and political relationships have had dramatic effects in Africa, Asia and Latin America. In some countries, rapid industrialisation and social change have taken place, leading to the emergence of 'newly industrialising countries' (NICs). In the oil-rich OPEC countries, reinvestment of oil profits after 1973 led to industrialisation and social change. But in large areas of Africa, Latin America and Asia, post-colonial development strategies have failed. Many countries are marked by rapid population growth, overuse and destruction of natural resources, uncontrolled urbanisation, political instability, falling living standards, poverty and even famine. Thus the idea of the 'third world' as an area with common economic problems and development perspectives has lost its meaning, and has largely been replaced by the idea of a 'South–North divide'. Economic crisis and social change in the South is generating new pressures for migration to the North.

These developments have led to considerable shifts in existing migratory patterns as well as to new forms of migration. Main trends include:

● decline of labour migration to Western Europe;
● family reunion of former foreign workers and colonial workers, and formation of new ethnic minorities;
● transition of some Southern European countries from countries of emigration to countries of immigration;
● continuation of mainly economically motivated migration to the 'classical immigration countries' of North America and Oceania, but with considerable shifts in the areas of origin and the forms of migration;
● new migratory movements (both internal and international) connected with economic and social change in the newly industrialising countries;
● recruitment of foreign labour, mainly from less-developed countries, by oil-rich countries;
● development of mass movements of refugees and asylum-seekers, generally moving from South to North, but also (especially after the collapse of the Soviet Bloc) from East to West;[8]
● increasing international mobility of highly-qualified personnel, in both temporary and permanent flows.

These movements will be examined in more detail below. However it is important to realise that administrative classifications of migratory movements can be misleading. Chain migrations often cut across a whole range of definitions, and migrants may move from one category to another. The main population flows of the post-1973 period are shown in Map 1.1 on page 6.

Migrants and minorities in Western Europe

The post-1973 period was one of consolidation and demographic normalisation of immigrant populations in Western Europe. Recruitment of both foreign workers and colonial workers largely ceased, especially between the mid-1970s and the mid-1980s. For colonial migrants in Britain, France and the Netherlands, trends to family reunion and permanent settlement continued. Socioeconomic disadvantage, discrimination and racism tended to constitute these groups as ethnic minorities, partially excluded from the mainstream of society. At the same time, the settlement process and the emergence of second and third generations, born in Western Europe, led to internal differentiation and the development of community structures and consciousness. By the 1980s, colonial migrants and their descendants had become clearly visible social groups.

Permanent settlement had not been envisaged for the foreign workers. When the German federal government stopped recruitment in 1973 and other governments followed suit, they hoped that the now unwanted 'guests' would go away. In fact some foreign workers did go home, but many stayed. Governments generally were unable to stop the process of family reunion. Foreign populations changed in structure. In the FRG, for instance, the number of foreign men declined slightly between 1974 and 1981, but the number of foreign women increased by 12 per cent, while the number of children aged up to 15 grew by 52 per cent (Castles *et al.*, 1984: 102). Instead of declining, as policy-makers had expected, the total foreign population of the FRG remained fairly constant at about four million in the late 1970s, only to increase again to 4.5 million in the early 1980s and over five million by 1990.

Trends were similar in other countries. By 1991 the total foreign population of Western European countries was estimated by the ILO to be 18 million, 13 million of whom were in EC member states; of these eight million were non-EC citizens, with about a quarter coming from Turkey and a further quarter from North Africa. If British citizens originating from the Indian sub-continent are included, there were 5–5.5 million Muslims in Western Europe. It was also estimated that around 2.6 million foreigners were in irregular or undocumented situations in 1991 (Böhning, 1991a).

Moreover the foreigners who left after 1973 were mainly those from the most developed countries, where there was some prospect of work for returnees. Those who stayed were from more distant and underdeveloped areas, in particular Turkey and North Africa. The stopping of labour migration thus helped increase the non-European share of immigrant populations. It was above all the non-European groups who experienced socioeconomic exclusion through discrimination and racism, like the former colonial worker groups. The mechanisms of marginalisation varied with, for example employment preference for nationals over foreigners in one case, informal discrimination against black workers in the other, but the consequences were the same – low-grade jobs and high unemployment rates for immigrants.

Some intra-European Community movement did continue after 1973. It was increasingly an individual migration, generally of skilled workers or highly-qualified personnel. By the late 1980s it was becoming customary to treat the EC as a single labour market, and to see intra-EC mobility as analagous to internal migration within a national economy. Table 4.2 gives information on the foreign population of some European immigration countries.

TABLE 4.2

Foreign resident population in selected OECD countries (thousands)

Country	1980	1985	1990	Per cent of total population 1990
Austria	283	272	413	5.3
Belgium		845	905	9.1
Denmark	102	117	161	3.1
France	3 714*		3 608	6.4
Germany	4453	4 379	5 242	8.2
Italy	299	423	781	1.4
Luxembourg	94	98		27.5**
Netherlands	521	553	692	4.6
Norway	83	102	143	3.4
Sweden	422	389	484	5.6
Switzerland	893	940	1 100	16.3
United Kingdom		1 731	1 875	3.3

Notes: * Figure for 1982. ** Figure for 1989.
These figures are for foreign population. They therefore exclude naturalised immigrants (particularly important for France, the United Kingdom and Sweden). They also exclude immigrants from colonies or former colonies with the citizenship of the immigration country (particularly important for France, the Netherlands and the United Kingdom). The figures for the UK in this table are not comparable with the birthplace figures given in Table 4.1.
Source: OECD SOPEMI, 1992: 131.

Southern Europe

Italy, Greece, Spain and Portugal have long histories of emigration. After 1973, they all experienced some return migration from former labour-recruiting countries. However, by the 1980s, a major reversal of historical patterns had developed, with the Southern European countries becoming receivers of immigrants from Africa and Asia. The causes were economic development and declining demographic growth in Southern Europe. In Italy, for instance, the total fertility rate[9] had fallen to 1.3 by the late 1980s (as low as in the FRG).

In Italy, the legal foreign population grew from 299 000 in 1980 to 781 000 in 1990 (OECD SOPEMI, 1992). This figure is unreliable because of lack of accurate data on illegal immigrants, who were estimated at between 150 000 and 250 000 in 1988. Main immigrant groups consisting mainly of males include Moroccans, Ethiopians, Egyptians and Senegalese, while migrants from the Philippines and Sri Lanka are mainly women, often employed in domestic service. Many migrants work legally in manufacturing and other sectors, but others are employed illegally in agriculture, domestic service and informal-sector jobs, or are engaged in peddling and other marginal activities. Legal changes, including amnesties for over 300 000 illegal entrants in 1986 and 1990, have done little to resolve the situation. Policy-makers have been caught by surprise by the rapid change from being a country of emigration to one of immigration, and there is a lack of clear policy, although Italy's first Immigration Minister was appointed in 1991.

Other Southern European countries have experienced similar developments. In Spain the official number of foreign residents doubled from about 200 000 in 1980 to 400 000 in 1989. In Portugal there were about 100 000 foreign residents in 1989. Estimates for Greece are very vague. Many recent entrants from the former Soviet Union or from Cyprus and Turkey are of Greek ethnicity. All the Southern European countries still have some emigration to other European countries, as well as increasing numbers of immigrants. The European immigrant flows are partly the result of increasing European integration and include relatively high income groups such as professionals or people attracted by the life style. Other immigrants come because of the crises in Eastern Europe (as with Albanians moving to Greece). The migrations from outside Europe are partly connected with former colonial links (for example Latin Americans in Spain, people from former African colonies in Portugal), but there are increasing spontaneous movements of unskilled migrant workers from North Africa and Asia (OECD SOPEMI, 1991, 21–5).

North America and Australia

Migration to the USA continued to grow throughout the 1970s, with intakes averaging 450 000 per year, and the 1980s, with intakes of about 600 000 per year. Some 40 per cent of US population growth in the 1970s came through immigration. By 1980 there were 13.9 million foreign-born people in the USA, 6.2 per cent of total population. The largest concentrations were in New York State (13.4 per cent of the state's population) and California (14.8 per cent of population) (Briggs, 1984: 77).

The entry system established by the 1965 amendments had unexpected results (see Borjas, 1990: 26–39). People of Latin American and Asian origin in the USA were able to use family reunion provisions to initiate processes of chain migration, which brought about a major shift in ethnic composition. In the 1951–60 period, Europeans made up 53 per cent of immigrants, compared with 40 per cent from the Americas and only 8 per cent from Asia. During 1971–80, Europeans constituted 18 per cent of new entrants, compared with 44 per cent from the Americas and 35 per cent from Asia. By the 1981–6 period, Europeans had declined to 11 per cent of entrants, while 38 per cent came from the Americas and 47 per cent from Asia. Concern was expressed that the immigration rules made it difficult for people to enter from Europe, leading to calls for the admission of people from 'traditional source countries' (such as Ireland) under special provisions. In 1990, Congress passed new legislation to increase the number of immigrants coming from Europe. The new law also increased the number of immigrants admitted on the basis of skills, leading to an overall increase in intakes.

The movement of temporary migrant workers to the USA has also continued, much of it in the form of illegal migration across the southern border. Mexican farmworkers have long played a crucial role for US agribusiness, which has opposed any measures for effective control-such as sanctions against employers of illegal workers. The number of undocumented workers is thought to be at least three to four million, though some estimates are as high as 10 million. The

Immigration Reform and Control Act of 1986 (IRCA) introduced a limited amnesty for undocumented workers. Approximately three million persons (over 70 per cent of them Mexicans) applied for amnesty (Borjas, 1990: 61–74). Most applicants were granted resident alien status, swelling the number of aliens admitted to the USA as permanent residents to more than 1.5 million in 1990 and 1.8 million in 1991. IRCA also imposed sanctions against employers of illegal workers, as well as authorising a Replenishment Agricultural Workers (RAW) Program to bring in legal 'guestworkers' if a shortage of labour should develop. However illegal immigration continued and the ease of falsifying identification documents undercut enforcement of employers sanctions, so that no shortage materialised.

In Canada, the overall number of entries increased considerably: the total was 89 000 in 1983, but 192 000 in 1989. Entries from Asia, Africa and the Middle East, and from the Caribbean and Latin America have grown rapidly, while European migration has declined. In 1989, about 40 per cent of immigrants came from Asia and the Pacific, 27 per cent from Europe, 16 per cent from Africa and the Middle East, 13.5 per cent from the Caribbean and Latin America and under 5 per cent from the USA. Hong Kong was the biggest single source country, followed by Poland (OECD SOPEMI, 1991: 44, 173). In 1990, the Canadian government announced a five-year immigration plan, designed to maintain the principles of family reunion and support for refugees, while at the same time increasing entries of skilled workers. The plan aimed to raise total entries to 220 000 for 1991 and then to 250 000 per year during 1992–95.

When the world recession of the 1970s hit Australia, the Labor Party government drastically cut immigration: the average level was 56 000 per year from 1971 to 1976. It also finally abolished the White Australia Policy, introducing entry criteria which did not discriminate on the basis of race, ethnicity, religion or national origin. The succeeding Liberal–Country Party government increased immigration to around 100 000 per year in the late 1970s and early 1980s. At the same time, the Indo-Chinese crisis led to the arrival of refugee boats from Vietnam. To prevent spontaneous and potentially uncontrollable entries of boat-people, Australia agreed to join the international relief effort. This led to the entry of large numbers of Vietnamese refugees, soon followed by refugees from the civil war in Lebanon. Australian openness to family reunion led to enduring patterns of chain migration from these areas. Recent immigration levels have fluctuated according to economic conditions. They were low (60 000–100 000 per year) in the recession of the early 1980s, high in the late 1980s (up to 140 000 per year) and declined again in the recession of 1991–2. Immigration from Asia (particularly Southeast Asia and the Indian sub-continent) is now the largest component of entry, making up 35–45 per cent of total intakes. A large proportion of entrants continue to come from Britain and New Zealand. Recently there has been an upsurge in applications for migration to Australia from Russia and other Eastern European countries.

Refugees and asylum-seekers

The current world refugee crisis began to develop in the mid-1970s, with mass departures from Vietnam, Kampuchea and Laos. Soon after, large numbers of refugees had to leave Lebanon and Afghanistan. In Africa, thousands fled from Zaire, Uganda, Namibia and South Africa. In Latin America, the suppression of democracy in countries such as Chile and Argentina led to exoduses. Political, ethnic and religious persecution seemed to be an almost inevitable accompaniment of political and economic change in poor countries, while the intervention of the leading Cold War powers often made human rights violations even worse. The number of refugees worldwide grew from 8.2 million in 1980 to 15 million by the end of the decade. Some estimates put the number at 20 million in 1992. A new phenomenon developed: the so-called 'jet-age asylum-seekers', who arrive by air or other means and ask for asylum once in the country. Many states have introduced complex, costly and long-drawn-out procedures to assess whether such claimants are really victims of persecution or simply economically motivated migrants (NPC, 1991).

The number of new asylum seekers in European OECD countries increased from 116 000 in 1981 to 541 000 in 1991. The events of 1989–91 led to an upsurge in movements of asylum-seekers from Eastern Europe to the West, but the numbers coming from Africa and Asia also grew. Germany had the biggest increase, with 256 000 new entrants in 1991, compared with 49 000 in 1981 (OECD SOPEMI, 1992: 132). By August 1992, the 1991 total for Germany had already been overtaken, and up to half a million asylum-seekers were predicted for the year. The disintegration of Yugoslavia exacerbated the situation: of the 256 112 asylum-seekers who entered

Germany from January to August 1992, 74 854 were from the former Yugoslavia. A further 57 463 were from Romania. Most of the Romanians and many of the Yugoslavs were gypsies – a group with a long history of discrimination and persecution in Germany too. They became the main targets of the neo-Nazi riots of August–September 1992 (*Der Spiegel*, 37/1992).

Another major flow following the collapse of the Soviet Bloc was of persons of German descent from the former Soviet Union and other Eastern European countries to the FRG, where they had a right to entry and citizenship (377 000 persons in 1989) (OECD SOPEMI, 1990: 4). Similarly many Jews left the former Soviet Union for Israel and the USA.

The USA has been a major refugee-receiving country for many years: altogether more than two million permanent residents entered as refugees between 1946 and the late 1980s. The largest refugee flows came from Cuba (473 000) and Vietnam (411 000). Refugee entry is closely linked to foreign policy. Prior to 1980, the US regarded virtually all persons fleeing a communist country as refugees. In 1980, the Refugee Act changed the definition of refugees (Borjas, 1990: 33), bringing it into line with that of the United Nations Convention on Refugees: that is, a person residing outside his or her country of nationality, who is unable or unwilling to return because of a 'well-founded fear of persecution on account of race, religion, nationality, membership in a particular social group, or political opinion'. The USA admitted about 84 000 refugees in 1989, compared with 110 000 in 1988 and 96 000 in 1987. In the 1980s around one-sixth of all new entrants were refugees (OECD SOPEMI, 1991: 178).

Canada, too, has an increasing number of refugees. An estimated 33 500 people were granted refugee status in 1991. Of these 7000 were asylum-seekers who applied after landing in Canada. The main countries of origin were Sri Lanka, Somalia, the USSR, China and Iran. Annual target figures for refugee admissions in the five-year immigration plan range from 46 500 to 58 000 (Immigration Canada, 1991). Canada has a lengthy and costly process for determination of refugee status, with a high acceptance rate.

Australia began to take in refugees from Indo-China in the late 1970s – a major factor in the growth of Asian immigration. Today Australia sets an annual quota for refugees as part of its general immigration policy. About 12 000 persons were admitted through the refugee and humanitarian category each year in the latter half of the

1980s. However the figure was cut to 10 000 in the 1992–3 migration programme. Since the mid-1980s a large proportion have been admitted under the Special Humanitarian Programme, (SHP) which allows selection of people who had fled their countries, but who could not satisfy the strict criteria of individual persecution laid down by the United Nations High Commission for Refugees (UNHCR) definitions. The SHP also includes 'in-country refugees': persecuted people still in countries of origin, such as Poland, El Salvador, Chile, Lebanon and Sri Lanka.

Until recently the USA, Canada and Australia mainly admitted refugees selected in camps in countries of first asylum, such as Thailand and Malaysia. Today increasing numbers of people enter the USA, Canada and Australia on tourist or other temporary visas, and then seek refugee status. For Western European countries, the entry of asylum-seekers in this way is the rule. By the beginning of the 1990s, asylum-seekers – from both the South and the East – had become the largest entry category in several countries, including Germany, France and Sweden. This led to complicated assessment procedures, and the need to provide maintenance for applicants during the waiting period. The FRG, which has the largest number of asylum-seekers in Western Europe because its Basic Law guarantees legal process to applicants, rejects over 95 per cent of all applications. Yet up to two-thirds of those rejected remain, owing to practical and legal difficulties in repatriating them. It is widely believed in Western Europe that many asylum-seekers are really economic migrants, using claims of persecution as a way of evading immigration restrictions. This has led to popular resentment and extreme-right campaigns against asylum-seekers. There was an upsurge in racist violence in Germany in 1991 and 1992, and many other countries also reported attacks on asylum-seekers. Demands for tougher measures are to be heard throughout Europe, and refugee regulations have been tightened up in several countries. Sweden, for instance, modified its liberal admission procedures in 1989.

Italy experienced two sudden influxes of Albanian asylum-seekers in 1991. Most were young men, and there was a widespread belief that they were really job-seekers or, as some people said, 'economic refugees' escaping poverty, rather than political refugees fleeing persecution. The first group, in March, met with a fairly friendly reception, while the second group, in August, were rounded up, confined in football stadiums and then deported.

Yet refugee movements to Western Europe have been small compared with movements between countries of the South. The International Organisation for Migration puts the number of refugees and asylum-seekers who have been forced to leave their countries worldwide at about 15 million. A further 14 million have been displaced from their homes, but remain within their countries of origin. Over nine million people are dispersed throughout Asia and the Middle East, four to six million in Africa and over a million in Central America (IOM, 1990). It is still the poorer countries who bear the brunt of the world refugee crisis.

Highly-qualified migrants

Improved transport and communications, together with internationalisation of production, trade and finance, are leading to increased mobility of highly-qualified personnel. Appleyard (1989: 32) has coined the phrase 'professional transients' to refer to executives and professionals sent by their companies to overseas branches or joint ventures, or experts sent overseas by international organisations. Much highly-skilled migration is between the industrialised countries, and special entry regulations and work permits have been introduced to facilitate the movements. The move to a common labour market within the European Community is designed to encourage interchange of qualified personnel.

Some migration of highly-skilled personnel is the result of capital investment by companies from industrialised countries in less-developed areas. For example, Japanese overseas investment has led to large movements of managers and technicians. The professional transients may stay only for short periods, but can have a considerable economic and cultural impact on the country where they work. Such migration can contribute to the development of migration networks which encourage movements of lower-skilled workers in the opposite direction. Temporary migration of highly-qualified workers can help change the sending society too. Just as European cultures were profoundly affected by the experiences of colonists in an earlier period, Japan is being changed today by the exposure of its executives and technicians to other cultures. The large number of workers sent overseas by their companies come back with new experiences and needs, which are helping to open up Japanese society to outside influences. This aspect of 'internationalisation' is widely regarded by Japanese observers as a cause of cultural change (Suzuki, 1988).

Much migration of qualified personnel is from less-developed to highly-developed countries: the so-called 'brain drain'. North America, Australia and Western Europe have obtained thousands of doctors, nurses, engineers and other university-trained professionals from India, Malaysia and other less-developed countries of the South. For example, public hospitals in Britain are heavily dependent on doctors and nurses from Africa and Asia. Currently figures on the skill levels of foreign worker entrants are only provided by a few countries, such as Australia, Canada, the USA and Britain. In these cases there is a clear trend towards increased immigration of highly-skilled workers. All these countries have modified their immigration policies in order to attract more qualified personnel. In Britain, 85 per cent of work permits issued by the government in the late 1980s went to professional and managerial workers, and about two-thirds of all employed immigrants (including EC nationals) were in these categories (Salt, 1989: 450). The 'brain drain' can represent a serious loss of skilled personnel and training resources for the poorer countries. On the other hand, many of the migrants were unable to find work in their home countries. Their remittances may be seen as a benefit, and many return eventually with additional training and experience, which can facilitate technology transfer (Appleyard, 1989).

Migration control and the state

Until the 1970s the policies of Western European governments were mainly concerned with recruitment of labour, while North America and Australia had policies designed to control and facilitate permanent immigration. In both cases the focus shifted in the 1980s to prevention of illegal migration, management of refugee and asylum-seeker movements, and finding the right balance between worker and family migrations. There is a convergence in approaches between countries which have pursued very different policies in the past. Even former 'guestworker' recruitment countries are now moving towards acceptance of the need for comprehensive immigration policies and international co-operation.

Labour market versus family reunification criteria

Immigration policies are often torn between the competing goals of facilitation of family reunification and responsiveness to labour market needs. In Australia, Canada, the United States and Western Europe, most legal immigration today is based on family reunification criteria. Several Western European countries tried to stop continuing family immigration after 1974, but found it difficult in view of legal obligations and social realities. French governmental efforts to staunch it, for instance, failed because family immigration rights were established by bilateral labour agreements and France's signature of international instruments such as the European Social Charter.

Swiss immigration statistics for 1989 testify to the preponderance of family immigration. In that year a total of 80 937 aliens were admitted to residency. Of these immigrants, 32 701 entered on family reunification criteria, including 5614 who also took up employment in Switzerland. About 80 per cent of family reunification immigration was estimated to result from seasonal workers transforming their status to resident aliens and then bringing in their families. Since the 1974 recruitment curb, family immigration (which means the entry not only of non-working dependants, but also of men and women eager to join the labour force) has provided a steady inflow of additional foreign workers throughout Western Europe. This inflow and the entry into the labour market of children born to resident aliens has largely compensated for foreign workers returning home.

The US immigration system was revised by the Immigration Act of 1990. In the fiscal years 1992 to 1994, 465 000 of the total of 714 000 numerically limited visas are allotted for family members, with an additional 55 000 set aside each year for spouses and children of aliens legalised under the provisions of the Immigration Reform and Control Act (IRCA) of 1986. Beginning in fiscal year 1995, a minimum of 675 000 immigrants are to be admitted, among them 480 000 family immigrants. But that minimum number can be exceeded to accommodate growth in immigration by immediate relatives of US citizens whose entry is not numerically restricted. Immediate relatives are defined as the children and spouses of US citizens and parents of US citizens aged 21 or older.

Canada has two family visa categories: family class visas for close relatives and assisted relative visas for distant relatives. In the 1980s, these two visa categories comprised over half of all landings or immigrant admissions to Canada. The assisted relative class is subject to a points system for determining allocation of visas. Family class relatives are not subject to the points system. They can enter as long as they are sponsored by a relative who meets an income requirement and is willing to guarantee financial support for a period of up to 10 years. Family-based immigration also constitutes the single largest component of legal immigration to Australia, as will be discussed in Chapter 5.

In all three countries, however, the priority accorded family-based immigration was challenged by advocacy of increased immigration based on economic criteria in the late 1980s. The US Immigration Act of 1990 diminished somewhat the predominance of family-based immigration in favour of business, investor and employment-related immigration, but it did so by raising overall numbers, rather than cutting family entries. Similarly Canada raised its skilled and entrepreneurial migrant intakes in the five-year plan announced in 1990, but did not reduce family and refugee categories. Australia also increased skilled and business migration in the late 1980s, but then cut all types of migration in 1991 and 1992 owing to the severe recession.

The significance of family-based immigration in the policies of Western democracies stems from the priority accorded humanitarian and human rights considerations. It also reflects the power of immigrant-origin minorities in democratic political systems. But family-based immigration also facilitates integration of immigrants. Indeed one of the most striking features of the US immigration system is its benign neglect of immigrants. It relies on families and ethnic communities to incorporate them. As a rule, US Federal government-funded services have only been provided to refugees. Hence, in sharp contrast to Western Europe and Australia, the USA lacks specific social policies for immigrants (see Chapter 8).

Illegal migration

Illegal migration is, by definition, a product of the laws made to control migration. Until the late nineteenth century, workers and their families could freely enter the USA, Canada, Australia and most

Western European countries. From the 1880s, governments began to impose restrictions on the basis of race or national origin, or according to labour market criteria. Ever since, there has been illegal immigration: some aliens enter clandestinely without going through required immigration procedures. Others enter legally but violate the terms of their entry, by overstaying their permit or working without permission.

Illegal immigration and employment has long been fairly widespread in Western Europe. As described above, the French government attempted to regulate labour migration, but many foreign workers found employment outside legal procedures and were subsequently legalised. In 1973, illegal immigrants were thought to make up about 10 per cent of the total foreign population of Western Europe. Illegal immigration was also substantial in the USA, as evidenced by the over one million Mexican nationals repatriated by Operation Wetback in 1954.

Attitudes to illegal migration varied. In France and the USA it was generally viewed as benign as long as there was high demand for unskilled labour. The FRG and Switzerland, with much stronger traditions of police control of foreigners, did not openly tolerate illegal entries but, even there, some spontaneous entrants managed to stay on and work. Official views on illegal immigration changed dramatically as economic conditions worsened, unemployment increased and anti-immigrant political movements began to attract support. The growing apprehension about illegal entries was linked to a broader politicisation of immigration issues. There was a general tightening up of controls in the 1970s and 1980s.

Most states enacted or reinforced sanctions punishing illegal employment of aliens. Penalties included deportation of workers, and fines against employers. The USA did not introduce sanctions against employers of illegal immigrants until the 1986 IRCA. Enactment of employer sanctions, however, was extremely controversial. Many Hispanics opposed them, as they feared that they would result in additional employment discrimination. A Government Accounting Office report issued in 1991 concluded that imposition of employer sanctions had indeed resulted in a significant pattern of additional employment discrimination against Hispanics. This points to a general dilemma: immigration control measures generally penalise individual workers, who are fined, imprisoned or deported. Thus far, they have had insufficient effect on the employers who benefit from exploiting the workers. Document fraud has also stymied effective enforcement, particularly in the USA.

Sanctions against employers of illegal immigrants are part of broader strategies to curb illegal immigration. Other measures include border controls, penalties against airlines which bring in unauthorised aliens, penalties for violations of social security, tax and housing regulations and stricter visa regulations. Many industrial countries have also had legalisation programmes, which offered an amnesty and legal status to illegal migrants, providing they came forward by a certain date and satisfied certain criteria, such as having work. By far the largest legalisation programme was that of the United States pursuant to IRCA in 1986 (which is described earlier in this chapter). Italy and France probably ranked second and third in numbers of aliens legalised. Other Western democracies that legalised illegal immigrants between 1970 and 1991 include Australia, Canada, the United Kingdom, Belgium, the Netherlands, Austria, Spain and Sweden. Not all states, however, gave illegal aliens the opportunity to legalise. Germany eschewed legalisation on the grounds that it would serve to attract even more illegal immigrants.

Restriction and 'root causes'

Despite regulatory measures, illegal immigration to industrial countries certainly increased over the 1970–90 period. Together with the upsurge in refugee and asylum-seeker entries from the mid-1980s, illegal migration became a focus for aggressive campaigns from the extreme right. This contributed to the overall politicisation of migration issues, and helped increase the pressure for migration control. There has been a flurry of international meetings and diplomatic activity concerned with migration issues. Current political initiatives take two forms: one is further tightening of restrictive measures, the other is the attempt to address what is often referred to as the 'root causes' of mass migration – the South–North divide.

From the mid-1980s, the Commission of the European Community repeatedly discussed migration, but failed to come up with a common policy towards entrants from non-Community countries. This meant that inter-state co-operation was largely left to ad hoc groups. The most important was that established at a meeting in Schengen on

June 1985: Germany, France and the Benelux countries signed an agreement on the removal of controls on their common borders and a joint policy on entrants from third countries. The 'Schengen Group' became the focus of efforts to tighten border controls and introduce tougher entry requirements for migrants from the South (Callovi, 1992).

The collapse of the Soviet Bloc made regulation of migration even more urgent. In December 1989, the 12 member states of the EC affirmed their 'right and duty to combat illegal migration'. In June 1990 the European Council agreed on the Dublin Convention, which set out rules for determining refugee status, to prevent asylum-seekers making multiple applications in different countries. However, by mid-1992, an insufficient number of governments had ratified the agreement, so it had yet to come into force. Also in June 1990, the Schengen Group (in the meantime joined by Italy, Spain and Portugal) signed an agreement laying down measures of external border control needed before checks between member countries could be abolished (Callovi, 1992).

The European Convention on Security and Cooperation in Europe (ECSC), signed in Paris in June of 1991, was intended to create a zone in which basic human rights as well as minimum living standards were respected. The idea was to create a zone from which individuals would have no basis to apply for asylum. The model in this regard was Poland, from which so many asylum-seekers had come in the 1980s. By the 1990s, it was considered that requests by Poles for asylum could be uniformly denied. Further agreements were made in 1991–2 with Eastern European countries, such as Hungary and Poland, on preventing use of their countries for transit of illegal migrants to Western Europe. At the same time, these countries signed the United Nations Refugee Convention and themselves began receiving asylum-seekers. The ECSC was supposed to prevent developments in Europe which would lead to mass population movements. The outbreak of inter-ethnic fighting in Yugoslavia, which produced hundreds of thousands of refugees, provided a quick test for the embryonic ECSC, which appeared wanting as a mechanism to ensure security.

In the international debates on mass migration there has been growing agreement that entry restrictions could have only limited success. The amount of control and surveillance needed to make borders impenetrable is inconsistent with the trend towards increased

interchange and communication, and would mean serious impinge-
ment on civil liberties, especially for existing minorities. Moreover the
disparity between economic and social conditions in the South and
the North is such that illegal migration is likely to grow whatever the
barriers. There is therefore an emerging consensus about the need to
address the 'root causes' of mass migration, by supporting development efforts in the countries of origin. However, despite much
rhetoric, little has so far been done to achieve the necessary changes.

Measures to reduce migration do not just mean development aid,
but foreign and trade policy initiatives, designed to bring about
sustainable development, and to improve political stability and
human rights. It has long been understood in the United States, for
example, that ultimately the key to stemming inflows of illegal
immigrants lies in improving socioeconomic and political conditions
in less developed societies. During the Reagan presidency from 1980
to 1988, however, US foreign policy was hostile to the North–South
dialogue (Miller, 1991: 36). US involvement in various insurgencies
and civil wars at times seemed to exacerbate political instability,
thereby generating additional international migrants. Ironically US
intervention, specifically in Central America, was partly justified by
what was termed 'the fear of brown bodies'. In other words, if the
USA did not quell insurgencies, they might succeed and the result
would be millions of additional refugees from the new regimes – the
Cuba scenario. The Haitian refugee emergency of 1992, in which
thousands of boat-people were turned back on the high seas by the
US Coastguard, showed that concern for human rights could take
second place to fears of the political repercussions of a mass influx.

One indication of a changing approach was the conclusion drawn
by a US federal study commission in 1990 that 'development and the
availability of new and better jobs at home is the only way to
diminish migratory pressures over time' (Report, Unauthorized
Migration: An Economic Development Response: xiii). But the
report also found that development would increase international
migration to the USA over the short to medium term. What had
changed was confidence in the ability of policies like legalisation,
employer sanctions and border enforcement to keep illegal migration
under control. The persistence of illegal migration to the USA despite
the legalisation and the imposition of employer sanctions was taken
by many as proof that a new strategy of 'abatement' was needed to
replace or complement a strategy of deterrence.

The onset of negotiations in 1991 between Mexico and the United States on the North American Free Trade Agreement, which would also include Canada, seemed to exemplify the new approach. While the main motives concerned trade and investment, immigration policy concerns also played a role. Nonetheless labour mobility was explicitly removed from discussion – it was viewed as a 'poison pill' by US negotiators (Weintraub, 1990: 127 and 1991: 64–74). A provision granting Mexican workers freedom of entry into the US labour market was viewed as politically unacceptable and as certain to fail to gain ratification by the US Congress. As far as US immigration policy was concerned, it was felt that a free trade agreement would spur investment and job creation in Mexico, reducing emigration to the USA. But it was clear that it would take years, even decades, for economic and demographic pressures behind Mexican emigration to abate. Moreover the effect of a free trade agreement over the short to medium term might actually be greater emigration. Hence there would be a continuing need for deterrent measures such as enforcement of employer sanctions and border controls.

In Western Europe too, immigration concerns loomed much more prominently in foreign policy debates than they had in the past. In late 1991, the EC signed an important agreement with the European Free Trade Agreement countries (the main ones being Sweden, Switzerland and Austria) integrating them into the European economic space. However there was concern in Eastern Europe and North Africa that the Single European Market would create greater barriers to external trade, thus keeping out products from less-developed areas.

Three types of international co-operation that might abate migration to Europe have been suggested (Böhning, 1991b: 14–15). The first is trade liberalisation. The problem is that the Western European industries that would be most affected by trade liberalisation, such as agriculture and textiles, are precisely those which have been highly protected. Therefore it would appear that Western European governments possess only a limited capacity to liberalise trade, a conclusion confirmed by the trade dispute between the USA and the EC during the Uruguay Round of the General Agreement on Tariffs and Trade (GATT) negotiations. The second means of international co-operation is direct foreign investment. But governments exercise little control over investors, who follow considerations of profit. Then there is foreign aid, which could abate international migration if designed to rapidly improve economic and social conditions for people otherwise likely to depart. However, in the past, foreign aid has generally done little to improve average living conditions. If it is to help reduce migration, future aid policy will have to be much more concerned with social and demographic issues. Above all, a halt to military aid is essential.

Conclusion

This overview of international migration to developed countries since 1945 can lay no claim to completeness. Rather we have tried to show some of the main trends, and to link them to the political economy of the world market in different phases. Many of the large-scale migrations have been primarily economic in their motivations. Labour recruitment and spontaneous labour migration were particularly significant in the 1945–73 period. In the years following other types of migration, such as family reunion and refugee and asylum-seeker movement took on great importance. Even migration in which non-economic motivations have been predominant have had significant effects on the labour markets and economies of both sending and receiving areas. But it is equally true that no migration can ever be adequately understood solely on the basis of economic criteria. Economic causes of migration have their roots in processes of social, cultural and political change. And the effect on both sending and receiving societies is always more than just economic: immigration changes demographic and social structures, affects political institutions and helps to reshape cultures.

Again it is worth looking back at the four-stage model of the migratory process put forward in Chapter 2. It works very well as an explanatory model for the transition of Western Europe 'guestworker' migrations into permanent settlement. It also applies fairly well to the movements from colonies and former colonies to Britain, France and the Netherlands. Here too initial labour movements led to settlement and formation of ethnic groups. The model appears less applicable to permanent movements to North America and Australia, where family migration and permanent settlement were always the intention of a large proportion of migrants. But in these cases, too, the four-stage model has explanatory value, as will be discussed in detail in Chapter 5. As for current flows, such as refugee and asylum-seekers or 'professional transients', time has yet to show what character processes of settlement and ethnic group formation will take.

The upsurge in migratory movements in the post-1945 period, and particularly in the 1980s, indicates that international migration is increasing in significance. It is linked to the internationalisation of production, distribution and investment and, equally important, to the globalisation of culture. Even countries like Japan, which have tried to close themselves off to foreign influences, are finding that they cannot participate in the international economy without being drawn into international cultural relationships.

Most recently the ending of the Cold War and the collapse of the Soviet bloc have added new dimensions to global restructuring. One is the redirection of investment of the advanced capitalist countries away from the South towards Eastern Europe. Another dimension is the growth of East–West migration, with previously isolated countries entering global migratory flows: Albania is the most dramatic example, with large-scale illegal movements to Italy and Greece since 1989. Just a few years ago a distinguished observer of migration could write in an article in *International Migration Review*'s Special Silver Anniversary edition: 'If the world consisted of Albania on the one hand and Japan on the other, there would be no *International Migration Review* at all (Zolberg, 1989: 405). Today both those countries have entered the international migration arena. There can be few areas today which are not profoundly affected by the growing global migratory flows.

5

The Migratory Process: A Comparison of Australia and Germany

The previous chapter described post-1945 migration to developed countries in general terms. This chapter will present two examples in more detail. The aim is to examine the dynamics of the migratory process in its various stages (as discussed theoretically in Chapter 2) in two countries with very different traditions and institutional frameworks. As will become apparent, there are significant parallels in the development of migration and ethnic diversity. This leads to the conjecture that the dynamics of the migratory process can be powerful enough to override political structures, government policies and subjective intentions of the migrants. This does not mean, however, that these factors are unimportant: as the chapter shows, settlement and ethnic group formation have taken place in both cases, but under very different conditions. This has led to differing outcomes, which can be briefly characterised as the formation of ethnic *communities* in the Australian case, as against ethnic *minorities* in Germany.

Australia and Germany: two opposing cases?

Australia and the Federal Republic of Germany (FRG)[1] have both experienced mass population movements since 1945. In both cases, movements started through the state recruitment of migrant workers.

In some periods, the areas of origin of migrants have been the same. However there the similarities seem to end, and the two countries are often seen as opposite poles on the migration spectrum.

Australia is considered one of the 'classical countries of immigration', a new nation which has been built through colonisation and migration over the last two centuries. Like the USA and Canada, it is part of the 'new world', a sparsely populated country open to settlement from Europe and, more recently, from other continents too. Since 1947, there has been a continuous policy of planned immigration, designed both to build population and to bring about economic growth. Immigration has been mainly a permanent family movement of future citizens and has made Australia into a country of great ethnic diversity, with official policies of multiculturalism.

Germany, by contrast, is generally seen as an historical nation, with roots that go back many centuries, even though unification as a state was not achieved until 1871. Post-1945 policies emphasised the recruitment of temporary 'guestworkers', although there have also been large influxes of refugees and 'ethnic Germans' from Eastern Europe. Today leaders still claim that Germany is 'not a country of immigration'. The end of the Cold War and German reunification have led to massive new population movements since 1989, making immigration and ethnic diversity into central political issues.

In comparing the two countries, we shall look at the way the migratory process is determined by various factors, grouped under the following heads:

- origins and development of the migratory movements;
- labour market incorporation;
- community development on the part of immigrants;
- the role of legal frameworks and government policies;
- interaction with the society of the receiving country.

Tables 5.1 and 5.2 give the most recent available figures on the composition of the immigrant population in the two countries. The figures for Australia are birthplace figures, for many overseas-born people have become citizens. About 23 per cent of the total population were overseas-born in 1991. What the Table 5.1 does not show is that about 20 per cent of those born in Australia had at least one immigrant parent. Over four out of ten residents of Australia thus have close links with the migratory process. The figures for the FRG show the foreign resident population for 1990:

TABLE 5.1

Australia: immigrant population by birthplace (thousands)

Country	1971	1981	1986	1991
Europe	2 197	2 233	2 222	2 410
United Kingdom & Ireland	1 088	1 133	1 127	1 222
Italy	290	276	262	262
Yugoslavia	130	149	150	167
Greece	160	147	138	146
Germany	111	111	115	121
Other Europe	418	418	430	493
Asia	167	372	536	898
New Zealand	81	177	212	288
Africa	62	90	109	186
America	56	96	117	158
Other and not stated	18	36	53	–
TOTAL	2 579	3 004	3 247	3 941

Note: Data for 1971, 1981 and 1986 are from the Census, 1991 data are provisional estimates.
Source: OECD SOPEMI, 1992: Table 26.

TABLE 5.2

Foreign residents in Germany (thousands)

Country	1980	1985	1990	Of which, females 1990
Turkey	1 462	1 402	1 675	745
Yugoslavia	632	591	652	295
Italy	618	531	548	216
Greece	298	281	315	142
Poland	–	105	241	106
Austria	173	173	181	80
Spain	180	153	135	60
Netherlands	–	108	111	52
United Kingdom	–	88	95	40
Iran	–	51	90	33
France	–	75	83	44
Portugal	112	77	85	39
Morocco	36	48	68	27
Romania	–	14	53	23
Hungary	–	21	35	13
Tunisia	23	23	26	10
Other countries	921	638	849	373
Total	4 453	4 379	5 242	2 296
Of which EC	–	1 357	–	–

Note: Figures refer to Western Germany.
Source: OECD SOPEMI, 1992, Table 10.

over 5.2 million people, who make up 8.2 per cent of the total population. In addition, Germany has large numbers of 'ethnic German' immigrants with a claim to German citizenship. The figures also omit foreign settlers who have become citizens. However this is a small group, since naturalisation rates are low (see below).

Origins and development of the migratory movements: Australia

After the Second World War, the Australian government started a large-scale immigration programme, designed to increase the population and stimulate the development of manufacturing industry. The Australian government was eager to recruit British migrants, but not enough were willing to come. In the late 1940s, a large proportion of migrants came from Eastern and North-western Europe; in the 1950s and 1960s, Southern Europeans predominated; in the 1970s and 1980s, the collapse of the White Australia Policy opened the way for non-European migrants, mainly from Asia, but also from the Middle East and Latin America. By the late 1980s, there were far more Asian than European immigrants. Table 5.3 illustrates how the areas of origin changed over time.

TABLE 5.3

Australia: settler arrivals: top 10 countries of birth, 1966–7 and 1990–91

1966–7 Country of birth	Number	Per cent	1990–91 Country of birth	Number	Per cent
UK & Ireland	75 510	54.4	UK & Ireland	21 860	18.0
Italy	12 890	9.3	Hong Kong	13 540	11.1
Greece	9 830	7.1	Vietnam	13 250	10.9
Yugoslavia	7 550	5.4	New Zealand	7 470	6.1
Germany	3 410	2.5	China	6 750	5.5
New Zealand	2 750	2.0	Philippines	6 390	5.3
USA	2 340	1.7	Malaysia	5 740	4.7
Netherlands	1 870	1.3	India	5 080	4.2
Lebanon	1 720	1.2	Sri Lanka	3 270	2.7
India	1 650	1.2	Lebanon	2 890	2.4
Sub Total	119 520	86.1	Sub Total	86 240	70.9
Other	19 160	13.9	Other	35 450	29.1
TOTAL	138 680	100.0	TOTAL	121 690	100.0

Source: BIR, 1991.

Migration from Britain and New Zealand was the result of historical and cultural links with Australia. For Southern Europeans the main causes for migration were, on the one hand, rapid demographic growth, poverty, unemployment and poor prospects for rural workers in the area of origin; on the other, the desire of Australian employers and authorities for low-skilled workers. The linkage was provided at first by Australian labour recruitment mechanisms, then by 'chain migration', the process by which early migrants encouraged and helped relatives, friends and fellow villagers to come and join them.

The first main wave of Asian migration to Australia in the post-war years had its origins in a foreign policy linkage: Australian troops had fought alongside the USA in Vietnam. When Vietnamese boat-people started coming to Australia in the mid-1970s it was hard to deny some historical responsibility. Australia admitted 10 000 to 15 000 Indo-Chinese refugees per year from 1978 to 1982. Family reunion and chain migration led to continued migration and a growing Indo-Chinese population. For other Asian source countries, such as the Philippines, Malaysia or Korea, the links are more tenuous: Australia's growing trade relationships with Asia can be seen as a factor, but not a very direct one.

Currently there are signs of change in the character of migration. Temporary movements to Australia have increased from 568 000 persons in 1984 to 1 689 800 in 1990. The 1990 total included 1 458 700 visitors, 82 100 students and 149 000 temporary residents (executives, specialists, working holidaymakers and sportspeople) (PIC, 1992: 7). Increased student intakes are the result of efforts to market Australian education in Asia. Many students enter the labour market, and a certain number stay permanently. After the Tiananmen Square Massacre of 1989, many Chinese students sought change to refugee status, and were granted special four year residence permits. The growing number of temporary residents represents increasing internationalisation of the economy, but it leads to unplanned settlement.

The number of refugees admitted to Australia has been at a fairly constant level of about 12 000 per year since the mid-1980s. Australia has selected refugees using UNHCR criteria, usually in refugee camps, but in the last few years there has been a dramatic increase of people entering Australia as visitors and seeking asylum. The number of applications received by the Determination of Refugees

Status (DORS) Committee increased from 167 in 1984 to over 10 000 in 1990–91 (NPC, 1991: 124). Australia, like other countries, is likely to find it impossible to deport rejected applicants, so that asylum-seeker movements look set to develop into a new form of immigration.

The overall picture since 1945 has been of a planned policy of permanent immigration, with control facilitated by Australia's isolated geographical position. Migration has nonetheless had unforeseen consequences: the ethnic composition of migrant intakes has changed in a way that was neither predicted nor desired by the architects of the migration programme. This has been partly because the need for labour during expansionary phases has dictated changes in recruitment policies. It has also been due to the way chain migration has led to self-sustaining migratory processes. Australia's population is still growing faster than any other OECD country except Turkey, and half the growth is due to immigration (PIC, 1992: 4). The dramatic economic and demographic developments in Asia are sure to further change migratory patterns.

Origins and development of the migratory movements: Germany

Germany has had several major migratory movements since 1945. The first and largest was that of over eight million expellees (*Heimatvertriebene*) from the lost eastern parts of the *Reich* and three million refugees (*Flüchtlinge*) who came to the FRG from the GDR up to 1961. These people were of German ethnicity, and immediately became citizens of the FRG. Despite initial strains, these immigrants were absorbed into the population of the FRG, providing a willing source of labour which contributed much to Germany's 'economic miracle' (Kindleberger, 1967).

The next major movement – that of 'guestworkers' from the Mediterranean area – started with the signing of a recruitment agreement with Italy in 1955. Further agreements were signed with Spain and Greece (1960), Turkey (1961 and 1964), Morocco (1963), Portugal (1964), Tunisia (1965) and Yugoslavia (1968). Historical links played some part: trade and migration between Central and Eastern Europe and the Balkans have been significant since the Middle Ages. German employers brought in workers from Southern and Eastern Europe (especially Poland) in the late nineteenth century. Labour recruitment, often by force, was significant in both world wars. In the 1950s the Cold War made recruitment from Poland impractical, but Southern Europe and Turkey appeared as natural labour reserves. However the central determinant of 'guest-worker' migration was systematic recruitment by the German Federal Labour Office working closely with the authorities of the countries of origin (Castles and Kosack, 1973: 39–43).

The majority of the 'guestworkers' were men, but there was always a substantial female minority. Employers at textile and clothing factories, electrical assembly plants and food processing enterprises often preferred female labour. At a time when it was very hard for spouses to enter the country as dependants, getting the partner in as a worker was often a form of family reunion. In Turkey, the waiting list for male workers was so long that women came first, then tried to get their husbands recruited. Where the woman was an equal – or even the only – breadwinner, the impact on patriarchal family structures was often dramatic (Morokvasic, 1984).

Most migration to Germany in the 1960s was from Southern Europe, but in the early 1970s Turkish workers became the largest single group. The decline of Southern European emigration in the 1970s was partly due to falling labour demand in destination countries, but was also a result of declining birth rates and improving living standards in the areas of origin. These develop-ments paved the way for access to the European Community (EC) by Spain, Portugal and Greece (Italy of course being a founding member), leading to a privileged status for workers from these countries in Germany. Turkey had no tradition of international labour migration. Organised movement was started by the agreement between the German and Turkish governments in 1961. The Turkish government hoped to relieve domestic unemployment and to obtain foreign exchange through worker remittances. The migrants them-selves sought an escape from poverty, unemployment and depen-dence on semi-feudal landowners. There was an expectation that money earned and skills gained abroad would encourage economic development. The Turkish government also hoped to gain access to the European Community.

But things did not turn out as planned. The German government stopped labour recruitment in 1973, hoping that surplus workers would leave. In fact, many Turks stayed, and family reunion continued. By 1974, there were just over one million Turkish residents (including family members) out of a total foreign population of 4.1 million. Their number grew to 1.6 million by 1982, and has remained at that level. In 1990, they were still the largest foreign group, followed by Yugoslavs. Family reunion was not the only form of continued migration: political unrest, leading up to the military coup of 1980, generated waves of asylum-seekers, who found shelter in the Turkish communities in Germany. Clearly the chain migration process was more powerful than German government policies. Mass deportation, though debated, was never a real option for a democratic state, committed to a wide range of international agreements. With family reunion and permanent settlement, the Turks lost their attractiveness as a flexible labour force that made few demands on social capital. Now they needed housing, schools and social amenities.

Turkish expectations of the benefits of labour migration were also disappointed. Many of the migrants selected by the German recruitment offices were not unemployed 'surplus population' but skilled workers. Since they were generally given unskilled jobs in Germany, they gained few qualifications relevant to Turkish industrialisation. Worker remittances, which ran at US$1.5 to 2 billion per year in the 1980s, certainly helped the Turkish balance of payments, but they were mainly used for consumption or for the establishment of small tertiary sector businesses (taxis, cafes and shops) rather than for productive investment (Martin, 1991a: 33–42). The provisions for association with the EC never came into force, owing to economic problems in Turkey and the military coup. When Turkey applied for full EC membership, in 1987, there were strong reactions in Germany, because of fears of an uncontrolled flood of workers. EC membership was refused in 1989.

Since 1973, there have been other major migrations to Germany:

● East–West movements, both of asylum-seekers and of economic migrants, which have grown dramatically as a result of political changes since 1989.
● mass migration from the GDR to the FRG, especially in 1989–90. this movement has continued as internal migration since reunification in 1990.
● migration of 'ethnic Germans' from the former Soviet Union, Poland, Romania and other Eastern European countries to the FRG; these *Aussiedler* have the right to German citizenship.

Germany's Basic Law lays down a right for victims of persecution to seek asylum. Anybody who arrives in the FRG and claims to be an asylum-seeker is permitted to stay pending an official decision on refugee status. The complex judicial procedure can take several years. The South–North asylum-seeker movement became significant in the late 1970s, with about a quarter of a million entrants from Turkey, Eritrea, Afghanistan, India, Pakistan, Vietnam, Chile and Argentina between 1979 and 1981. Following anti-refugee campaigns by extreme-right organisations, measures such as refusing permission to work and confinement in isolated reception centres were taken to deter asylum-seekers (Castles *et al.*, 1984: 75, 200). Asylum-seeker inflows declined temporarily, but then started to increase, reaching 100 000 in 1986, 193 000 in 1990 and 256 000 in 1991 (OECD SOPEMI, 1992: 132). By August 1992 the 1991 figure had already been surpassed, and a total of 500 000 for the year was predicted. Fears of a mass South–North migration of desperate and impoverished people were seized on by the extreme right, and there was an upsurge in racist incidents. In 1990, 96 per cent of applications were rejected. However legal and practical difficulties precluded deportation of most rejected applicants; presumably most of them stayed on illegally (Pro Asyl, 1991).

Events in Eastern Europe since 1989 have led to an upsurge of migration to the FRG. The fear of a South–north invasion has been overlaid with the idea of a new East–West mass movement. In fact, the expected exodus from the Soviet Union has not taken place, although the potential still exists. Most East–west migrants belong to ethnic minorities, including Jews and gypsies (OECD SOPEMI, 1991: 8–18). Large groups of asylum-seekers have come from Poland, Romania and Yugoslavia. Poles were the largest group among asylum-seekers in 1988 (29 023 persons) and 1989 (26 092). Even in 1990, after the change in government, there were 9155 Polish asylum-seekers (Manfrass, 1992). It is hard to separate this movement from the simultaneous growth of temporary labour migration (mostly short-term and on tourist visas) from Poland. These workers now play a major role in building, domestic work and other informal sector activities in Germany – a resumption of historical patterns going back to the nineteenth century. In 1992, there was an upsurge in asylum-seekers from war zones of the former Yugoslavia. However many asylum-seekers from this area were in fact gypsies, as were the majority of those from Romania. This ethnic group became the main target of racist violence in mid-1992.

The *Aussiedler* are people of German origin whose ancestors have lived in Russia, Poland, Romania and other areas of Eastern Europe for centuries. The number of *Aussiedler* rose from 86 000 in 1987, to 203 000 in 1988, 377 000 in 1989 and 397 000 in 1990. In the latter year, 148 000 were from the Soviet Union, 134 000 from Poland and 111 150 from Romania. Like the post-1945 expellees, the *Aussiedler* have the right to enter Germany and can immediately claim citizenship. They are highly privileged compared with other migrants. *Aussiedler* are generally of rural origin, and have considerable problems of social adaptation and labour market entry.

Altogether around 20 million people have migrated into Germany since 1945, over two million of them in the last three years. The neat categories of the 'guestworker system' have completely broken down. Current movements are volatile and unpredictable. Their causes lie in a mixture of long-standing historical patterns, new political constellations, emerging economic interests, uncertain social developments and complicated ethnic conflicts. German industrialists are currently rushing to take control of investment, industry and trade throughout the former Eastern Bloc, thus realising the age-old dream of building a sphere of German influence. The financial and communicative links which this is creating are certain to encourage future migrations.

Labour market incorporation

Up to about 1973, both Australian and German immigration policies were concerned with the recruitment of a manual labour force for construction and manufacturing. Non-British migrants who received assisted passages to Australia were directed into jobs on large construction sites such as the Snowy Mountains Hydro-electric Scheme, in heavy industry, or in factories (Collins, 1991). Similarly the German Federal Labour Office channelled foreign workers into unskilled and semi-skilled jobs on building sites and in factories, and used restrictionary labour permit rules to keep them there as long as possible. Foreign workers were attractive to employers. A manager of Australia's largest steel company, BHP, described Italians as a 'hardworking race, especially those in the unskilled category', while company records showed a preference for Southern Europeans who were seen as 'readily available, eager to migrate and less reluctant to undertake hazardous, dirty and enervating jobs' (Lever-Tracy and Quinlan, 1988: 47–8). In Germany, economists suggested that failure to recruit foreign workers would lead to increased upward wage pressure and a decline in the competitivity of German industry (Castles and Kosack, 1973: 378).

The pre-1973 movements were mainly rural–urban migration: Mediterranean farmers and rural workers emigrated because of poverty, population growth, breakdown of social structures through war, and decline of local industries. Many intended to work temporarily in industrial economies, in order to use their earnings to improve their farms or set up small businesses upon return. In the German case, this expectation matched the policies of the recruiting agencies. Even in Australia, many Southern European workers expected to return home, and indeed did so in the 1960s and 1970s, as conditions improved in their countries of origin. However this apparent agreement of interests between migrant workers and employers was neither complete nor durable. Some migrants were skilled, but in both countries there was a widespread policy of refusing to recognise their qualifications, compelling them to start off in low-skilled manual jobs. Once workers in Australia had spent two years in the workplaces they were directed to, many moved out to better jobs. In Germany, workers were generally allowed to change jobs after one year. In time, many migrant workers' intentions changed: it became clear that it would not be possible to achieve their objectives in the home country as quickly as originally expected. Sometimes a failed attempt to set up a business at home led to remigration. The result was an increasing orientation towards long-term work and upward mobility in the immigration country (a trend which went hand-in-hand with family reunion) (Piore, 1979: 50ff).

As perspectives changed, the discriminatory nature of the recruitment process was resented all the more. Workers found that, having entered the labour market at the bottom, it was hard to gain the education and training needed for promotion. Certain types of work turned into a 'Southern European occupational ghetto' (Lever-Tracy and Quinlan, 1988: 82) or into *Gastarbeiterbeschäftigungen* (guestworker jobs). Typical of such jobs for men were car assembly lines, construction sites and foundry work and, for women, clothing, textiles and food processing. Services occupations such as catering, refuse collection, office cleaning and unskilled jobs in public utilities also became known as 'migrant work' (see Collins, 1991; Castles *et al.*, 1984).

The structural factors and discriminatory rules which led to initial low status caused enduring patterns of labour market segmentation. Even gaining full labour market rights (in the case of workers who have been in Germany for many years) or citizenship (in the case of Australia) did not necessarily lead to an improved work situation. Two decades on, the migrant workers of the early waves remained highly concentrated in the original sectors (Funcke, 1991: 9; Collins, 1991). This applied particularly to migrant women, whose situation was affected both by patriarchal structures in the countries of origin and gender discrimination in the country of immigration. Their situation in terms of occupational status, wages and conditions was invariably the worst of all groups in the labour market (Morokvasic, 1984; Phizacklea, 1983 and 1990).

Economic restructuring since the early 1970s has brought significant changes. In both countries the pre-1973 entrants bore the brunt of restructuring, as the number of low-skilled manual jobs in manufacturing declined. The result was high rates of unemployment and early retirement from the workforce. As for newer migrants, there has been a differentiation in qualification and occupational status. A growing proportion have high qualifications, and seek employment as skilled workers, executives and technicians. But people who come through family reunion or as refugees often lack skills and education. Such job-seekers have high rates of unemployment or find themselves in insecure and poorly-paid casual or informal-sector employment. Even highly-skilled migrants experience above average unemployment, especially where recognition of their qualifications is hindered by prejudice or institutional barriers.

At the same time, migrant workers have become a structural factor in the labour market. Segmentation into specific forms of work means that they cannot be replaced by local labour, even at times of high unemployment. In Germany, at least until the events of 1989, the low birth rates of the 1970s and 1980s were leading to new demands by employers for migrant workers (Tichy, 1990). In Australia, too, new migrants are needed to make up for skill deficits. In this situation some immigrant workers have been able to achieve promotion from unskilled to skilled or white-collar work. In many cases there has been intergenerational mobility, as children of migrants who have obtained education and vocational training in the immigration country secure better jobs than their parents. There is strong statistical evidence of such mobility in Australia (Hugo, 1986: 225). In Germany, the situation is less clear-cut: until recently not many foreign children were succeeding at school, while few employers were willing to give training places to them (Castles *et al.*, 1984: Chapter 6). More recently school participation and achievement rates have improved, while the declining availability of young Germans owing to demographic factors should make it easier to get apprenticeships. However, even now many young foreigners are refused training places because of prejudice (Funcke, 1991: 11).

One route out of factory work is self-employment: 'ethnic small business' has become significant in virtually all industrial countries (Waldinger *et al.*, 1990). In Australia, some migrant groups have higher rates of self-employment or business ownership than locally born people. However many small businesses fail, and the rate of self-exploitation (long working hours, poor conditions, use of family labour power, insecurity) is high even in those which succeed (Castles *et al.*, 1991). In Germany, the move into small business was delayed for non-EC migrants by refusal of official permission to become self-employed. Turkish or Yugoslav entrepreneurs often had to pay a German or EC citizen to be the front for a business. This obstacle is less significant today, as many immigrants now have the long-term residence permits needed to establish a business. As in other countries, they are concentrated in 'ethnic niches' such as retail trade, catering, construction and transport (Waldinger *et al.*, 1990). By 1990, it was estimated that 150 000 foreigners (of whom 100 000 came from Mediterranean countries) had set up businesses. In catering they were estimated to make up 26 per cent of all business owners (Funcke, 1991: 10).

Community development

Most migrants found their first jobs in industrial towns or in working-class areas of big cities. In Germany, many foreign workers were at first housed by employers in hostels or camps near the work site. In Australia, the Department of Immigration provided hostels for new arrivals, and they often sought work and longer-term housing around these. As relatives and friends arrived through chain migration, they tended to go where the earlier arrivals could give them support and help.

In both countries the growing need for family accommodation meant that migrants had to enter the general housing market. Several factors put migrants at a disadvantage. Most had low incomes and few savings. Early arrivals lacked the local knowledge and contacts needed to find housing through informal networks. There was often a good deal of discrimination against migrants: some landlords refused to rent to them, while others made a business out of it, taking high rents for substandard and overcrowded accommodation. In some cases there was discrimination in the allocation of public housing, with rules that effectively excluded migrants, or put them at the end of long waiting lists (see Castles and Kosack, 1973: Chapter 7). Migrants therefore tended to become concentrated in the inner city or industrial areas where relatively low-cost housing was available. The quality of the accommodation and of the local social amenities (such as schools, health care facilities and recreational facilities) was often poor.

In Germany, concentration in low-quality housing has persisted long after settlement. According to an official report, the housing situation of foreign residents was 'generally bad' in 1991. They tended to have rented accommodation in low-standard or derelict housing, and were often rejected by German landlords because of prejudice. Public housing authorities often denied housing even to 'well-integrated foreigners' (Funcke, 1991: 11). In Australia, where there is a strong tradition of owner-occupation, many migrants were able to improve their situation over time. By the 1986 Census, most Southern Europeans owned their own homes, and their rate of owner-occupation was higher than for the Australian-born population (ABS, 1989). Nonetheless many still remained in the original areas of settlement, though some had moved to outer suburbs. Newer groups, such as Indo-Chinese immigrants seem to be following the same trajectory, which, however, requires considerable time and thrift.

There has been much debate in both countries about the formation of 'ethnic ghettoes'. In fact, unlike the USA, there are very few areas with predominantly migrant populations. Rather we find class-based segregation, with migrants sharing certain areas with disadvantaged groups of the local population: low-income workers, the unemployed, social security recipients and pensioners (see Castles *et al.*, 1984: 117–20). However there are neighbourhoods where a specific ethnic group is large enough to have a decisive effect on the appearance, culture and social structure. The Turkish community of Kreuzberg in West Berlin is a well-known example.[2] Areas with a visible Turkish, Greek, Yugoslav or Italian presence (or a mixture of all of these) can be found in most German cities. In Australia, a strong Italian flavour can be found in the Carlton area of Melbourne, or in the Leichhardt and Fairfield areas of Sydney. There are Chinatowns in the centre of Melbourne and Sydney, and more recently Indo-Chinese neighbourhoods have developed in Richmond (Melbourne) and Cabramatta (Sydney).

Residential segregation of migrants has a double character: on the one hand, it can mean poor housing and social amenities, as well as relative isolation from the majority population; on the other hand, it offers the opportunity for community formation and the development of ethnic infrastructure and institutions. The most visible sign of this is the establishment of shops, cafes, and agencies which cater for migrants' special needs. 'Ethnic professionals' – health practitioners, lawyers, accountants – also find opportunities in such areas. Ethnic businesses and services offer meeting places and opportunities to communicate and organise, in a setting protected from the sometimes hostile gaze of the majority population. A further development was the establishment of newspapers in migrant languages, followed (at least in Australia) by the setting up of ethnic radio stations.

Small business owners and professionals form the core of ethnic middle classes, and take on leadership roles in various associations. Welfare organisations cater for special needs of specific migrant groups, sometimes compensating for gaps in existing social services. Social associations set up meeting places for their own groups, such as the large sports and recreation clubs of Italian, Greek and other communities in Australia; these often have significant cultural and political functions too (Alcorso *et al.*, 1992). Cultural associations aim to preserve homeland languages, folklore and tradition, and often set up mother-tongue or religious classes. Political associations of all complexions struggle for influence within the community. Often their starting-point is political and class divisions in the country of origin, but with increasing length of stay their aims become more oriented to the situation in the country of immigration.

Religion also plays a part in community formation. Sometimes migrants can link up with existing structures: for instance many Southern Europeans in Germany and Australia entered the Catholic Church. However they often found that religion was practised in different ways, and that the German clergy or the predominantly Irish clergy in Australia were not always sensitive to their needs (Alcorso *et al.*, 1992: 110–12). In many cases, priests or religious orders (such as the Scalabrinians from Italy) accompanied the migrants, giving churches in areas of migrant settlement a new character. Orthodox Christians from Greece, Yugoslavia and Eastern Europe had to establish their own churches and religious communities. In recent years, the most significant religious development has been connected with migrations of Muslims: Turks and North Africans to Germany; Lebanese, Turks and Malaysians to Australia. The establishment of mosques and religious associations has had a high priority. Bhuddist, Hindu and Bahai temples can also be found in what were formerly almost exclusively Christian countries.

The developments described for Australia and Germany can be found in all countries of immigration. They are at the nexus of the migratory process, where transitory migrant groups metamorphose into ethnic communities. Thus the establishment of Italian neighbourhoods in Australian cities could be taken as the attempt to create a specifically Italo-Australian space. Establishing community networks and institutions means an at least partially conscious decision to start 'placemaking' and building a new identity (Pascoe, 1992). Community formation is linked to awareness of long-term or permanent stay, to the birth and schooling of children in the country of immigration, to the role of women as 'cultural custodians' and above all to the coming of age of the second generation (Vasta, 1992). Similarly, in Germany, growing awareness of the long-term nature of stay led to formation of associations by Turks. Though many had an Islamic character, they were increasingly aimed at obtaining social and political rights in Germany. Moreover they were linked to a new collective identity which found expression in the demand for dual citizenship, that is the recognition of being both Turkish and German.

The concept of the ethnic community plays a central part in debates on assimilation and multiculturalism. Community formation is not a mechanistic or predetermined process and the communities that emerge are neither static nor homogeneous. Not all migrants form communities, at least in the sense of having a tangible form or a geographical location (for instance, one cannot speak meaningfully of an English community in Australia, nor an Austrian community in Germany). Communities are based not just on cultural difference, but also on socioeconomic differentiation (labour market segmentation and housing segregation) and on discrimination (legal disadvantage, racist attitudes and behaviour). Community formation is not just concerned with cultural maintenance, but is a strategy which emerges to cope with disadvantage, to improve life chances and to provide protection from racism.

The relationships and institutions which make up the community are initially based simply on individual and group needs. However, as economic enterprises, cultural and social associations, and religious and political groups develop, a consciousness of the community emerges. This is in no way homogeneous; rather it is based on struggles for power, prestige and control. The form and outcome of these conflicts depend both on internal factors and on interaction with the wider society and, above all, with the state. The ethnic community can best be conceived as a changing, complex and contradictory network. The network is most intense and easily identifiable at the local level (for example, 'the Italian community of Fairfield' or the 'Turkish community of Kreuzberg'), but is in turn linked in many ways to wider networks: co-ethnics in the same country, the social groups and the state of the immigration country, and finally the social groups and the state of the country of origin.

Legal frameworks and government policies

There are important parallels in the migratory process in Australia and Germany, but the laws and policies regulating migration have been very different. Australian governments aimed to attract permanent settlers from Britain and, as a second best, other Europeans. According to Immigration Minister Harold Holt, speaking in 1950, this was the only way to hold Australia against 'the hungry millions of people in the resurgent continent of Asia' (Vasta, 1991). However, by the 1960s, changes in Australia's international position led to abolition of the White Australia Policy, opening the door to Asian immigration. Family reunion was accepted from the outset, so primary migration led quickly to migratory chains and to community formation. Newcomers were encouraged to become Australian citizens. The initial five-year waiting period for naturalisation was reduced to three and then two years. Moreover the privileged status of British immigrants was abolished in 1973. The 1986 Census showed that 59 per cent of overseas-born people had become Australian citizens.[3] Citizenship is based on the *ius soli* (law of the soil) principle, so that children born to legal immigrants in Australia are automatically citizens. The Australian model embodies an inclusionary concept of the nation: if immigration policy allows someone to become a member of the civil society (that is a participant in economic and social relationships), then citizenship policy allows him or her to become a member of the political community (or state) and of the nation (or people).

For Germany there are two separate legal frameworks: the first applies to people who can claim German *Volkszugehörigkeit* (ethnicity), that is, post-1945 expellees and refugees and current *Aussiedler*. They have a right to citizenship, and are not considered foreigners, nor even immigrants. Their total number since 1945 is about 15 million. The second framework applies to foreign workers and their families, and non-German refugees. The German government still clings to the idea that these groups (about five million people at present) are temporary entrants. Naturalisation is extremely hard to obtain. By the mid-1980s, over three million foreigners in the FRG fulfilled the ten year residence qualification, but only about 14 000 per year actually obtained citizenship (Funcke, 1991). Nor do children born in Germany to foreign parents have any automatic right to citizenship, although the Foreigners Law of 1990 has made it somewhat easier. Even second-generation immigrants live in a state of insecurity and can, under certain circumstances (such as conviction for criminal offences or long-term unemployment), be deported to the country of origin of their parents.

The difference between Australian and German policies is connected with different historical experiences of nation-state formation. Australia is a new nation, built on immigration, which is now consciously moving away from British antecedents. Citizenship is based not on ethnicity or culture, but on the principle of territoriality, that is, residence on the territory of the Australian state.

By contrast, Germans see themselves as part of an historical nation, with roots which go back many centuries. When the German *Reich* emerged as the first modern German state in 1871, nationality was defined, not through territoriality, but through ethnicity as shown by language and culture. A person could only obtain German nationality by being born into the German community, so that 'blood' became a label for ethnicity. When Hitler annexed Austria, in 1938, he could claim that its people were coming 'home to the Reich', though they had never actually belonged to it. The same principle was used to take citizenship away from Jews and gypsies whose ancestors had lived on German soil for centuries: they allegedly lacked 'German blood'. Today German citizenship is still based on *ius sanguinis* (law of the blood). The German model is an exclusionary one. Millions of foreigners have become part of civil society, but they are excluded from the state and nation. This is the rationale behind the seemingly absurd slogan 'the FRG is not a country of immigration' (see Hoffmann, 1990).

This fundamental difference affects all aspects of public policy towards immigrants and minorities. The Australian model for managing diversity has had two main stages. Once it became clear that mass non-British immigration was taking place in the 1950s, the government introduced a policy of *assimilationism*, based on the doctrine that immigrants could be culturally and socially absorbed, and become indistinguishable from the Anglo-Australian population (Wilton and Bosworth, 1984). Measures to encourage successful settlement included some special services for new arrivals. But the centrepiece of assimilationism was the treatment of migrants as 'New Australians', who were to live and work with Anglo-Australians and rapidly become citizens. There was no special educational provision for migrant children, who were to be brought up as Australians. Cultural pluralism and the formation of 'ethnic ghettoes' were to be avoided at all costs.

By the 1960s, it became clear that assimilationism was not working, owing to the processes of labour market segmentation, residential segregation and community formation already discussed. By the 1970s, political parties were also beginning to discover the political potential of the 'ethnic vote'. The result was the abandonment of assimilationism and the shift to *multiculturalism*. This is based on the idea that ethnic communities, which maintain the languages and cultures of the areas of origin, are legitimate and consistent with Australian citizenship, as long as certain principles (such as respect for basic institutions and democratic principles) are adhered to. In addition, multiculturalism means recognition of the need for special laws, institutions and social policies to overcome barriers to full participation of various ethnic groups in society (Castles *et al.*, 1990).

In Germany there was no question of assimilation in the early years. The idea was that most workers would only stay for two to five years. This 'rotation' was encouraged in order to keep workers mobile and flexible. Foreign workers were controlled by a network of bureaucracies. The Federal Labour Office organised recruitment and granted work permits. The *Auslènderpolizei* (foreigners' police) issued temporary residence permits, kept foreign workers under surveillance and deported those who offended against the rules (for instance by changing to a better-paid job without permission). The personnel departments of the employers provided some basic social services and managed company hostels. To deal with personal or family problems of foreign workers, the government provided funding to church and private welfare bodies (see Castles and Kosack, 1973).

By the 1970s, foreign children were entering German schools in large numbers. The educational authorities worked out a 'dual strategy' designed both to integrate foreign children temporarily during their stay in Germany, and to prepare them for return to their country of origin. The result was a system of 'national classes', 'preparatory classes' and 'mother-tongue classes' which separated foreign from German students, and prevented many foreign children from achieving educational success (see Castles *et al.*, 1984: Chapter 6). Family reunion also meant that workers were leaving company accommodation and seeking housing in the inner cities. The result was a public outcry about the emergence of 'ghettoes' and a debate on 'foreigners policy' which was to continue up to the present.

There are three recurring positions in the debate: firstly, the call for a continuation of exclusionary policies, including restriction of family entry, limitation of rights for immigrants and widespread use of deportation powers. This has been the position of the extreme right, but also of much of the ruling Christian Democratic Union (CDU). The second position recognises that settlement is irreversible, and calls for policies of assimilation or integration. This is sometimes coupled with the idea that some people (Europeans) can be integrated, while others (Turks and other non-Europeans) cannot. Such positions have been associated with the Social Democrats (SPD), but also with some sections of the CDU. The third and most recent position is one that holds that assimilation is no longer possible in view of the emergence of ethnic communities, and that multicultural models are the only solution. This view is held in the Green Party, some parts of the SPD, the churches and the trade unions (Castles, 1985; Leggewie, 1990; Tichy, 1990).

Government policies remain contradictory. The myth of temporary residence shapes the legal status of foreigners, except those from EC countries, who largely enjoy social and economic parity with German citizens. For the largest immigrant groups – the Turks and the Yugoslavs – this means an insecure and marginal position. Foreign residents are excluded from a whole range of rights and services, and denied political participation and representation. Even the proposal for allowing long-standing foreign residents voting rights for local government has been rejected by the Federal Constitutional Court. Yet the state cannot altogether escape the realities of settlement. A market economy requires mobility and flexibility, as well as certain standards of welfare. Democratic societies cannot function well if large sections of the population are excluded from participation. Such contradictions indicate that the current German model is not stable, and that a move towards recognition of settlement and the introduction of some elements of multicultural policy is probable in the long run.

Interaction with the society of the receiving country

The attitudes and actions of the population and state of the country of immigration have crucial effects on the migratory process. In turn, migrant community formation may modify or reinforce these effects. In both countries the control of migrant labour by the state, and its incorporation by employers, set the conditions for settlement processes. Discrimination in hiring and promotion, non-recognition of skills and regulations explicitly designed to limit migrant workers' right to equal treatment in the labour market can be seen as forms of institutional racism.[4]

Local workers and their unions generally supported such discrimination, at least at the beginning of the movement. In both countries there were strong traditions of opposition to foreign labour. In Australia, the labour movement supported the White Australia Policy and was hostile to all non-British immigration. German workers had been exposed to Nazi ideologies, and many had participated in racism towards Jews and Polish, Russian and other forced labourers in the Second World War. Australian unions only agreed to recruitment of Eastern and Southern Europeans in the 1940s after getting official guarantees that they would not compete with local workers for jobs and housing (Collins, 1991: 22–3). German unions demanded that foreign workers should get the same work and conditions as Germans doing the same jobs, but otherwise supported discriminatory 'guestworker' regulations, which ensured that most foreigners got inferior positions (Castles and Kosack, 1973: 129). Later on the unions in both countries realised that a split in the working class harmed local workers too, and made efforts to organise migrants and to fight the more blatant forms of exploitation, but by then discriminatory attitudes and structures were well established.

The attitude of local workers towards migrants was part of a wider picture. Up to the 1960s, many Australians were highly suspicious of foreigners. In everyday terms this meant reluctance to rent to migrants or to have them as neighbours, hostility towards anyone speaking a foreign language in public, mistrust of visible foreign groups and resentment towards foreign children at school. The 1960s and the 1970s were a period of growing acceptance of difference and decline in open racism, no doubt owing to the relative prosperity of the period and the widely recognised contribution of immigration to economic growth. This permitted such dramatic changes as the abolition of the White Australia Policy, the first large-scale Asian entries (through the Indo-Chinese refugee programme) and the introduction of multicultural polices. In the 1980s, there was a resurgence of racism, with increasing public polemics against immigration (particularly from Asia) and multiculturalism, and a growth in racist violence, both organised and spontaneous (HREOC, 1991).

In Germany, most social groups supported the 'guestworker' system and there was little public hostility or racist violence in the early stages, although there was informal discrimination, such as refusal to rent to foreigners, or exclusion from bars and dance halls. In the late 1960s, the extreme-right National Democratic Party began campaigning against foreigners. The real escalation of racism came in the late 1970s: the recession had led to unemployment of Germans for the first time since the 'economic miracle', the foreign workers were not going home as expected but instead were bringing in their families. The Turks had become the largest and most visible group, and fear of Islam remains a powerful historical image in central European cultures. The upsurge of third-world refugee entries was exploited by the extreme right, and anti-immigrant themes were soon taken up by the leadership of the Christian Democratic Party (Castles *et al.*, 1984: Chapter 7; Castles, 1985). Reunification in 1990 was accompanied by vast population movements and by growing economic and social uncertainty, particularly in the area of the former GDR. The result was widespread hostility towards immigrants and an upsurge of organised racist violence.

These tendencies reinforced and shaped the processes of community formation described above. It is important to realise that the development of ethnic communities has reciprocal effects on the attitude and behaviour of the population, as well as on state policies. For people who fear the competition of migrants or who feel threatened by difference, the visible existence of such communities may confirm the idea that 'they are taking over'. Ethnic areas can become the target for organised racist attacks, and ethnic minorities can become the focus for extreme right mobilisation. On the other hand, contact with new cultures and some of their more accessible symbols, such as food and entertainment, may break down prejudices. Where ethnic small business and community efforts rehabilitate inner city neighbourhoods, good inter-group relationships may develop.

Complex links emerge between ethnic communities and the wider society. Political parties seek co-operation with ethnic political groups of similar complexion. Local party branches in ethnic community areas need foreign members, and must take account of their needs in order to attract them. For instance, the Australian Labor Party set up Greek branches in Melbourne in the 1970s. Unions have a need to organise immigrant workers. In inner city areas, churches find that they must overcome barriers on both sides, and work with mosques and Islamic associations, if they are to continue to carry out their traditional social role. Artists and cultural workers of minorities and the majority find they can enrich their creativity by learning from each other. Multifaceted new social networks develop in the ethnic community areas of the cities. These give members of the majority population greater understanding of the social situation and culture of the minorities, and form the basis for movements opposed to exploitation and racism (Castles *et al.*, 1984, Chapter 8).

Similar tendencies prevail in the public sector. Both the German and the Australian state have experimented with using ethnic associations as instruments for delivery of social services, such as counselling, family welfare and youth work. Education authorities work with ethnic parents' organisations. The relationship is often an uneasy one, for aims and methods can differ widely. Government agencies may see traditionalist ethnic organisations with petit-bourgeois leaderships as effective instruments of social control of workers, young people or women. On the other hand, ethnic leaders may use their new role to preserve traditional authority, and slow down cultural and political change. The state can choose which ethnic leaders it wants to work with, and reward desired behaviour by providing patronage and funding (Castles *et al.*, 1990: 65–71; Jakubowicz, 1989). But co-option is a two-way process: state agencies try to use ethnic community structures and associations, but have to make concessions in return.

Co-option has gone much further in Australia than in Germany, because of the acceptance of permanent settlement and the granting of citizenship. Here ethnic leaderships have a power base which is important to the state and the 'ethnic vote' is thought to affect the outcome of elections (Castles *et al.*, 1992: 131–3). Members of ethnic communities are accepted as members of the wider society, who may have special needs or interests. In Germany, members of ethnic communities lack political clout and are perceived as not really belonging to society. Indeed recognition of ethnic community leaderships has often been seen as a way of maintaining migrants' capability of return to the country of origin – however illusory that might be.

The main expression of the Australian approach is to be found in the policy of multiculturalism, with its wide-flung network of consultative bodies, special agencies and equal opportunities legislation. In Germany, links between state and ethnic communities are far less developed. The office of the 'Plenipotentary of the Federal Government for the Integration of Foreign Workers and their Families' is a powerless husk, with virtually no staff or funds. Indeed its long-time head, Liselotte Funcke, resigned in despair in mid-1991 (Nirumand, 1992: 214–8). But in the big cities with large ethnic community populations, the need for co-operation cannot be denied. In Berlin, Frankfurt and elsewhere 'commissions for foreigners' or 'offices for multicultural affairs' have been set up. These are actively seeking to build structures to work with ethnic community groups and to propagate legal and administrative reforms which will recognise the legitimacy of such co-operation.

Conclusions

Many people reject the validity of a comparison between Australia
and Germany, arguing that Australia is a 'classical country of
immigration', which set out to build its economy and nation through
settlement from overseas, while Germany is an 'historical nation'
which has recruited temporary workers and is not a 'country of
immigration'. This argument does stand up to analysis. Both
countries have had mass immigration. Germany has had around 20
million immigrants since 1945, one of the biggest population
movements to any country ever. Australia – with immigration of
over five million people since 1945 – has had a very high inflow
relative to its fairly small population. Both countries recruited
migrant workers in roughly the same areas at the same time.
Whatever the intentions of policy-makers, both movements led to
similar patterns of labour market segmentation, residential segregation and ethnic group formation. In both cases, racist attitudes and
behaviour on the part of some sections of the receiving population
have been problems for settlers.

Thus there are great similarities in the migratory process, despite
the differences in migration policies and attitudes towards permanent
settlement. In both countries we can observe the four stages of the
migratory process outlined in Chapter 2. The initial stage was one of
labour recruitment, although with differing expectations: temporary
sojourn in the German case, a high degree of settlement in the
Australian one. The second stage was one of prolonging of stay and
the emergence of social networks for mutual assistance among
migrants. The third stage was that of family reunion, increasing
orientation towards the receiving country and emergence of ethnic
community institutions. In fact it is hard to clearly separate these two
stages: in Australia especially, family reunion often came fairly early
in the process. The fourth stage, that of permanent settlement, was
reached in the 1970s in both countries.

The parallels in the migratory process in Australia and Germany
are important because, if these apparently opposing examples show
corresponding patterns, it should be possible also to find them for
other countries, which are somewhere between these cases on the
migration spectrum. But the differences are also significant and
require analysis. They go back to the different historical concepts of
the nation and to the intentions of the post-war migration

programmes. The Australian authorities wanted permanent settlement, and went to considerable lengths to persuade the public of the need for this. Chain migration and family reunion were therefore seen as legitimate, and the model for settlement was based on citizenship, full rights and assimilation. Assimilationism eventually failed in its declared goal of cultural homogenisation, but it did provide the conditions for successful settlement and the later shift to multiculturalism.

The German government planned temporary labour recruitment without settlement, and passed this expectation on to the public. Official policies were unable to prevent settlement and the emergence of ethnic communities. But these policies (and the persistent failure to adapt them to changing conditions) did ensure that such developments took place under conditions of marginalisation and exclusion. The results could be summed up by saying that the Australian model led to the formation of ethnic communities which are seen as an integral part of a changing nation, while the German model led to ethnic minorities, which are not seen as a legitimate part of a nation unwilling to accept a change in its identity.

Herein lies the usefulness of the concept of the migratory process. It means looking at all the dimensions of migration and settlement, in relation to political, economic, social and cultural practices and structures in the societies concerned. The grasp of these complex dynamics can help us understand specific problems and events, in a way which transcends short-term and local considerations. If the architects of the post-war European 'guestworker systems' had studied the migratory process in their own histories or elsewhere, they would never have held the naive belief that they could turn flows of migrant labour on and off as if with a tap. They would have understood that movement of workers almost always leads to family reunion and permanent settlement. The very fears of permanent ethnic minorities held by some governments turned into self-fulfilling prophecies: by denying legitimacy to family reunion and settlement, governments made sure that these processes would take place under the most unfavourable circumstances, leading to the creation of minorities and to deep divisions in society.

6

The Next Waves:
The Globalisation of
International Migration

The North–South gap – the differentials in life expectancy, demography, economic structure, social conditions and political stability between the industrial democracies and most of the rest of the world – looms as a major barrier to the creation of a peaceful and prosperous global society. International migration is a major consequence of the North–South gap. However the world can no longer be simply divided up between rich and poor nations. Long before the end of the Cold War, new poles of financial, manufacturing and technological power had emerged in the oil-rich Arab states and in East Asia. Oil-producing areas outside the Arab region, such as Nigeria, Venezuela and Brunei, have also become important areas of immigration. A wide range of industries attract migrant workers – agriculture, construction, manufacturing, domestic services and more.

Chapter 3 dealt with some of the migrations of the colonial period. Chapters 4 and 5 concentrated on immigration to developed countries since 1945, but touched on the causes of emigration from less-developed areas. The focus of this chapter is upon current trends in international migration to, from and within Eastern European, Arab, African, Asian and Latin American countries. The next waves of migrants will mainly come from these areas. Much of the international migration will continue to be intra-regional, but many migrants will also desire to go to Western Europe, Australia or North

America. Understanding migration within the South is an essential precondition for formulating the future policies of the developed countries.

Eastern Europe

By 1990, a new spectre haunted Europe: that of an influx from the East. In Western Europe, there was speculation about mass migration on a scale not seen since the collapse of the Roman Empire. The disintegration of the Communist Bloc and of the USSR was accompanied by mounting economic chaos, massive unemployment and political strife. One study predicted that nearly one-quarter of Eastern Europe's labour force (excluding the USSR) could be unemployed by 1994 – some 14 million persons. An additional 30 to 40 million persons in the area of the former USSR were seen as threatened by unemployment (Szoke, 1992). However it was far from certain that the political turmoil and economic collapse would lead to massive 'unwanted' emigration outside the region. There were obvious limits to the outflows of Jews to Israel, Germans to Germany and Greeks to Greece, although it appears that some non-Jews and non-Germans claimed those ethnicities in order to emigrate. There undoubtedly were many people who wanted to emigrate but who lacked 'privileged' ethnic background. There were several reasons why fears of mass emigration from the former Communist Bloc area appeared exaggerated.

Firstly, the Cold War had sealed off these states from the rest of the world. There were significant outflows of refugees from the Warsaw Pact area in 1956, 1968 and during the 1970s. But, by and large, ordinary Russians or Romanians did not have networks that would enable them to find work and establish residence in Western Europe or North America outside of legal channels. Moreover, several of the countries nearest to Western Europe have demographic structures that are not unlike those characteristic of Western Europe. Demographic pressure to emigrate is not found in much of the ex-Warsaw Pact area, save for cases like Romania, as it is found, say, in North Africa or in Central America. Surveys reveal that most Hungarians, for example, do not expect or wish to emigrate. The government of Hungary is much less concerned about prospects for emigration than it is about 'unwanted' immigration (Szoke, 1992).

126

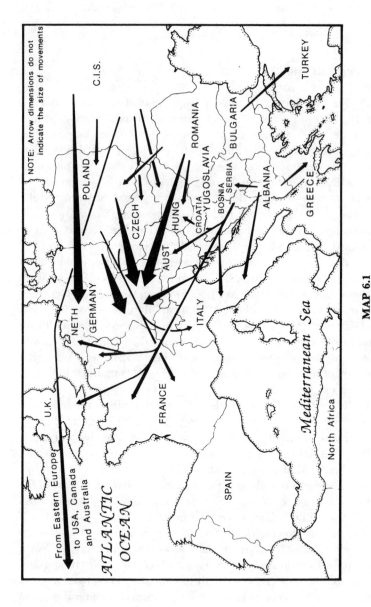

MAP 6.1

Migrations from Eastern to Western Europe since 1989

Hungary, Poland and the Czech and Slovak Republics appear unlikely to generate large numbers of emigrants except if their economies collapse totally. Instead they are fated by geography to be the most proximate areas of relative affluence and perhaps political stability for the areas to their south and east, which appear more likely to generate large numbers of refugees and would-be emigrants. In the space of a few years, they have become lands of immigration. Over 40 years of Soviet domination left them poorly prepared to cope with the novel situation (Toth, 1992); they have had to enact laws and develop institutions to regulate international migration almost overnight.

By 1991, Hungary possessed a substantial foreign population of refugees, quasi-refugees and foreign workers, both legal and illegal. Hungary served as an important transit point for migrants wishing to go to Western Europe. As many aliens travelling through Hungary were turned back at the border, Hungary had to provide for many of the aliens not permitted to enter Austria. One camp housed some 4451 such aliens, at significant cost to the financially constrained Hungarian government (Szoke, 1992). To slow the inflow of aliens desiring to pass through Hungary for points West, the Hungarian government announced new rules: from October of 1991, aliens were required to have the equivalent of US$13 for each day of planned stay in Hungary, in addition to a sum necessary to cover the cost of return to the aliens' country of citizenship. In the first three days after the new regulations took effect, some 46 000 aliens were refused entry (Szoke, 1992).

Hungary, Poland and the Czech and Slovak Republics could become an immigration buffer zone for Western Europe. It is these four states that are the most directly affected by political instability and economic chaos in Eastern Europe. They regard prospects for their own political stability and economic development as contingent upon developing a capacity to regulate international migration and to prevent mass 'unwanted' entry. The 1991 signature of agreements between Poland and the so-called Schengen Group (France, the FRG, Italy and the Benelux countries) helped establish the ground-work for future co-operation on regulation of international migration. The agreement granted Poles the opportunity for visa-less entry into the Schengen Group states for periods up to three months. Hungarians and Czechoslovaks similarly enjoy visa-free entry. The Polish government agreed in return to accept the repatriation of its citizens who violate the terms of their entry – for example, through illegal employment. The Poles also agreed to accept the return of 'third country' nationals who cross Poland and then enter the Schengen area illegally. In other words, the Poles agreed to accept the return of Russians or Ukrainians who enter Germany illegally.

While many Poles were working illegally in Dutch or German agriculture, tens of thousands of Russians and Ukrainians found work, also generally illegally, in Polish agriculture and construction. Ukrainians and Russians frequently agreed to work for wages well below those paid to Polish citizens. Tens of thousands of would-be asylum-seekers in Western Europe also entered, many of them Romanian gypsies. Some estimates placed the number of foreign workers in Poland at 700 000 in 1991. In addition Poland was receiving huge influxes of border-crossers from the ex-USSR who would enter for a few days in order to barter and then return home with hard-to-find goods or hard currency. Delays at border crossing points on Poland's eastern frontier lasted for days.

All along the former frontier between Eastern and Western Europe, migrants from Eastern Europe, and from other areas of the world as well, attempt to enter countries like Austria and Germany illegally. The Czech border with the German state of Bavaria has become a major entry point for aliens entering in violation of German immigration law. Hungary, Poland and the Czech and Slovak Republics were all granted associate status by the European Communities in 1991. While their full integration into the EC appears decades away, association should facilitate economic restructuring. This, in the long run, should lessen the huge gap separating their economies from those to the West.

Mass emigration is far more likely in the areas to the South and East. But even if those uprooted by conflict or economic chaos wanted to emigrate to the West, it would be quite difficult for most of them to do so. A more reasonable scenario is to expect large-scale population movements between the successor states to the USSR and several Eastern European states.

One of the major consequences of emigration from the successor states to the Soviet Union and other Eastern European states will be the loss of highly skilled and professional manpower. This was apparent in the extraordinary skills brought to Israel by many Soviet Jews. It was feared that the loss of highly skilled people to Israel, Western Europe and North America could have crippling economic effects and prolong the painful transition period from command to more capitalistic economies (Shevtsova, 1992). Prospects for emigration by highly skilled, workers were much brighter than for the less skilled as both Western Europe and North America were experiencing shortages of highly skilled workers by 1990.

The future of international migration in this area hinged on general economic and political developments. Much would depend on whether the new governments could offer their citizens hope of a better life in the future. There was reason to be profoundly pessimistic about long-term prospects for the area's economies and politics, especially if the West were to provide little assistance. There is a long and terrible history of Eastern European governments resorting to forced emigration to resolve the region's complicated ethnic problems (Stola, 1992). But, even in the worst scenarios, mass 'unwanted' migration of East Europeans to Western Europe seemed improbable.

Most likely, the next waves will be predominantly intra-regional, although there may also be considerable emigration to the South. The mass departure of over 350 000 Bulgarian Turks may well be a harbinger of the future. Over half of the Bulgarian Turks returned home once the repressive policies against them there ceased (Vasileva, 1992). If human rights are protected, emigration from the area will decrease. Already by 1991, it had become virtually impossible for Poles to be accorded political asylum in Western Europe, although some still attempted to obtain it. One of the goals of the Convention of European Co-operation and Security signed in Paris in June of 1991 was to create a European space from the Atlantic to the Urals in which people would be afforded minimum living standards and human rights. The sooner the spirit of that convention can be translated into practice, the less likely regional instability will be and with it prospects for 'unwanted' mass human migration.

The Arab Region[1]

The area from the Atlantic beaches of Morocco to the Western borders of Afghanistan and Pakistan is one of enormous diversity. Within it there are four key migratory patterns: emigration from the Mediterranean littoral to Western Europe, Arab labour migration to oil-producing states, Arab migration to non-oil producing Arab

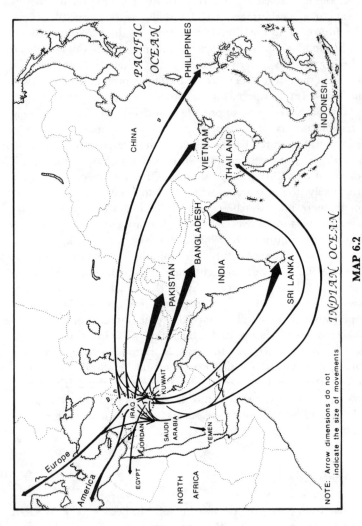

MAP 6.2

Return migration from the Gulf during the 1990–91 Kuwait crisis

NOTE: Arrow dimensions do not
indicate the size of movements

states, and East and South Asian labour migration to oil-producing states. The first three movements will be dealt with here, while Asian migration to the oil states will be discussed later in the section on the Asia–Pacific region.

Demographically the Arab region contains extreme contrasts. The swath from Morocco to Turkey is one of the world's most fertile areas. There is enormous population growth and most of the population is young. Areas like Beirut, Gaza and the lower Nile Valley are very densely populated. Population density and the gap between job creation and the entry of new cohorts into the labour market propels emigration. Nearby, however, are lightly populated desert wastelands and zones of rapid economic growth which are made possible only through massive recruitment of foreign labour. The first major forms of international migration within the region in modern times were shaped by European powers that controlled most of the Arab region until the Second World War and even later.

North Africa and Turkey: still Western Europe's labour reservoir?

The legacy of colonialism is most apparent in North Africa. Algeria was long an integral part of France and much of the interdependency between the two societies stems from this historical relationship. But international migration helped sustain and nurture further interdependence after 1962 (Miller, 1979: 328–41). The Franco-Algerian nexus illustrates a more general factor, the growing tissue of interdependency, that helps generate international migration worldwide and is central to understanding the potential for future migration.

During the First World War and thereafter, Algerian Muslims were recruited for employment in metropolitan France. After the Second World War, barriers to emigration to mainland France were removed and Algerian Muslims were made French citizens. Hundreds of thousands moved to the mainland, especially after the outbreak of the war of Algerian national liberation in 1954. When Algeria was granted independence in 1962, persons of Algerian background in mainland France could opt for French or Algerian citizenship. Most chose Algerian, but a significant minority became French citizens, especially so-called Harkis: Algerian Muslim soldiers who had served with the French army. Following independence, labour emigration to France continued. By 1970, Algerians comprised the largest immigrant community in France, numbering almost one million.

Algerians were a predominantly blue-collar workforce concentrated in the most poorly paid, dangerous and physically exhausting work in French industry, particularly construction and motor manufacturing. Independence did little to change this. What changed was legal status: Algerians became foreign workers but their legal status was special and remains so to this day. Unlike most other foreign workers, Algerians were not admitted to France after 1962 through normal National Immigration Office channels. A yearly quota of Algerians as determined by Franco-Algerian bilateral labour agreements could enter France and find employment. Hence the population of Algerians employed in France grew after independence and many workers were joined by family members. Under French law, children born in France to parents who themselves were born in France are automatically French citizens. Since most Algerian nationals were born in France, as Algeria was part of France up to 1962, their children if born in France were French citizens, even though the parents were not. Algeria simultaneously regarded many of these children as Algerian citizens (Costa-Lascoux, 1983: 299–320).

A long legal controversy between France and Algeria over the citizenship of the offspring of many post-independence emigrants exemplified the transnational nature of significant segments of both French and Algerian society. The constant flow of labour and dependants across the Mediterranean sustained multiple political, socioeconomic and cultural linkages between the two societies which in turn created an environment propitious to further emigration. By the early 1970s, however, tensions surrounding the presence of North Africans in France increased and Algerians became targets of racist attacks. This prompted an Algerian government decision to suspend further labour emigration to France in 1973. In all likelihood, this migration would have ended soon anyway, as France suspended most recruitment of foreign labour in 1974.

By the 1980s, Algerians were outnumbered by Portuguese migrants. Nonetheless, the existence of a sizable expatriate community in France continued to critically affect the Algerian economy and society. Entire regions were dependent on income derived from wage remittances from Algerians abroad. France continued to function as a safety valve of sorts for a society confronted with mass unemployment and a staggering rate of demographic growth. Family reunification permitted some Algerians to become legally employed in France while others worked illegally. The Algerian community in France participated directly and indirectly in Algerian politics. As in the past, anti-status quo groups found greater freedom of expression and organisation on the mainland than in Algeria itself.[2]

The repercussions of the Gulf War were felt in Algeria, where the government and the great mass of the population sided with the Iraqis. The war contributed to the growing appeal of a fundamentalist movement that favours the imposition of Islamic law. After the December 1991 elections, the major Muslim fundamentalist party came close to winning a majority of seats in the Algerian legislature. In January 1992, the Algerian president resigned and the army intervened to stop a second round of elections that appeared destined to give the fundamentalists a large majority. The French, Italian and Spanish governments feared that Algerian instability would lead to mass emigration. The events were viewed with particular gravity by France because of the high level of political tension surrounding immigration issues there, especially with regard to North Africans. Mainstream political parties feared that events in Algeria would increase the appeal of the anti-immigrant National Front, and endanger French political stability – a fear confirmed by the results of regional elections in March 1992.

Support for the Islamic fundamentalist movement in Algeria and elsewhere in North Africa had been growing long before the Gulf War, but the war strengthened the appeal of fundamentalism. France had desperately sought to avoid military conflict in the Gulf, but, in the end, it sided with the USA to maintain Western unity. The point is that major events in international relations increasingly involve migration either directly, as in the case of the five million people displaced by the Gulf War, or indirectly, as in the case of French fears of political instability in Algeria, with its possible effects upon French domestic politics. The interdependency created by decades of trans-Mediterranean migration meant that the mounting political instability would be likely to affect France directly, particularly through increased emigration by Algerians fleeing either life under military dictatorship or Islamic fundamentalist rule.

Morocco and Tunisia, by contrast, had merely been French protectorates. Far fewer Moroccans and Tunisians were uprooted by the arrival of European settlers and confiscation of their land. Hence emigration to the mainland was less extensive and significant than in the Algerian case. Unlike Algerians, Tunisians and Moroccans were recruited for labour in France through the National Immigration Office. Moroccan and Tunisian labour emigration to France became significant only in the 1960s, although as early as 1936 there was a legalisation of Moroccans working illegally in France (Weil, 1991a: 149–50).

Some measure of the enormous significance of labour emigration to North African societies can be found in the size of wage remittance flows and revenue flows from France. Officially recorded revenue transfers nearly quintupled between 1974 and 1981, before slowing somewhat. By 1981, they represented nearly one-third of global transfers received by the three countries. Moroccans and Tunisians seemed to evidence a greater propensity to transfer savings than Algerians. In part this was due to the more recent arrival of Tunisians and Moroccans, the ageing of the Algerian work-force and its vulnerability to unemployment, and to the progression of family reunification. But the gap was mainly due to Algerians transferring money and goods back home through means that are not recorded statistically. Simon estimates total transfers resulting from North African emigration to Europe at between 20 and 22 billion francs in 1985, roughly US$4–5 billion (Simon, 1990: 29).

Turkey is the other principal source of emigrants from the Arab region to Europe (Martin, 1991a). Since 1972, Turkey has been an associate member state of the EC, but the EC declined to accept full accession by Turkey in 1989. Immigration concerns were the principal reason behind the EC decision, although other factors, such as human rights violations and the recent history of military intervention in government, also played a role. By the year 2000, Turkey is expected to be the most populous North Atlantic Treaty Organisation (NATO) state after the USA. Turkey has millions of emigrants already established in Western Europe. The village and family networks that have developed since the recruitment era will make it potentially more difficult to stop migration from Turkey than from many Eastern European countries.

At the same time, however, Mediterranean littoral countries such as Turkey and Morocco are alarmed that Western Europeans will prefer Eastern European migration to largely Islamic migration from the South. These fears have some basis in fact. It is not unusual to hear French business and governmental officials speak of the desirability of reorienting international migration to the East in order to attenuate integration problems. Significantly Switzerland by 1991 defined both Turkey and Yugoslavia as belonging to the 'Third Circle' of nations from which labour recruitment is not allowed. Central European countries like Poland, Hungary and the Czech and Slovak Republics, on the other hand, were defined to be part of the 'Second Circle' of states from which foreign labour could be recruited. Current debates on immigration in Western Europe are often dominated by fears of a mass influx from Turkey and North Africa, where population growth rates are very high while economic growth is sluggish.

Concern over the future of international migration was also a major factor in mounting apprehensions in Mediterranean littoral countries over the consequences of the creation of a single European market. The worst of these fears were exaggerated: residents from countries like Morocco and Turkey would not be forced to repatriate, and better integration of resident alien populations would continue to be a priority. The interdependency woven by decades of international migration meant that Western European and Mediterranean littoral states share a common future that would be jeopardised by short-sighted discriminatory or repressive measures aimed essentially at Muslim immigrants. A high degree of trans-Mediterranean tensions over international migration will persist. Only time will tell whether these tensions, which are at the front line of the global North–South divide, will be attenuated through skilful government or exacerbated by the absence thereof.

Arab migration to oil-rich Arab states

The role of migrant workers in the Arab oil states in the 1991 Gulf War was mentioned in Chapter 1. Movements, mainly of male workers, from the poorer to the richer Arab states have taken on enormous political significance in this volatile region. Libya has admitted large numbers of migrant workers from neighbouring states, principally Egypt and Tunisia. When Egyptian–Libyan relations soured as Egyptian President Anwar el-Sadat reoriented foreign policy towards the West, tens of thousands of Egyptians were expelled. Similarly, during periods of Libyan–Tunisian tension, Tunisian migrants were deported. Since 1990, citizens of the four other Maghreb Union states (Morocco, Tunisia, Mauritania and Algeria) have been able to enter Libya freely. For many years there was a significant illegal resident population there from Tunisia, but the advent of freedom of movement has normalised their legal status. Libya provides an extreme example of the interconnection between international migration and foreign policy issues. The mass expulsions also testify to the disregard of Libyan authorities for Arab League and International Labour Organisation (ILO) standards. As the Moroccan scholar Abdellah Boudahrain has argued, disregard for the rights of migrants is commonplace in the Arab world despite the existence of treaties designed to ensure protection (Boudahrain, 1985: 103–64).

Like Libya, Iraq has been governed since 1968 by a revolutionary regime embracing pan-Arabism. The ruling Ba'ath Party in Iraq regards freedom of entry, residence and employment for non-Iraqi Arabs as consistent with the ideal of Arab unity and nationhood. The Iraqi government declared that fellow Arabs would not be treated as just another category of foreigners, as the Iraqis claimed was the case in other Gulf states. However there have also been Persian as well as South and Southeast Asian migrants in Iraq. By the late 1970s, the Iraqi government grew increasingly critical of the growing proportion of non-Arab workers employed in nearby states, which it regarded as a threat to the Arab character of the Gulf (Roussillon,1985: 650–55). By the late 1970s, the number of Asian migrants in Iraq was declining in favour of Arab migrants, while the opposite trend was occurring in the oil-rich Gulf states to the South. The openness of Iraq to migrants from other Arab states helps explain the sympathy felt for Iraq during the Gulf crisis virtually throughout the Arab world.

Estimates of the number of migrants in Iraq are sketchy at best. The Secretary of State for Egyptians Abroad estimated that there were 1.25 million Egyptians working in Iraq in 1983 (Roussillon, 1985: 642). The significance of migration of Arabs to Iraq increased during the long and terrible Iraq–Iran war. In the late 1980s, reports of tensions between Egyptian migrants and the indigenous population became frequent. Moreover Ba'athist rhetoric against non-Arab migrants intensified. Frictions apparently increased with the onset of the Kuwait crisis and undoubtedly contributed to the massive exodus of migrants from Iraq in late 1990 and early 1991. Many migrants, however, stayed on despite the hardships and threats to their lives.

Arab migration to the oil-rich states of the Arabian Peninsula was even larger in volume. Some areas, like Kuwait, developed immigrant labour policies under British rule. Workers from British possessions in South Asia, particularly present-day India and Pakistan, figured prominently in them. Significant East Asian migration to the Gulf also began long before 1975 (Seccombe and Lawless, 1986: 548–74). Those areas under American domination, particularly Saudi Arabia, developed quite different foreign man-power policies: labour migration developed during the 1950s and 1960s; Westerners and Palestinian refugees often provided the skilled labour required for oil production. In the wake of the 1967 and 1973 Arab–Israeli wars, labour migration rocketed as the rising price of oil financed ambitious development projects. Between 1970 and 1980, oil revenue in the Arab states belonging to OPEC (the Gulf states plus Iraq and Libya) increased from five million to 200 billion dollars. Saudi revenues alone increased from one to one hundred billion dollars (Fergany, 1985: 587).

From the mid-1960s to mid-1970s, the majority of international migrants to the Gulf states were Arabs, mainly Egyptians, Yemenis, Palestinians and Jordanians, Lebanese and Sudanese. During the 1970s, however, the Gulf monarchies grew increasingly worried about the possible political repercussions of massive labour migration. Palestinians, in particular, were viewed as politically subversive. They were involved in efforts to organise strikes in Saudi oil fields and in civil strife in nearby Jordan and Lebanon. Yemenis were implicated in various anti-regime activities (Halliday, 1985: 674). Foreign Arabs were involved in the bloody 1979 attack on Mecca which was subdued only after the intervention of French troops. One result of such events was increased recruitment of workers from South and Southeast Asia, who were seen as less likely to get involved in politics, and easier to control. Whereas Arab migrant workers were predominantly male, there was a substantial and increasing propor-tion of women among workers from the Philippines and Sri Lanka. They worked as domestic servants and nurses, and in other service occupations.

By the mid-1980s, the price of oil had plummeted and some observers, like the CIA, concluded that the epoch of massive migration to the Arabian Peninsula had come to an end (Miller, J. 1985). Hundreds of thousands of Arab, South and East Asian workers did lose their jobs and return home. It was feared that the decline in foreign worker employment would adversely affect political stability and strengthen the appeal of Islamic fundamentalism. But the conclusion that massive labour migration to the oil-rich states had come to an end was premature. The Kuwaiti case revealed that migrant labour had become an irreplaceable component of the labour force (Birks *et al.*, 1986: 799–814). Despite government efforts to reduce dependency upon foreign labour, including mass expulsions of illegal aliens, foreigners continued to constitute the bulk of the Kuwait labour force on the eve of the Iraqi invasion. While the government announced plans to reduce its dependency on foreign labour in the wake of the Iraqi defeat, it remains difficult to imagine Kuwait rebuilding without a massive influx of migrant labour.

In 1991 and 1992, hundreds of thousands of Egyptians began to take the place of politically suspect populations like the Yemenis and Palestinians expelled from Saudi Arabia during the crisis (Miller, J., 1991), but, judging from press reports on the return of migrant workers to Kuwait and other small Arab monarchies, there was an increased proportion of South and East Asian workers in their migrant workforces. Despite the military victory over Iraq, the Gulf monarchies had further eroded their legitimacy in most of the Arab world. This made even their key ally, Egypt, increasingly unattractive as a source of migrant labour.

With a population of over 55 million, Egypt is by far the most populous of Arab states and it has been the most affected by intra-regional labour migration. The evolution of Egyptian labour migration correlated not only with the ups and downs of oil revenues in nearby oil-producing states but also with changes in Egyptian domestic and foreign policies. Dramatic increases in emigration followed the death of President Nasser in 1970 and the waning of the appeal of his mildly socialistic and pan-Arab policies. His successor Sadat proclaimed the *infitah*, or opening toward the West, and more liberal economic policies. Following the 1973 war with Israel, Sadat pursued a decidedly pro-Western foreign policy which included signature of a peace treaty with Israel. Remittance of wages from Egyptians working abroad became a crucial economic concern as entire villages and regions depended on them for consumption and investment (Fadil, 1985).

Emigration greatly affected the fabric of life in many villages as peasants, craftsmen and highly-skilled professionals were lured away by wages many times higher than they could expect to earn at home

(Singaby, 1985: 523–32). Labour emigration undoubtedly relieved chronic unemployment and underemployment, but it also stripped Egypt of much-needed skilled workers and disrupted, for better or worse, traditional village and family structures. Among the many significant effects of the massive emigration was growing Egyptian dependency upon regional political and economic developments: there were returning waves of migrants from Libya at the height of Egyptian differences with Colonel Khadaffi, during the oil price drop of the mid-1980s and, most recently, during the Gulf crisis.

Arab migration to non-oil producing states

Arab migration to non-oil producing states within the Arab region is quantitatively and geopolitically less significant than migration to the oil-producing states, but is nonetheless important. In this movement it is hard to differentiate between labour and refugee flows.

Jordan is a premier example of a non-oil producing Arab state greatly affected by international migration. By the mid-1970s, perhaps 40 per cent of the domestic workforce was employed abroad, primarily in the Gulf (Seccombe, 1986: 378). This outflow prompted what is called replacement migration, the arrival of foreign workers in Jordan who substituted for Jordanians and Palestinian residents of Jordan who emigrated abroad. However a great deal of foreign labour arriving in Jordan has not taken the place of expatriate labour. Much of the Jordanian labour that went abroad was skilled. Much of the labour that Jordan receives is skilled as well, but there is also a big inflow of unskilled Egyptians and Syrians. In the 1980s, this inflow is thought to have contributed to growing unemployment amongst Jordanian citizens and resident aliens. Wages in industries heavily affected by foreign workers have also declined (Seccombe, 1986: 384–5).

Another important migrant labour pattern involved Palestinian Arab residents of the territories occupied by Israel in the 1967 war. The Israeli labour market was opened up to workers from Gaza and the West Bank. This was part of an Israeli strategy aimed at integrating the occupied territories into the Israeli economy (Aronson, 1990b). Most workers from Gaza and the West Bank had to commute daily to work in Israel and were required to leave each evening. Palestinian migrants found jobs primarily in construction, agriculture, hotels and restaurants and domestic services

(Semyonov and Lewin-Epstein, 1987). Illegal employment of Palestinians from the territories was fairly widespread (Binur, 1990). In 1984, some 87 000 workers from the occupied territories were employed in Israel, about 36 per cent of the total workforce of the occupied territories.

By 1991, Soviet Jewish emigration had affected employment opportunities in Israel for Arabs. The Israeli government clearly preferred to see Soviet Jews employed in construction or agriculture, rather than Palestinians. Yet some of its efforts to employ Soviet Jews in construction, agriculture and other typically Arab jobs met with little or no success. Either the Soviet Jewish immigrants desired different jobs or the pay and working conditions were unsatisfactory. Nonetheless the massive arrival of Soviet Jews in Israel undoubtedly displaced some Palestinian workers. It was extremely difficult to measure the displacement because other factors also affected employment of West Bank and Gazan Palestinians in Israel. The Gulf War heightened animosities and there was a wave of attacks by Arabs from the occupied territories on Jews in Israel. In the wake of the war, Israeli authorities introduced new and more restrictive regulations and admission procedures, aimed at weakening the Intifada, as well as ensuring greater security. A combination of all these elements resulted in a sharp decline in employment of Palestinian workers from the occupied territories in 1991.

Sub-Saharan Africa

With one-quarter of the world's land mass and a tenth of its population, Africa is the region most affected by refugees. About half of the world's refugees are found in Africa. Most have fled political and ethnic conflict, but Africa also has environmental refugees, such as the people of Mauritania and Mali, forced by drought to flee their homelands for points south.

Sub-Saharan Africa generates significant outflows of intercontinental migrants, mainly to Western Europe but also to North America and the Middle East. These outflows were traditionally directed primarily to former colonial powers, for example, Zairians emigrating to Belgium, Senegalese to France or Nigerians to the United Kingdom. Many emigrants are college-educated and the loss of scarce human capital though the 'brain drain' has been a long-

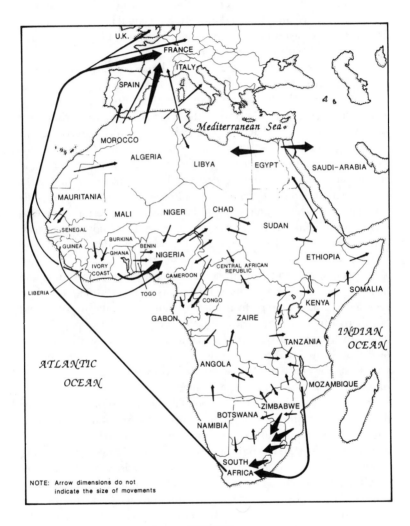

MAP 6.3
Migrations within and from Africa

standing African concern. Intercontinental migration has diversified, however, and increasingly includes poorly educated labour migrants. Sub-Saharan Africans are emigrating in significant numbers to countries like Spain, Switzerland, Italy, Canada and the United States. But the vast bulk of international migration from sub-Saharan countries stays within the continent.

As in the Arab region, European colonialism has left a legacy which still strongly influences migratory patterns. The European presence shifted the locus of economic activity and trade to coastal areas, producing migrations from the interior to the coast that have persisted after independence. The colonial powers carved up the continent into politico-administrative entities (which later became independent states) with little regard for the congruence of ethnic and territorial boundaries. Members of an ethnic group are often citizens of two or more adjoining or nearby states, while many states include members of several ethnic groups. This leads to confusion over legal status or national identity as well as to traditions of movement across international boundaries that are often poorly demarcated and controlled.

The colonial period brought not only European administrators and farmers, but also Syro-Lebanese merchants to West Africa, as well as merchants and workers from the Indian Peninsula to East and Southern Africa. In the post-independence period, these populations generally became privileged but vulnerable minorities. European-origin settler populations often departed en masse at independence, with disastrous economic consequences, as they had played key roles in agriculture, business and government.

In the post-independence period, labour migration and refugee flows have been the predominant forms of international migrations within sub-Saharan Africa. The area includes a large share of the world's poorest states. Migration is often a way to escape crushing poverty, even death due to starvation or malnourishment. Population statistics leave much to be desired: some of the states have never had a census. The paucity of elementary information on citizen and resident alien populations, the frequent absence of identity documents and the ability of some individuals to declare themselves to be nationals of one state when, in fact, they are citizens of another, makes analysis of international migration in sub-Saharan Africa particularly difficult.

Sub-Saharan Africa has witnessed the proclamation of numerous international organisations for the purpose of removing barriers to trade and the free movement of goods, capital and people. Generally these agreements have been poorly implemented or contradicted by policies and practices in member states (Ricca, 1990: 108–34). Despite the existence of many zones in which there is nominally freedom of movement by nationals of signatories to these agreements, there is nonetheless a great deal of illegal migration.

Illegal migration within sub-Saharan Africa is extremely variegated and complex. It is often tolerated in periods of good relations and economic prosperity, only to be repressed during economic downturns or periods of international tensions. The mass expulsions from Nigeria in 1983 and 1985 were the most significant in terms of persons uprooted – as many as two million – but they are part of a much broader pattern. Tens of thousands of Senegalese have been forced to flee violence in Mauritania, while many Mauritanians had to flee Senegal in 1989 (Fritscher, 1989). In late 1991, tens of thousands of Zairians living in Congo were expelled. The director of Congo's Air and Border Police predicted that three-quarters of the million or so Zairians in Congo would be expelled (Noble, 1991). Tensions over the unregulated arrival of Zairians and other aliens had been building for some time in Congo. Aliens' were seen as contributing to rapid population growth in sprawling suburban areas and as overtaxing resources. Zairians were singled out by one specialist as contributing to vice (Loutete-Dangui, 1988: 224–6).

This situation contrasted with the Nigerian case where technically illegal employment of aliens primarily from the Economic Community of West African States (ECOWAS) was looked upon benignly by the Nigerian government during a period of economic expansion. In the mid-1970s, many Ghanaians entered and found work in construction and the services. Most did not understand the limitations on the free movement of persons within ECOWAS and assumed that the agreement afforded them unlimited stay and access to employment in Nigeria (Andepoju, 1988: 77). A downturn in the economy coupled with Nigerian governmental instability and deteriorating relations between Nigeria and Ghana prompted a new, stricter policy.

The best-known and most politically important case of organised labour migration in sub-Saharan Africa, involves the Republic of South Africa's (RSA's) recruitment of foreign labour from adjacent predominantly black African states. The roots of this recruitment can be traced back to the colonial period. Most legally recruited foreign workers from Mozambique, Botswana, Lesotho, Swaziland and Malawi work in gold mines, with less than 10 per cent finding employment in agriculture and other non-mining industries. There also is some illegal immigration from countries like Mozambique, which mainly affects the RSA's agricultural sector, but reinforced controls since the 1970s have apparently diminished this.

Foreign worker recruitment to the RSA illustrates well the connection between labour migration and broader economic and political dependency. Lesotho and Swaziland, for example, are landlocked states which border on the Republic of South Africa. Lesotho is in fact completely surrounded by the RSA, while Swaziland also borders on Mozambique. Their populations can barely eke out a living from agriculture. The absence of economic opportunities makes employment in RSA mines the only alternative for them, despite the well-known rigours of employment in the mines and the high risk of injury or death.

Recruitment from Lesotho, Swaziland and the other states supplying foreign workers to the RSA is highly organised. Candidates for the mines are subjected to a battery of physical and aptitude tests, and many are rejected. The successful ones are transported by air, rail or bus to the mines where they live in hostels. Virtually only males are hired and most of them are young. They are given contracts which require them to return home after one or two years of work. The RSA foreign worker policy, therefore, has not led to settlement as expected by the migratory chain theory, because of the prevention of family reunion and other strict conditions enforced on the workers.

In 1960, there were about 600 000 foreign workers in the RSA. By 1975, there were 485 000 and by 1986, 378 000. Between 1975 and 1983 alone, the foreign workforce declined by 40 per cent (Ricca, 1990: 226). In 1973, the share of foreigners in the black miner workforce stood at 79 per cent. By 1985, it had been reduced almost by half and stood at only 40 per cent. In between, recruitment of indigenous South African blacks from the 'homelands' increased roughly inversely to the decline in foreign worker employment. There was a clear shift away from recruitment of foreign workers from internationally recognised independent but economically dependent states, in favour of increased recruitment from the newly fashioned 'black homelands', which were not recognised by the international community. The change arose partly from the South African regime's fear of being deprived of foreign labour from nearby states as a result of anti-apartheid policies (Ricca, 1990: 226–8).

RSA displeasure and unease over regional labour development were also manifest in the 1984 decision to expel migrant workers from Mozambique. The expulsion underscored the continuing dependence of the suppliers of foreign labour upon the RSA. However other factors had undermined the status quo. Chief among these was the emergence of a powerful black miners union, the National Union of Mine Workers. Moreover political factors forced the Chamber of Mines to adopt a new approach to industrial relations. The price of gold declined while production costs increased. By 1990, half of the Chamber of Mines gold mines were operating at a loss. This and a need to modernise gold production technology raised the spectre of large-scale layoffs in South African mines, which would probably affect foreign workers most.

With the renunciation of the apartheid system, a new era is unfolding in the RSA. The 'internalisation' of employment in the mines seems likely to continue. With the homeland areas faced with crushing poverty and malnourishment, there will be no shortage of potential workers. Certainly the future of employment in the mining industry is a vital issue for the emerging political system in the RSA and for the region as a whole. The eclipse of apartheid creates a prospect for normalisation of long disrupted diplomatic and economic relations. The confrontation with apartheid had displaced hundreds of thousands of people, but now there is hope that the violence will end and refugees will be able to return home.

Overall, however, there are reasons for deep pessimism concerning the future of African migration. Standards of living are falling and political instability appears endemic in many areas. In 1960, there were 300 000 refugees throughout Africa. By 1970, there were a million. Since then the number has quintupled with no easing of the background conditions giving rise to refugees in sight (Ricca, 1990: 220). The huge number of refugees in Africa is a symptom of the nation-building and state formation process (Zolberg, 1983; Zolberg *et al.*, 1989) which can be compared to similar processes in Europe from the sixteenth to the twentieth centuries. There, too, ethnic and religious minorities faced persecution, and war and economic dislocation were rampant. Western European states took centuries to resolve basic issues of national identity and governmental legitimacy. Sub-Saharan Africa, like much of the former colonised world, has had to confront a broad spectrum of modernisation issues in the decades since independence. This is the underlying cause of the proliferation of refugees and there is no end in sight. The increasing number of environmental disasters threatens to swell the ranks of sub-Saharan African refugees further. But, thus far, relatively few African refugees have left the continent. In view of the considerable resources – both financial and cultural – needed to move to developed countries, and the considerable barriers erected by potential receiving areas, the likelihood that large numbers of African refugees could leave in the future appears small.

Latin America and the Caribbean: from an immigration to an emigration region

The vast and highly diverse area to the south of the USA is sometimes portrayed as consisting of four principal areas. The Southern Cone comprises Brazil, Argentina, Chile, Uruguay and Paraguay – all societies in which a majority of the population is of European origin. This was an area of massive immigrant settlement from Europe until the 1930s. Some European immigration continued after the Second World War, as with the arrival of some 500 000 Italians in Argentina from 1947 to 1955. There were also inflows from elsewhere: for example Brazil received African slaves up to the nineteenth century and Japanese workers from the late nineteenth century until the 1950s. The Andean area to the north and west differs in that Indians and *mestizos* (persons of mixed European–Indian background) comprise the bulk of the population. Immigration from Europe during the nineteenth and twentieth centuries was less significant. Central America comprises a third distinctive area; again societies are largely comprised of persons of Indian and *mestizo* background, although there are exceptions, such as Costa Rica. The fourth area is the Caribbean, comprised mainly of people of African origin. Quite a number of countries do not fit neatly into these four areas, but the categorisation serves to underscore how immigration since 1492 has differentially affected the area as a whole and how many of these societies were forged by immigration.

Indeed, Lattes and de Lattes (1991) estimate that Latin America and the Caribbean received about 21 million immigrants from 1800

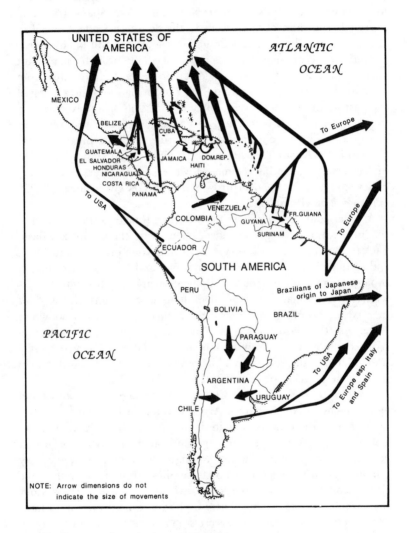

MAP 6.4
Migrations within and from Latin America

to 1970. Of the multiple immigration flows during this period, the single largest one was the estimated three million Italians who went to Argentina. The bulk of immigrants came from Spain, Italy and Portugal, and most of them went to the Southern Cone. States like Argentina and Uruguay encouraged immigration until the inter-war period. The economic depression of the 1930s brought significant changes in immigration policies. Apart from the Italian influx from 1947 to 1955, mass immigration from Europe had become a thing of the past by the 1930s (Barlan, 1988: 6–7). A significant exception to this general pattern was Venezuela, which had received very few European-origin immigrants until the rule of Perez Jimenez, from 1950 to 1958. About 332 000 persons, mainly of Italian origin, settled in Venezuela under his regime. However the so-called open doors policy stopped with the overthrow of the military government in 1958 (Picquet *et al.*, 1986: 25–9).

As inter-continental inflows from Europe waned, intra-continental (or intra-regional) migrations developed. As in the Caribbean Basin back in the nineteenth century, labour migration predominated. The end of the Chaco War between Paraguay and Bolivia, for example, brought significant numbers of Bolivian army deserters into North-western Argentina. Some of them took jobs in agriculture. This marked the beginning of a seasonal labour migration from Bolivia to Argentina that lasted for over three decades, until mechanisation reduced the need for Bolivian labour. This labour flow was largely unregulated until 1958 when a bilateral agreement was signed to help protect the Bolivian migrants (Barlán, 1988: 8–9).

Similarly Paraguayan and Chilean labour migrants began to find employment in North-eastern Argentina and in Patagonia, respectively. These labour flows grew in significance in the 1950s and 1960s. Foreign workers spread from agricultural areas to major urban centres. Single, mainly male, immigrants were soon joined by families, creating neighbourhoods of illegal immigrants in some cities. Most Chileans entered legally with visitor or tourist visas but then would overstay. Their entry and employment appear to have been tolerated, as long as they were seen as contributing to economic growth and prosperity, a view challenged only in the 1970s (Sanz, 1989: 233–48). Beginning in 1948, the Argentine government adjusted laws and policies to enable illegal foreign workers to rectify their status. Reinhard Lohrmann has observed that irregular or illegal migration is the predominant form of migration in Latin

America, but that this was not viewed as a problem until the late 1960s and early 1970s (Lohrman, 1987: 258).

The Argentine legalisations of 1949, 1958, 1964 and 1974 have been extensively scrutinised by scholars and governments contemplating legalisation policies in their own countries (Meissner *et al.*, 1987). Venezuela is another country where legalisation was deemed necessary. With the slowing of immigration from Europe and with oil-related economic growth, millions of Colombians flocked to Venezuela. They often entered and took up employment illegally. Many arrived via the *caminos verdes* – the green highways – over which a guide would steer them across the frontiers (Mann, 1979). Other Colombians arrived as tourists and overstayed. By the late 1970s, several million Colombians were thought to be residing illegally in Venezuela. Not only the oil industry but also agriculture, construction and a host of other industries attracted migrants. Declining incomes in Colombia and the attraction of the stronger Venezuelan currency were significant factors making work in Venezuela attractive (Martinez, 1989: 203–5). Most Colombians emigrated to areas close to the Venezuelan–Columbian frontier and many were short-term migrants (Pelligrino, 1984: 748–66).

Colombian seasonal workers traditionally helped harvest the coffee crop. Bilateral labour accords between Columbia and Venezuela were signed in 1951 and 1952. The Treaty of Tonchala in 1959 obliged the Colombian and Venezuelan governments to legalise illegally employed nationals from the other country if licit employment could be found. This accord led to the establishment of a temporary permit system for seasonal workers, with permits valid for six months. In 1979, the Andean Pact was signed, obliging member states to legalise illegally resident nationals from other member states (Picquet *et al.*, 1986: 30). It was on the basis of this diplomatic engagement that the Venezuelan legalisation of 1980 was authorised. Despite estimates ranging from 1.2 to 3.5 million illegal residents out of a total Venezuelan population of some 13.5 million, only some 280 000 to 350 000 aliens were legalised (Meissner *et al.*, 1987: 11). Either the estimates were much too high, which seems likely, or the legalisation programme did not succeed in transforming the status of many illegal residents.

The legalisation policies implemented in Argentina and Colombia testified to the changing character of migration within South America. Intra-regional labour migrations had supplanted immigration from Europe. Much of it began as temporary labour migration of agricultural workers which led to diffusion of foreign worker employment into other industries and settlement in urban areas according to the chain migration pattern.

There were other significant migrations between Latin American and Caribbean countries. Perhaps the most notorious was the employment of tens of thousands of Haitian *braceros* (strong armed ones) in the Dominican Republic's sugar cane harvest. Every year between November and May, tens of thousands of Haitians entered for harvest-related employment, both legally and illegally. These workers were predominantly men, but some families followed, and settlement took place. In the early 1980s, the sugar crop represented only 12 per cent of cultivated land in the Dominican Republic but half of all exports and one-fifth of the revenue received by the government. Despite high unemployment and underemployment in the Dominican Republic, practically all the sugar crop was harvested by Haitians. For critics of the *bracero* policy, one reason for the disaffection of Dominicans for agricultural employment was the horrific working conditions and pay of Haitian *braceros*. In 1979, the London-based Anti-Slavery Society described the Haitian sugar cane workers' plight as slavery (Péan, 1982: 10).

Every year, the government of the Dominican Republic would make a payment to the Haitian government for the provision of *braceros*. In 1980–81, US$2.9 million were paid for 16 000 *braceros*. In 1983, the sum was US$2.25 million (French, 1990). This arrangement lapsed only in 1986 when the Haitian dictator 'Baby Doc' Duvalier was forced into his sumptuous exile in France. Since then, sugar interests in the Dominican Republic have relied increasingly on recruiters to find the estimated 40 000 workers needed for the harvest. In 1991, following democratic elections in Haiti and growing international criticism of the plight of Haitian workers in the Dominican Republic, the Dominican Republic's government ordered a mass expulsion of Haitians. Of the more than 10 000 individuals expelled, many were persons of Haitian extraction who had long resided in the Dominican Republic or who had been born there (French, 1991: 15). The mass expulsion of Haitians contributed to the destabilisation of the fragile Haitian democracy. The overthrow of the democratically elected President Aristide in September 1991 led to a renewed outflow of Haitian emigrants to the USA. Most of them were intercepted by the US Coastguard and detained at the

US naval installation at Guantanamo Bay in Cuba before being repatriated.

The Haitian outflow to the USA was part of the broader shift in the Latin American and Caribbean countries. By the 1970s, the region was a net exporter of people. The underlying reasons for this historic change are many, and the transition did not occur overnight. Since the colonial period, Caribbean migrants had been arriving on the eastern and southern shores of what is now the USA. These northward flows were accentuated during the Second World War, when Caribbean workers were recruited for defence-related employment in US Caribbean possessions, specifically the Virgin Islands, and for agricultural work on the US mainland. The origins of the British West Indies' temporary foreign worker programme, which recruited thousands of workers annually for employment in US agriculture, and which continued in to the 1990s as the so-called H-2A programme, were not unlike the far larger temporary foreign worker programme established between Mexico and the USA.

Temporary labour recruitment helped set in motion the massive northward flows of legal and illegal immigrants from Latin America and the Caribbean to the United States and Canada after 1970. But the causes of the shift are to be found in other factors as well – the declining economic fortunes of the region, its demographic explosion, rural – urban migration, political instability and warfare. Many of these additional factors cannot be viewed as strictly internal. Policies pursued by the USA, such as its intervention in Central America, clearly played a role in the sea-change that saw the area become a net area of emigration.

Probably the single most important factor behind the rise in emigration from the Latin American and Caribbean countries has been the declining level of economic performance. Gross domestic product per capita fell in the 1980s. Between 1940 and 1980 in Mexico, the annual average rate of growth was 6 per cent, which enabled the economy to absorb most of a rapidly growing workforce. Much the same was true of the Caribbean and Central American countries, but the declines of the 1980s undid those gains (CSIMCED, 1990: 13–14). A major problem affecting overall economic performance was the burden of repaying and financing debts contracted in the 1970s and 1980s.

The downturn in economic performance exacerbated employment problems linked in part to rapid growth of labour forces. Many Latin

American and Caribbean countries experienced exponential population growth following the Second World War, in part as the result of improvements in public health which lowered mortality. Mexico's population tripled from 20 million in 1940 to more than 67 million in 1980, and its population grew by an estimated 21 million during the 1980s. In Central America, the population grew from 9 million in 1950 to 28 million in 1990 (CSIMCED, 1990: 11). Mexican fertility is now dropping. It declined 40 per cent from 1970 to 1989 but Mexico's population increased as much in 1990 as it did in 1970 (CSIMCED, 1990: 12). This suggests that rapid growth of the labour force will continue long into the future, virtually ensuring that international migration will remain a key issue in coming decades.

Political instability and strife have also contributed to increasing emigration, particularly from Central America. In the 1980s, about two million Central Americans were uprooted, mainly Guatemalans, Salvadorans and Nicaraguans (Gallagher and Diller, 1990: 3). Only some 150 000 of these were recognised by the United Nations High Commissioner for Refugees (UNHCR) as refugees. Hundreds of thousands of individuals fleeing Central America entered the United States and Canada, most of them illegally.

The Asia–Pacific Region

Over half the world's population and nearly two-thirds of the world's workforce lives in the Asia–Pacific region (Hugo, 1990). In the 1970s and 1980s international migration from Asia grew dramatically.[3] The main destinations were the Middle East, North America and Australia. At the beginning of the 1990s, the major growth has been in migration within Asia, particularly from less-developed countries with massive labour surpluses to fast growing newly-industrialising countries (NICs). The international movements are often linked to large-scale internal migrations, resulting from economic, social and political change. For example, recent investment by Hong Kong in the Special Economic Zone of Shenzhen in southern China has created two million manufacturing jobs, leading to mass rural–urban migration, especially of women (Skeldon, 1992: 44). Indonesia's *transmigrasi* programme is estimated to have shifted 6.5 million people from densely populated Java to more sparsely populated

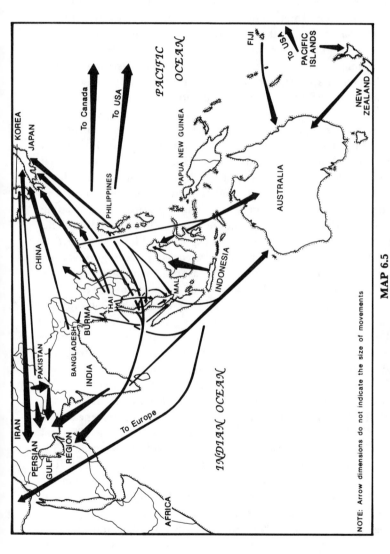

MAP 6.5
Migrations within the Asia–Pacific region

NOTE: Arrow dimensions do not indicate the size of movements

islands like Sumatra, Sulawesi and Irian Jaya since 1968 (*Time*, 11 November 1991). There are also large internal refugee movements of people fleeing volcanic eruptions, flood, earthquakes and political or ethnic persecution. Internal migration will not be dealt with here, but it is important to realise that it is often the first step in a process that leads to international movement.

Asian migration is not new: westward movements from Central Asia helped shape European history in the middle ages, while southward movement of Chinese people to Southeast Asia goes back centuries. In the colonial period indentured workers were recruited, often by force (see Chapter 3). The British took workers from India to the Caribbean and to Africa, as well as to Fiji. The Dutch recruited Chinese workers for construction work in Java. The British colonial administration in Malaya brought in Chinese, Indians and Indonesians to work in the tin mines and plantations. Chinese settlers in Southeast Asian countries and South Asians in Africa became trading minorities with an important middleman role for colonialism. This often led to hostility – and even mass expulsion – after independence. In the nineteenth century there was also considerable migration from China and Japan to the USA, Canada and Australia. In all three countries, discriminatory legislation was enacted to prevent these movements and to restrict the rights of those who had already migrated.

Migration from Asia was low in the early part of the twentieth century owing to restrictive policies by immigration countries and colonial powers.[4] Movements started to grow in the 1960s, reaching high levels in the 1970s and 1980s. The reasons were complex (compare Skeldon, 1992: 20–22; Hugo, 1990; Fawcett and Cariño, 1987). Discriminatory rules against Asian entries were repealed in Canada (1962 and 1976), the USA (1965) and Australia (1966 and 1972). Increased investment and trade, particularly with the USA, helped create the communicative networks needed for migration. The US military presence in Korea, Vietnam and other countries in the region also forged such links, as well as directly stimulating movement in the shape of GI brides. The Vietnam War gave rise to large-scale refugee movements. The openness of the USA, Canada and Australia to family migration meant that primary movements, whatever their cause, gave rise to continuing entries of permanent settlers. The huge construction projects in the Middle East oil countries caused mass recruitment of temporary contract workers from several Asian countries. Rapid economic growth in several Asian countries led to movements of both highly-skilled and unskilled workers.

Asia's sudden and massive entry onto the world migration stage can be seen as the result of the opening up of the continent to economic and political relationships with the industrialised countries in the post-colonial period. Western penetration through trade, aid and investment created the material means and the cultural capital necessary for migration. At the same time, the dislocation of existing forms of production and social structures through industrialisation, the 'Green Revolution' and wars (often encouraged by major powers as part of the Cold War) forced people to leave the countryside in search of better conditions in the growing cities or overseas. Later on, the rapid industrial take-off of some areas and the continuing stagnation or decline of others created new pressures for migration. Improved living standards in the industrialising areas were generally quickly followed by declines in fertility, creating both economic and demographic pull factors.

Asian migration can be examined in several ways. It is possible to differentiate between labour-importing countries (Japan, Singapore, Taiwan and Brunei), countries which import some types of labour but export others (Hong Kong, Thailand, Malaysia, Korea); and countries which are predominantly labour exporters (China, Philippines, India, Bangladesh, Pakistan, Sri Lanka, Indonesia) (compare Martin, 1991b: 187). An alternative approach – adopted here – is to look at migration according to the main types: movement to highly – developed western countries, contract labour to the Middle East, intra-Asian labour migration, movement of highly-skilled workers, student migration and refugee movements. It is important to realise that these categories, although useful for analytical and administrative purposes, are often hard to keep separate in practice. All but the first and the last categories are supposed to be temporary, but in fact many people in other categories stay on permanently. In addition, there is substantial illegal migration, often in the form of people on tourist visas who overstay their permits.

Migration to Western Europe, the USA, Canada and Australia

Three European countries with worldwide empires experienced Asian migrations connected with decolonisation: from the former Netherlands East Indies (Indonesia) to the Netherlands, from Vietnam to

France, and from the Indian sub-continent and Hong Kong to Britain.[5] These movements had virtually ceased by the late 1970s. More recently there has been some migration of highly-skilled workers from Asia to European countries, as well as recruitment of low-skilled workers, such as Filipino domestic servants in Italy.[6]

The largest movement was that to the USA after the 1965 Immigration Act. The number of migrants from Asia increased from 17 000 in 1965 to an average of more than a quarter of a million annually since 1981 (Arnold *et al.*, 1987). Most Asians came to the USA through family reunion provisions of the 1965 Act, though refugee or skilled worker movements were often the first link in the migratory chain. Since 1978, Asia has been the main source of migrants to the USA, making up 40–50 per cent of total immigration. By 1985, all of the top five source countries except Mexico were Asian. The main countries of origin were the Philippines (881 000 migrants from 1965 to 1989), China including Taiwan (624 000), South Korea (606 000), Vietnam (537 000) and India (Skeldon, 1992: 27). By 1990, there were 6.9 million Asian-Americans, and the number was expected to increase to over 10 million by the end of the century (Gardner, 1992: 93).

The picture for Canada and Australia is very similar. Asian immigration developed after the removal of restrictions in the 1960s and 1970s, with additional stimulus from Indo-Chinese refugee movement at the end of the 1970s. By the beginning of the 1990s, about half of new immigrants to Australia came from Asia. For the period 1988–91, seven of the top ten source countries were Asian: Vietnam, Hong Kong, Philippines, Malaysia, China, India and Sri Lanka. In 1991, it was estimated that 717 000 Asian-born people were permanent residents of Australia, making up 4 per cent of total population and 18 per cent of the overseas-born population. In Canada it was the 1976 Immigration Act, with its non-discriminatory provisions and its emphasis on family and refugee entry, which opened the door to Asian migration. By 1981, 424 000 Asians had entered Canada, and the 1981 Census showed the presence of 674 000 people of Asian ethnic origin (Kubat, 1987: 237). Asian immigration, particularly from China, Hong Kong, the Philippines and Vietnam, grew in the 1980s, making up about 40 per cent of all entries by the end of the decade. New Zealand, on the other hand, has had little immigration from Asia owing to restrictive regulations, although there has been a fair amount from some Pacific Islands which have close economic and political ties with New Zealand (Trlin, 1987).

The movements from Asia to the USA, Canada and Australia have certain common features. In all three countries, unexpectedly large movements have developed mainly through use of family reunion provisions. The countries of origin have been largely the same, with increasing participation of China and Hong Kong in recent years. Hugo (1990) notes a trend to feminisation of Asian migration to the USA and other developed countries, partly through family reunion, but also owing to the increasing number of women as primary migrants. A further trend is the growing involvement of brokers, agents, lawyers and middlemen of various types, who provide contacts and knowledge of immigration regulations (Hugo, 1990). In the last few years all three immigration countries have put increasing emphasis on skilled and business migrants, and have changed their regulations to encourage this category. In view of surplus highly-educated personnel in Asia, such policies will further encourage migration from the region. Currently an international labour market for highly-skilled personnel is emerging, with Asia as the main source, and immigration countries are competing to attract this group (compare Borjas, 1990: 199–228).

Contract labour migration to the Middle East

Large-scale migrations from Asia to the Middle East developed rapidly after the oil price rise of 1973. The main labour-sending countries were Bangladesh, India, Pakistan, Sri Lanka, Indonesia, Thailand and South Korea. Some workers also came from China, usually as a labour force for Chinese construction firms. Most women workers came from the Philippines, Indonesia, Thailand, Korea or Sri Lanka, while neither Pakistan nor Bangladesh sent females abroad (Martin, 1991b: 189; Skeldon, 1992: 40–1). Most migrants from South Asia were unskilled, but those from the Philippines and South Korea were often better educated; many took skilled jobs as drivers, carpenters, mechanics or building tradesmen. Some were professionals, especially engineers and medical practitioners. It is clear that labour migrants were often not part of a surplus population of the unemployed rural and urban poor, but rather skilled workers, whose departure could have a negative effect on the economy (Skeldon, 1992: 38).

Migration to the Middle East took place within rigid contract labour frameworks: workers were not allowed to settle or bring in dependants, and lacked civil or political rights. They were generally segregated in barracks. They could be deported for misconduct, and were often forced to work very long hours. Women domestic workers were often subjected to exploitation and sexual abuse. The big attraction for workers was the wages: often ten times as much as could be earned at home. However wage levels declined during the 1980s as labour demand fell, and competition between labour-sending nations increased. Many migrant workers were exploited by agents and other intermediaries, who took large fees (up to 25 per cent of their first year's pay). Agents sometimes failed to keep their promises of providing work and transport, and wages and working conditions were often considerably inferior to those originally offered.

The governments of labour-sending countries saw the migrations as vital to their development programmes, partly because they hoped they would reduce unemployment and provide training and industrial experience, but mainly because of the worker remittances. Billions of dollars were sent home by workers, making a vital contribution to the balance of payments of countries with severe trade deficits. For instance, Pakistani workers remitted over $2 billion in 1988, which covered 30 per cent of the cost of imports. Indian workers remitted $2.6 billion, the equivalent of 15 per cent of imports (ILO, 1991).[7] Millions of families became dependent on remittances, and had improved living standards because of them. However it is not clear what contribution migration actually makes to development, since money is often spent on luxury goods, dowries, housing or land, rather than on productive investments. In some cases the increased inflow of money has led to inflation, disadvantaging non-migrant families. Since the migrants generally come from the middle strata rather than the poorest groups in the areas of origin, remittances often exacerbate social inequality, and lead to increased concentration of land ownership.

Governments have attempted to regulate migration to protect workers and to ensure transfer of remittances through official channels. Control appears to have been most effective in Korea, where the majority of migrants are hired by Korean firms which have won construction contracts in the Middle East. Workers are provided with transport and accommodation, and earn up to three times what they could expect at home. However working hours are long (up to 60 hours a week) and conditions are highly regimented (Skeldon, 1992: 40). Regulation has been much less effective in other countries, leading to illegal migration and exploitation.

Labour migration within Asia

In recent years rapid economic growth and declining fertility have led to considerable demand for migrant labour in some Asian countries, including Japan, Hong Kong, Taiwan, Singapore and oil-rich Brunei. South Korea, Malaysia and Thailand have both emigration and immigration.

Japan has been experiencing severe labour shortages since the mid-1980s. Young, highly-educated Japanese are unwilling to take factory jobs, and there is little further potential for rural–urban movements or for increasing female labour force participation. The official answer is to increase capital investment overseas, that is to export labour-intensive workplaces. But there are limits to this: construction and services jobs cannot be relocated, and many factory jobs, such as car components, are part of complex supply chains which cannot easily be spatially divided. In the 1980s, increasing numbers of women were admitted, mainly from Pakistan, the Philippines, Bangladesh and Korea to work as dancers, waitresses and hostesses (often a euphemism for prostitution). They were followed by men from the same countries, who worked – generally illegally – as factory or construction workers (Sekine, 1990).

The Japanese government encouraged emigration after the Second World War, and is strongly opposed to immigration, owing to fears of overpopulation and concern to preserve ethnic homogeneity. There was considerable debate on the need for foreign labour in the late 1980s, with business associations favouring recruitment, while trade unions and the government were opposed (Sekine, 1990; Suzuki, 1988; Martin, 1991b). In 1990 revisions to the Immigration and Refugee Recognition Law introduced severe penalties for illegal foreign workers and their employers. However employment of unskilled foreigners of Japanese origin was permitted, leading to a scramble to recruit 'Japanese Brazilians'. Other ways of getting round the law are to employ 'trainees' from developing countries, or to give work to foreigners who register as students of Japanese language schools and are permitted to work 20 hours per week. Such schools are often mere fronts for illegal labour recruitment (*Look Japan*, October 1991) Today there are thought to be anything from 100 000 to 300 000 illegal foreign workers in Japan.

Singapore is heavily dependent on workers from Malaysia, Thailand, Indonesia and the Philippines for unskilled jobs. About 160 000 foreign workers make up 11 per cent of the labour force. They are strictly controlled. The government imposes a foreign worker levy (S$300 in 1990) to equalise the costs of foreign and domestic workers. Unskilled workers have to rotate every few years and are not permitted to settle or to bring in their families. Unskilled workers are forbidden to marry Singaporeans and women have to undergo regular pregnancy tests. In 1989, there was an amnesty for illegal workers, after which a mandatory punishment of three months' jail and three strokes of the cane were introduced. This led to strong protests from the Thai government. On the other hand, Singapore is eager to attract skilled and professional workers, particularly those of Chinese ethnicity from Hong Kong. They are encouraged to settle and quickly granted permanent resident status. (Martin, 1991b: 182–4; Skeldon, 1992: 44–6).

Malaysia, with its complex ethnic composition (56 per cent Malay, 33 per cent Chinese and 10 per cent Indian and other) is both an emigration and an immigration country. Over 80 000 mainly low-skilled Malays work in Singapore. Many ethnic Chinese migrate to Australia and other countries, since they feel disadvantaged by policies which encourage education and business activity for Malays. There are less than 100 000 legal foreign workers in peninsular Malaysia, but there are thought to be at least 400 000 illegals. Thais are employed in agriculture in the northern states, Indonesians in agriculture and construction and Filipinos in domestic service. The East Malaysian island states of Sabah and Sarawak are even more dependent on foreign workers, with over half a million Filipinos and Indonesians working on plantations and in construction. They account for up to half the population of Sabah (Stahl, 1990; Martin, 1991:b 186–7).

Fast-growing countries like Korea and Thailand are sending fewer workers abroad, as job opportunities open up locally. In 1983, 225 000 Korean workers were abroad, of whom 42 per cent were construction workers. By 1989, only 76 000 were abroad, of whom 10 per cent were construction workers. Korea is considering recruiting unskilled workers from China (Martin, 1991b: 188). In Thailand, Burmese and Cambodians work on the farms of the north-east, many of which belong to migrants who are in the Middle East (Martin, 1991b: 187). Brunei has about 40 000 foreign workers, over 40 per cent of the labour force (Stahl, 1990). Hong Kong has shortages of both skilled and unskilled workers. While many highly-qualified people leave for North America and Australia, unskilled workers from China enter illegally in large numbers. Taiwan is one of the world's most densely populated countries, yet economic growth has led to labour shortfalls. There are thought to be up to 300 000 illegal workers, and the government has recently decided to admit foreign workers on one-year visas (Stahl, 1990).

Highly-qualified migrants

Another growing movement is that of professionals, executives, technicians and other highly-skilled personnel. One form this takes is the 'brain drain': university-trained people moving from under-developed to highly-developed countries. Europe, North America and Australia have obtained thousands of doctors and engineers from India, Malaysia, Hong Kong and similar countries. This is a drain on the resources of the poorer countries, and may lead to bottlenecks in supply of skilled personnel. On the other hand, many of the skilled migrants are unable to find work in their countries of origin. If they succeed in finding work appropriate to their qualifications while away, their remittances may be beneficial, and many do return when opportunities become available, bringing with them new experience and sometimes additional training. Unfortunately many highly-skilled migrants find their entry to appropriate employment in highly-developed countries restricted by difficulty in securing recognition of their qualifications, or by discrimination in hiring and promotion practices. If they fail to get skilled jobs, their migration is both a loss to their countries of origin and a personal disaster.

Another form of highly-qualified migration is what Appleyard (1989: 32) calls 'professional transients' and Stahl (1990) calls 'capital-assisted migration'. This refers to executives and professionals sent by their companies to work in overseas branches or joint ventures, or experts sent by international organisations to work in aid programmes. Capital investment in less-developed countries may be seen as an alternative to low-skilled migration to developed countries, but it leads to movements of skilled personnel in the opposite direction. These migrations may be of considerable economic and cultural importance. For example, 83 000 Japanese were assigned to work in overseas branches of Japanese companies in 1988, while a further 29 000 (not including students) went overseas to engage in scientific study and research. Over one million Japanese went abroad in the same year for a 'short stay for business' (Skeldon, 1992: 42–3). Unfortunately there is little statistical information on such movements from other countries, but there is no doubt that professional transients from the 'four tigers' are playing an increasing role throughout Asia, alongside their counterparts from North America, Europe and Australia.

Capital investment from overseas is a catalyst for socioeconomic change and urbanisation, while professional transients are not only agents of economic change, but also bearers of new cultural values. The links they create may encourage people from the developing country to move to the investing country in search of training or work. The returning professional transients also bring new experiences and values with them. For instance, some Japanese observers see the stationing of highly-trained personnel overseas as part of the 'internationalisation' of Japan, and a powerful factor for cultural change (Suzuki, 1988: 41).

Students

Considerable numbers of Asians have gone to developed countries to study in recent years. By the late 1980s, there were 366 000 foreign students in the USA, of whom nearly half came from Asia. In the case of Canada, seven East and Southeast Asian countries made up 45 per cent of the 71 000 foreign students present in 1989 (Skeldon, 1992: 35). There was considerable competition among developed countries to market education to Asia, with a trend towards joint ventures with Asian universities to provide courses to fee-paying students.

Student movement to developed countries may be part of the brain drain, since many do not return. A study of Taiwanese students showed that only about 5 per cent returned home after studying overseas between 1960 and 1968. By the 1980s, the proportion of returnees had risen to a quarter (Skeldon, 1992: 35–7). However schemes to provide student scholarships as part of development aid often impose legal requirements to return home upon completing studies. Research in South Korea found that three quarters of those who studied abroad did return home; 20–30 per cent of that country's professionals were estimated to have been trained abroad, mainly in the USA and Japan. Movements of students need to be examined as part of the more general linkages which include professional migrations and capital flows. In the long term, it is likely that many do return, and that they play a role in both technology transfer and cultural change.

Refugees

About half the world's estimated 15 million refugees have their origins in Asia. The two largest forced exoduses have been from Indo-China and from Afghanistan.[8] Over two million people fled from Vietnam, Laos and Cambodia in the late 1970s and early 1980s, following the Vietnam War. Many left as 'boat-people', sailing long distances in overcrowded small boats, at risk of shipwreck and pirate attacks. Over a million have been resettled in the United States, with smaller numbers in Australia, Canada and Western European countries. China has accepted about 300 000 refugees, mainly of ethnic Chinese origin, for resettlement. Other Asian countries have been unwilling to accept permanent settlers. Over 400 000 refugees remain in camps in Thailand, Malaysia, Hong Kong, Indonesia and the Philippines, awaiting either resettlement or repatriation. In 1989, a 'Comprehensive Plan of Action' was adopted by the countries of origin, the countries of first asylum and the countries of resettlement. People already in the camps were to be resettled, while any new asylum seekers were to be screened to see if they were really victims of persecution. Those found to be economic migrants were to be repatriated. This led to voluntary or even forced repatriation, particularly from the overcrowded camps of Hong Kong. Vietnam introduced an 'Orderly Departure Programme' to permit legal emigration, particularly of people with relatives in overseas countries (Skeldon, 1992: 49–52; Hugo, 1990; UNHCR, 1991).

Up to a third of Afghanistan's population of 18 million fled the country in the years following the Soviet military intervention in 1979. The overwhelming majority remained in the neighbouring countries of Pakistan (3.6 million in 1989) and Iran (over two million). Unlike the Vietnamese case, there was hardly any resettlement overseas. The Afghan exodus came just after the Indo-Chinese refugee emergency, and there was little willingness in Western countries to provide homes for new waves of refugees. Moreover the war in Afghanistan continued, and the guerilla leaders wanted to use the refugee camps as bases for recruitment and training. For political, religious and cultural reasons, Pakistan and Iran were willing to provide refuge for extended periods. Pakistan received substantial compensation from the the USA in the form of military, economic and diplomatic support. With the end of the war in 1992, there were hopes for a large-scale return of refugees. However the outbreak of new conflicts and the devastated condition of the country seemed likely to delay this. The different handling of the Vietnamese and Afghan cases is an example of the way refugee movements can become part of wider foreign policy considerations for major powers (Suhrke and Klink, 1987).

Apart from these two huge refugee movements, there have been many smaller ones. They include Filipinos in Malaysia, Tibetans in India and Nepal, East Timorese in Australia and Portugal, and Fijian Indians in Australia. After the failure of the democracy movement in 1989, thousands of Chinese sought asylum in a wide range of countries. Most recently there have been large movements of refugees from Burma (Myanmar) into Thailand and Bangladesh. The latter case is especially poignant: one of the world's poorest countries, recently subject to catastrophic flooding, is now struggling to help political and ethnic refugees, with little support from the international community.

Perspectives for Asian migration

Migrations from and within Asia grew rapidly in the 1970s and 1980s, and there is enormous potential for further expansion. Between 1969 and 1989, an estimated 11.8 million Asians worked in other countries, mainly the Middle East, and in 1990 over three million were estimated to be working there (Appleyard, 1991: 36). In recent years, as expansion in Middle Eastern labour markets has slowed, intra-Asia movements have shown fast growth. The Indian sub-continent provides a vast reservoir of workers, while any opening up of China to emigration could provide enough workers to satisfy the rest of the world's need for unskilled labour. Economic and political reform in China could open the door for mass emigration, while setbacks to reform could lead to huge refugee movements. The fast-growing economies of East and Southeast Asia seem certain to pull in large numbers of migrant workers. Despite Japan's reluctance to allow entries of migrant workers, such movements seem inevitable. Japan looks set to follow the German path of becoming a country of immigration without being willing to admit it.

Conclusions

It is customary to differentiate between different categories of migrants, and regions of migration. But it is important to realise that all the movements have common roots, and that they are closely interrelated. Western penetration triggered off profound changes in other societies, first through colonisation, then through military involvement, political links, the Cold War, trade and investment. The upsurge in migration is due to rapid processes of economic, demographic, social, political, cultural and environmental change, which arise from decolonisation, modernisation and uneven development. These processes seem set to accelerate in the future, leading to even greater dislocations and changes in societies, and hence to even larger migrations.

Thus the entry of the countries of Eastern Europe and of the South into the international migration arena may be seen as an inevitable consequence of the increasing integration of these areas into the world economy and into global systems of international relations and cultural interchange. These new migratory movements are a continuation of historical processes that began in the fifteenth century with the European colonial expansion, and the ensuing diffusion of new philosophical values and economic and cultural practices around the globe.

The first effect of foreign investment and development is rural–urban migration, and the growth of cities. Leaving traditional forms of production and social relationships to move into burgeoning cities is the first stage of fundamental social, psychological and cultural changes, which create the predispositions for further migrations. To move from peasant agriculture into a city like Manila, São Paulo or Lagos may be a bigger step for many than the subsequent move to a 'global city' like Tokyo, Los Angeles or Sydney.

It is therefore impossible to analyse migration as an isolated phenomenon – it is one facet of societal change and global development. The different forms of migration – permanent emigration, contract labour, professional transients, students and refugees – all arise from these broader changes. The categories are interdependent: for instance, a refugee movement can start a permanent migration, or professional transients moving one way can encourage unskilled workers to move in the other direction along the migratory chain. Moreover large-scale illegal movements have developed on the periphery of the permitted categories.

Migrations arise from complex links between different societies, and help to create new links. Movements of professionals and students from developing countries to Western industrialised nations are sometimes part of the brain drain, but they also help to create cultural links, and may encourage technology transfer. The growing mobility of professionals is a development of great significance, which may in future help to weaken national boundaries. Although such movements are generally temporary in intention, permanent settlement does take place in some cases, helping to strengthen transnational networks based on kinship and culture, as well as economic activity.

Patterns of migration are highly complex. Some countries experience emigration of skilled workers and immigration of the unskilled, while in other countries unskilled nationals emigrate from one region while unskilled migrants enter a different one. Some countries are making a rapid transition from emigration to immigration. Even poor countries with mass departures of contract workers may bring in certain types of workers: for instance, middle-class Pakistanis are reported to be recruiting Filipinos and Sri Lankans as maids, and the Philippine embassy in Islamabad is said to have tried to stop the movement on account of frequent sexual abuse (*Malay Mail*, 14 November 1991).

One fairly general feature of labour migration systems, particularly in the Middle East and in Asian countries, is the attempt at rigid control of foreign workers, the prohibition of settlement and family reunion, and the denial of basic rights. Many of the governments concerned refer explicitly to the European experience, in which temporary guestworkers turned into settlers and new ethnic minorities. The strict regulatory systems are designed to prevent this. Will they succeed? Countries like Germany and Switzerland found it hard to implement rigid controls, because they contradicted both employers' interests in a stable labour force, and democratic traditions and human rights principles. It is easier for dictatorships to disregard human rights than it is for Western democracies, but there are some pressures for longer stay common to both situations: the increasing feminisation of migration makes family formation easier, and employers have an interest in retaining trained and experienced labour forces. It therefore seems reasonable to predict that countries everywhere will become more ethnically diverse and cosmopolitan through migration.

7

Migrants and Minorities in the Labour Force

Of the world's estimated 80 million recent international migrants, a quarter are thought to be legally admitted workers, another quarter illegally resident aliens, one-quarter spouses and children and the remainder refugees and asylum-seekers (Widgren, 1987: 4). In Western Europe, where employment of foreign labour generally had stagnated or declined between 1975 and 1985, significant growth in stocks of foreign labour was the pattern thereafter. The OECD reported that the largest proportional increases in the 1980s occurred in Luxembourg (47 per cent), Switzerland (33 per cent), Austria (32 per cent) and the United Kingdom (OECD SOPEMI, 1992: 23). In France, entries of new permanent foreign workers increased 44 per cent from 1989 to 1990, from 15 592 to 22 393 (Tribalat, 1992: 164). But inflows of foreign workers were still far below levels experienced in the 1960s. In 1970, for example, a record figure of nearly 175 000 permanent foreign workers entered France (*Office National d'Immigration*, 1981: 8).

In Australia, immigration accounted for one-third of the labour force increase in 1989 and 1990. By 1991, a quarter of Australia's workforce was foreign-born. Canada expected half of its labour force increase projected for the 1990s to be immigrants (OECD SOPEMI, 1992: 23). The pattern of growing alien employment by the 1990s probably affected other regions as well but was difficult to confirm owing to inadequate statistics in much of the rest of the world. Even within the OECD countries, however, levels of alien employment are often underestimated. The upsurge in alien employment in the OECD countries was both a cause and an effect of rising levels of immigration. By the 1990s, inflows of asylum-seekers had significant labour market effects. Many countries moved to prohibit employment of asylum applicants, as was done in the FRG in the early 1980s and France in 1991 (Tribalat, 1992: 153).

Nonetheless further increases in alien employment seemed inevitable whether authorised by governments or not. The OECD's 1986 Conference on the Future of Migration identified the underlying reasons for the long-term prospect for increasing alien employment: the ageing of Western societies, demographic imbalances between developed and developing regions in close proximity to each other, the North–South gap, continuing employer demand for foreign labour and the growth of illegal migration (OECD, 1987). Furthermore the conference stressed the necessity of understanding immigration in its global context and as something inextricably bound up with economic and foreign policies, developments in international trade and growing interdependence.

This book has shown how most of the post-1945 movements started as labour migration, often deliberately organised by employers and governments. We have also seen how the movements have changed in character, with increasing participation of non-economic migrants, including dependants and refugees. The economic migrants too have become differentiated, with increasing participation of highly-skilled personnel and entrepreneurs. The political economy-based theories of labour migration which developed in the 1960s and 1970s emphasised the crucial role of migrant workers in providing low-skilled labour for manufacturing industry and construction, and in restraining wage growth in these sectors. In the 1990s, there is a need to re-examine this political economy in the light of the shift from temporary labour to permanent settlement and the increasing economic differentiation of migrant workers. Obviously, the major changes in economic structure, such as the decline of manufacturing employment, the growth of the services and the trend towards casualisation of employment, have had a major effect on the work situation of migrants and ethnic minorities. Key questions to be asked include:

● What has been the impact of economic restructuring since the 1970s on migrant workers?

● Have the patterns of labour market segmentation by ethnic origin and gender which had emerged by the 1970s persisted, or have there been significant changes?

● What variations are there in employment patterns according to such criteria as ethnic background, gender, recentness of arrival, type of migration, legal status, education and training?

● What variations are to be found between immigration countries, and how are they to be explained (for example, through economic structure, patterns of discrimination, legal arrangements or government policies)?

● What is the situation of second and subsequent generation immigrants on the labour market (is disadvantage passed on from generation to generation)?

● Is institutional or informal discrimination a major determinant of employment and socioeconomic status?

● What strategies have migrants adopted to deal with the labour market disadvantage (for example, self-employment, small business, mutual aid, finding 'ethnic niches')?

This chapter addresses the above questions by reviewing some of the major theoretical and empirical findings concerning immigrants and labour markets since the 1970s. The growing complexity of immigrant labour market effects is examined, along with illustrative statistical and empirical material concerning cross-national trends in labour market segmentation, especially the growing polarisation of immigrant labour market characteristics. A case study of the evolution of foreign employment in the French motor and building industries is included to demonstrate the disproportionately adverse effects of economic restructuring since the early 1970s on foreign labour, and to illustrate in some detail processes of labour market segmentation affecting immigrants. The strikes by foreign car workers in France in the 1970s and early 1980s dramatically underscored the growing significance of immigrant labour in the international political economy.

Globalisation and international migration

The international migration and employment nexus has been the object of extensive but inconclusive scholarship and acrimonious political debate. A passage from a 1989 government report, *The*

Effects of Immigration in the US Economy and Labor Market, summarised
the state of knowledge in the USA as follows:

> The assessment of the effects of immigration on the US economy
> and labor market is a complex undertaking and a definite response
> remains essentially elusive. In addition to difficulties in isolating
> the labor market behaviour of such groups as illegal immigrants
> and non-immigrants, larger questions of data adequacy also
> conspire to make what is a particularly contentious analytical
> exercise even more so . . . few unequivocal answers can be offered
> regarding the role of the foreign born in the various US labor
> markets.
>
> The shortage of appropriate data allows the analysts' predis-
> positions to influence the outcome of the research to a significant
> degree. Differences in academic disciplines, for instance, influence
> the research questions asked and often dictate the choice both of
> the unit of analysis and the analytical tools used. Furthermore, the
> level of data aggregation, and the focus and location of the
> investigation, often lead to different findings and influence their
> interpretation. Finally, theoretical and philosophical differences
> often intrude to the point of creating an analytical and inter-
> pretative morass. (US Department of Labor, 1989: 179)

In spite of these caveats, the 227 page report went on to conclude that
immigration was increasingly important to understanding the US
economy and, on balance, had a slight but beneficial overall effect. It
noted, for instance, that the foreign-born constitute nearly 7 per cent
of all US workers and accounted for some 22 per cent of annual
growth of the workforce in the 1980s (US Department of Labor,
1989: xi). Its upbeat conclusion concerning the effects of international
migration influenced adoption of the Immigration Act of 1990 which
increased annual legal migration to the US by 35 per cent.

One of the principal themes emerging from the analysis of
international labour migration in the 1980s was its interconnections
with globalisation of the international economy. The US Department
of Labor report was emblematic:

> The underlying economic and social conditions that create,
> organise and sustain international migration result from the
> degree and manner in which regional economies become integ-
> rated, and not simply from stagnation or economic crisis found in

individual countries . . . To the extent that US policies and practices contribute to the pace and pattern of regional integration, they help organise the expansion of regional labour flows. International trade, investment, communication and transportation facilitate the narrowing of differences between regions and countries and contribute to the expansion of opportunities and . possibilities for international migration . . . Just as a firm expands from production for a local market to sell overseas in an international market, local labor markets are transformed through economic development into regional and international labor exchanges . . . The timing, direction, volume, and composition of international migration, therefore, are fundamentally rooted in the structure and growth of the regional economy in which the United States is most actively involved. Flows of labor occur within an international division of labour with increasingly integrated production, exchange and consumption processes that extend beyond national boundaries. (US Department of Labor, 1989: 5)

Other major factors affecting global patterns of immigrant employment include the decline in manufacturing employment in 'old' industrial areas, the rise of the 'newly industrialising countries' (NICs), the reorganisation of production and distribution within transnational corporations, more emphasis on control and communications using new technologies, the increased role of globally mobile financial capital and the emergence of 'global cities' as centres of corporate finance, marketing and design.

The growth of manufacturing in the NICs does not generally reduce labour emigration. Moreover a concomitant capitalist revolution in traditional agricultural societies has spurred massive rural–urban migration, bringing more peasants to urban areas than can be employed by new world market factories. Thus many of the exploding cities of Asia and Latin America become way stations on the road to urban centres in industrial democracies. Many of these new labour migrants confront an erosion of the relatively favourable and protected wages and employment conditions achieved by generations of blue-collar unionism. They take low-skilled non-unionised jobs where they have little bargaining power or security of employment. Hence new migrations and new patterns of ethnic segmentation have been hallmarks of the transformation of the global economy since the 1970s.

Growing fragmentation and polarisation of immigrant employment

The persistence of labour market segmentation of immigrants is a theme common to many of the more recent studies on immigrants and labour markets. Castles and Kosack demonstrated a general pattern of labour market segmentation between native and immigrant workers in Western Europe in the 1970s (Castles and Kosack, 1973). The Australian economist Jock Collins regards the 'impact of post-war immigration on the growth and fragmentation of the Australian working class' as 'one of the most salient aspects of the Australian immigration experience' (Collins, 1991: 87). The US Department of Labor report concluded:

> the most important current consequence of internationalisation, industrial restructuring, and the increase in the national origins and legal status of new immigrants is the dramatic diversification of conditions under which newcomers participate in the US labor market. Newcomers arrive in the United States with increasingly diverse skills, resources and motivations. In addition, on an increasing scale, they are arriving with distinct legal statuses. In turn, this proliferation of legal statuses may become a new source of social and economic stratification. (US Department of Labor, 1989: 18)

The range and significance of immigrant labour market diversity is obscured by policy and analytical perspectives that stress the homogeneity of competitive labour markets or sharp contrasts between primary and secondary labour markets (US Department of Labor, 1989: 18). It is often meaningless to generalise about average earnings and other labour market effects of immigration, just as it is meaningless to assume a general interest in discussions of immigration policy. Immigration has extremely unequal effects upon different social strata. Some groups clearly gain from policies facilitating large-scale expansion of foreign labour migration, while other groups lose. The winners are large investors and employers who favour expanded immigration as part of a strategy for deregulation of the labour market. The losers would be many of the migrants themselves, who would find themselves forced into insecure and exploitative jobs, with little chance of promotion. Among the losers would also be some existing members of the workforce, whose employment and social condition might be worsened by such policies.

As late as 1979, a US government task force concluded that: 'The precise impacts of immigration on the US economy, or any economy for that matter, have not been thoroughly studied because of the difficulty of isolating contributions of immigration from other factors' (Interagency Task Force on Immigration Policy, 1979: 257). Growing political controversy over immigration policies, which had spread across the world by the 1980s, has helped generate an outpouring of scholarship since then. One of the principal aims has been to examine empirically assumptions and deductions that have fuelled debates over immigration. Many of these pertain to the labour market role of immigrants – their effects upon wages and working conditions, welfare and unemployment. Much more is known about the labour market effects of international migration than was the case in the 1970s.

In the 1980s, awareness grew of a bifurcation in the labour market effects of immigration upon industrial democracies. Immigrant workforces became increasingly bipolar with clustering at the upper and lower levels of the labour market. The head of ILO's migrant workers section termed Western Europe's growing number of professionals, technicians and kindred foreign workers the 'highly invisible' migrants (Böhning, 1991: 10). He estimated that they comprised one-quarter of legally resident aliens living in the EC and included two million citizens of EFTA countries, which in 1993 is slated to join with the EC to create the world's most populous free trade zone, the European Economic Area. Americans, Canadians and Japanese comprised most of the remainder of the EC's highly invisible migrants. However resident alien populations, such as Turks in Germany, who are stereotypically seen as blue collar workers, also include surprising numbers of professionals and entrepreneurs.

The growing number of professional level foreign workers reflects the globalisation of the economy. The British geographer John Salt has documented how the proliferation of transnational firms and changing management needs and practices have contributed to growing professional level foreign worker populations worldwide (Salt, 1989). The expectation is for professional level, employment-related immigration to continue to grow as highly qualified employment represents a steadily expanding share of overall employment.

In Germany, for instance, the unqualified share of the workforce was expected to decline from 27 per cent in 1985 to 18 per cent in 2010, whereas the highly qualified component would expand from 28 to 39 per cent (Böhning, 1991b: 11; the figures are for the area of the former West Germany only). In a little over a generation, then, two million jobs for unskilled workers are expected to be eliminated while 3.4 million additional highly-skilled jobs will be created. While labour force need projections must be contemplated with caution, the unavoidable implication of the German projections is that there will be no resumption of large-scale recruitment of unskilled foreign workers as in the 1960s (Werner, 1992: 89). Some Germans, however, disagree and foresee a need for large-scale immigration on demographic grounds (Tichy, 1990). The economic research section of the German parliament concluded in 1992 that Germany would require an influx of 300 000 foreigners annually to maintain its labour force (*This Week in Germany*, 18 September 1992, 4). The trend away from unskilled, legal foreign worker employment and toward growing highly-skilled foreign employment was apparent in data compiled by Heinz Werner.

TABLE 7.1

Foreign employees in the Federal Republic of Germany, by occupational Qualification, 1977–89

Level of qualification	Total 1977	Total 1989	EC Nationals 1977	EC Nationals 1989
Trainees	87	197	92	82
Employees with low qualification	96	78	103	62
Middle-level qualification	93	92	94	80
Graduate employees	86	106	84	105
Total employees	95	87	100	68
Absolute numbers (thousands)	1 889	1 689	730	497

Note: index figures (1980 = 100)
Source: Werner, 1992.

For the EC as a whole, the Single European Act is expected to spur economic growth. Demand for labour is expected to exceed supply in most EC countries, save for Ireland and France. By the year 2000, unemployment is expected to decline considerably, although not be eliminated. Areas of high labour force increase will also experience high economic growth (Werner, 1992: 86–7). However experts like Werner expect little or no increase in migration between the EC member states after 1 January 1993, except at the highly-skilled, professional level. Consequently EC member states are likely to turn to the former EFTA states, Eastern Europe and elsewhere for highly qualified manpower. Several former communist states have eagerly sought to export labour and numerous agreements facilitating labour movement between Eastern and Western Europe have been signed (see Chapter 6). But these developments also sparked fears of a brain drain in the former Warsaw Bloc area. The loss of highly-skilled labour to the West was seen as a potentially severe hindrance to socioeconomic development in the post-Cold War period (Shevstova, 1992).

A bifurcation in the labour market characteristics of immigrants was apparent in the USA, Canada and Australia as well. George Borjas found an overall pattern of declining skills in post-1965 immigrant cohorts to the USA as compared to the pre-1965 immigrants. The fundamental explanation for this is to be found in the 1965 changes in US immigration law which removed the national origins restrictions and opened up the USA to immigration from around the world (see Chapter 4). As entries from Western Europe declined in favour of growing immigration from Asia and Latin America, the differences in the prevailing socioeconomic and educational standards between the regions were reflected in the declining skills and rising poverty of post-1965 immigrants (Borjas, 1990). The USA is far more attractive to poorer and less privileged Mexicans than it is to the Mexican middle and upper classes, who are little inclined to emigrate from a society marked by extreme inequality in income distribution and life chances (Borjas, 1990: 126). Hence it was scarcely surprising that the Mexican immigrants who were legalised in the late 1980s through the Special Agricultural Worker programme – nearly one million – on average possessed only four years of schooling. Borjas estimated that the decrease in the level of economic development and the increase in the income inequality in the countries sending immigrants to the USA, along with declining educational attainment, accounted for 60 per cent of the decrease in earnings between the immigrant cohorts of the 1950s and those of the 1970s.

The growing bifurcation of immigrants to the USA was apparent in sharply contrasting poverty rates of various national origin groups. The fraction of immigrants from Germany and Italy living in poverty was 8.2 per cent, whereas Chinese and Koreans had poverty rates of 12.5 and 13.5 per cent, respectively, and immigrants from the Dominican Republic and Mexico suffered poverty rates of 33.7 and 26 per cent (Borjas, 1990: 148). Similarly Borjas found a strong link between rising welfare utilisation by immigrants and the changing character of immigration to the USA (Borjas, 1990: 150–62). These trends prompted Borjas to advocate changes in US immigration law that would increase the skill levels of immigrants. The Immigration Act of 1990 included a number of provisions designed to accomplish that by nearly tripling the number of visas reserved for qualified workers from 54 000 to 140 000 yearly. Moreover 10 000 visas were set aside for investors annually – 7000 for foreign investors of at least US$1 million in urban areas and 3000 for investors of no less than US$500 000 in rural and high unemployment areas.

As in Western Europe, labour market projections for the USA forecast growing shortages of highly skilled, professional level and technical workers. Adoption of the Immigration Act of 1990 was designed to enhance US competitiveness in what was perceived as a global competition to attract highly skilled labour. One of the major challenges facing the USA in the future is finding gainful employment for existing and projected stocks of low and unskilled workers, many of whom are minorities. Nonetheless advocacy of temporary foreign worker recruitment for industries like agriculture, restaurants and hotels, and construction continues on both sides of the Atlantic and many employers complain about labour shortages despite relatively high unemployment rates. The North American Free Trade Agreement (NAFTA), which was initialled in August 1992, will, if ratified, create a free trade zone between the USA, Mexico and Canada. Even though labour migration is not included in NAFTA, implementation of the agreement is expected to stimulate migration of workers from Mexico, and therefore to exacerbate the employment difficulties of low-skilled workers in the USA and possibly Canada.

A sharp pattern of immigrant labour market segmentation is also apparent in Australia (see Chapter 5). In 1978, Collins identified four major groups: (1) men born in Australia or in English-speaking background countries and other male immigrants from Northern

Europe, who were disproportionally found in white-collar, highly skilled or supervisory jobs; (2) men from non-English speaking background countries who were highly concentrated in manual manufacturing jobs; (3) Australian and English speaking background women, disproportionally in sales and services; and (4) non-English-speaking background women who tended to get the worst jobs with the poorest conditions (Collins, 1978). For Collins: 'Perhaps the crucial point in understanding post-war Australian immigration is that [English speaking] and [non-English speaking] migrants have very different work experiences' (Collins, 1991: 87).

Significant immigrant labour market segmentation is thus evident in industrial democracies. Traditional gender divisions, which concentrated women in low-paid and low-status work, have been overlaid and reinforced by new divisions affecting immigrant workers of both sexes. As migration is globalised there are widening gaps both between immigrants and non-immigrants, and among different immigrant categories. Future trends in the labour market will favour highly-skilled immigration but the pool of aspiring low-skilled immigrants is enormous and will expand exponentially in coming years.

The processes of labour market segmentation lead to long-term marginalisation of certain groups, including many of the new immigrants from non-traditional sources. Generally there are not rigid divisions based on race, ethnicity or citizenship status. Rather certain groups have become over-represented in certain disadvantaged positions. Some individual members of disadvantaged groups do well in the labour market, but most do not. The causes for this are not only found in specific factors like education, length of residence, prior labour market experience or discrimination, much more complex explanations are usually required, ones which provide historical understanding of the processes of labour migration and settlement, along with its role in a changing world economy.

Global cities, ethnic entrepreneurs and immigrant women workers

Patterns of international migration and their labour market consequences are tightly bound up with the nature of capital flows, investment, international trade, direct and indirect foreign military intervention, diplomacy and cultural interaction. Recent work by Sassen (1988), for instance, has stressed how patterns of foreign investment and displacement of certain US manufacturing jobs abroad have fostered new migratory streams to the USA (or have tended to expand pre-existing flows). One consequence of US corporations moving manufacturing operations abroad in the quest for lower wages has been a concomitant increase in migratory inflows from the areas of investment. Sassen stresses the significance of the emergence of global cities, like New York or Los Angeles, in which immigrant workers continue to find employment in expanding service sectors and in industries characterised by sweatshops or extremely poorly paid labour, to understanding future patterns of international migration. Linkages between global cities and distant hinterlands create paradoxes wherein enormous wealth and highly skilled and remunerated professional employment uneasily coexist with growing low-paid and unskilled service industry employment and developing world-like employment conditions in underground industries.

The casualisation of labour and growing illegal alien employment are characteristic attributes of global cities. Considerable illegal employment of aliens often coincides with high unemployment of citizens and resident aliens, who are disproportionally likely to be minorities and have often been victims of job losses in industries that have shifted manufacturing operations abroad.

As noted in Chapters 3, 4, and 6, some immigrant groups have traditionally played key economic roles as middlemen traders and entrepreneurs. Since the 1970s recession, a growing body of research has examined immigrant entrepreneurship and its effects upon immigrants and immigration in general. Across industrial democracies, growing numbers of immigrants are self-employed and owners of small businesses (Waldinger *et al.*, 1990). Most typical are ethnic restaurants, 'mom and pop' food stores and convenience stores. Immigrant-owned businesses frequently employ family members and kinsfolk from the country of origin. Light and Bonacich, in their influential study, *Immigrant Entrepreneurs* (1988) which focused on Korean immigrant businesses in Los Angeles, traced the origins of the Korean community there to the circumstances of the Korean War which led to the establishment of extensive transnational ties and eventually migration between the Republic of Korea and the USA.

Recent studies in France similarly stress the complex historical genesis of immigrant entrepreneurship. Sayad noted that 'sleep merchants' who supplied lodging for illegal aliens, usually compatriots, figured among the first North African businessmen in France (Vaddamalay, 1990: 13). In Germany, there were 150 000 foreigner-owned businesses by 1992, including 33 000 owned by Turks. The Turkish-owned businesses generated 700 000 jobs in 1991 and recorded sales of DM 25 billion (about US$ 17 billion) and invested DM 6 million in Germany. (*This Week in Germany*, 18 September 1992: 4).

Some indication of the impact of immigrant entrepreneurs can be garnered from data compiled by the US Census Bureau indicating sharp increases in business firms owned by Asians and Hispanics in the 1980s. Firms owned by Asian Americans, Pacific Islanders, American Indians and Alaska natives increased 87 per cent from 1982 to 1987, from 201 264 to 376 711. This compared with a 14 per cent increase over the same period for all US firms (Census Bureau press release of 2 August 1991). Similarly Hispanic firms in the USA increased from 233 975 in 1982 to 422 373 in 1987, an 81 per cent increase (Census Bureau press release of 16 May 1991). Hispanic owned firms accounted for 3 per cent of all US firms and generated 1 per cent of gross receipts.

Immigrant entrepreneurship has been assessed divergently. Some scholars stress the economic dynamism of immigrant entrepreneurs with their positive effects upon economic growth and quality of life for consumers. A more critical viewpoint stresses the human suffering entailed by the intense competition involving many immigrant entrepreneurs, the long hours of work, exploitation of family labour and of illegally employed aliens, resultant social problems and so on. (Light and Bonacich, 1988: 425–36). The Los Angeles riots of 1992 revealed an undercurrent of tension between blacks and Korean businesspeople in Los Angeles. Tensions between urban black Americans and Korean entrepreneurs were manifested in other major US cities in the 1980s, frictions that were probably related to anti-Jewish business sentiments that were manifested when US ghettoes boiled over in the 1960s. The reality of these tensions again stresses the need for a broadgauged approach to apprehension of immigration.

Research in the 1980s also shed a great deal of additional light on the labour market role of immigrant women. Again broad developments in the international arena shaped their labour market effects. Houstoun *et al.* documented a female predominance in legal immigration to the US since 1930. They concluded that deployment of US military forces abroad played a significant role in this. They noted, for instance, that an estimated 200 000 Asian-born wives of USA servicemen resided in the US in the early 1980s. While working age immigrant men reported a labour force participation rate (77.4 per cent) similar to US men, female immigrants were less likely to report an occupation than US women. Only 34 per cent reported an occupation. The bifurcation pattern considered above was more pronounced with immigrant women. They were more concentrated in highly-skilled occupations (28.1 per cent) than US women but also more concentrated in low-status, white-collar clerical employment (18.0 per cent), semi-skilled blue-collar operation jobs (17.9 per cent) and in private household work (13.9 per cent). They were half as likely to be employed as private household workers at the bottom of the female job hierarchy (Houstoun *et al.*, 1984).

Data on female immigrant employment in Australia revealed sharp segmentation by nationality. Collins and Castles used 1986 Census data to examine the representation of women in manufacturing industry. The index figure 100 indicates average representation. They found high degrees of overrepresentation for women born in Vietnam (494), Turkey (437), Yugoslavia (358) and Greece (315). Women from the USA (63), Canada (68) and Australia (79) were underrepresented (Collins and Castles, 1991: 15). Female clustering in manufacturing industries undergoing restructuring rendered them disproportionally vulnerable to unemployment. Immigrant women of a non-English speaking background were thought to be overrepresented in outwork for industries such as textiles, footwear, electronics, packing and food and groceries. Collins and Castles considered these workers as perhaps the most exploited section of the Australian workforce (Collins and Castles, 1991: 19).

Morokvasic has argued that, in general, immigrant women from peripheral zones living in Western industrial democracies 'represent a ready made labour supply which is, at once, the most vulnerable, the most flexible and, at least in the beginning, the least demanding work force. They have been incorporated into sexually segregated labour markets at the lowest stratum in high technology industries or at the "cheapest" sectors in those industries which are labour intensive and employ the cheapest labour to remain competitive' (Morokvasic, 1984: 886). The emerging patterns of labour migration in the 1990s look set to continue this type of incorporation of women's labour, and to extend it to new areas of immigration, such as Southern Europe and Southeast Asia.

Labour market segmentation and industrial restructuring: foreign labour in France's car and building industries

In nearly all highly-developed countries, migrant workers have become highly concentrated in the motor and building industries. Employer recourse to foreign labour in these sectors has been particularly significant – both in quantitative and in political terms – in France. At the height of labour immigration in the early 1970s, some 500 000 foreigners were employed in the building industry. About one out of every three workers was a foreigner and roughly one out of every four foreigners employed in France was found to be in the building industry. In motor car construction, there were some 125 000 foreigners employed, representing one out of every four car workers. Only the sanitation services industry had a higher ratio of foreign to French employees by 1980 (Miller, 1984).

The disproportionate effects of the 1970s recession upon French and foreign workers in the car and building industries were incontrovertible. Although foreigners comprised one-third of building sector employees, they suffered nearly half of the total employment loss from 1973 to 1979, and declined to 17 per cent of the building industry workforce by 1989 (OECD SOPEMI, 1992: 24). In the car industry, where total employment actually grew over the same period, foreign workers were hard hit by layoffs. While the total employment increased by 13 000, 29 000 fewer foreigners were employed in the industry by 1979. During the 1980s, tens of thousands of additional jobs were lost, with aliens again being disproportionally affected.

A report compiled by the *Fédération Nationale du Bâtiment*, the main French building sector association, revealed that total employment in the building sector declined by 11.7 per cent from 1974 until 1981. But the reduction of the foreign employee component, some 150 000 jobs, represented a loss of 30 per cent of the 1974 foreign workforce, whereas the 45 000 decrease in the number of Frenchmen employed represented only a 3.9 per cent decline from 1974 employment levels.

In other words, three out of every four jobs lost in the building industry from 1974 to 1981 had been held by foreigners.

Foreign worker employment in the building and motor car construction industries reached its height in 1974 and then contracted sharply. Nonetheless, according to a Ministry of Labour survey, foreign workers comprised 28 and 18.6 per cent of the building and car construction industries workforces, respectively, in 1979. The continuing importance of foreign worker employment was all the more remarkable because, in addition to the halt in recruitment, the French government sought to reduce foreign worker employment through a programme offering a cash incentive for repatriation. There was also a *revalorisation du travail manuel* programme, which sought to substitute French for foreign workers through improving the conditions of manual jobs. Both the repatriation and *revalorisation* programmes fared poorly. However case studies in the 1980s indicated that some French firms were succeeding in reducing dependency on foreign labour (Merckling, 1987).

Foreign workers were routinely given jobs with unskilled or semi-skilled manual labour classifications which belied their actual level of training or the skill required to perform the job. In both industries it was often charged that there was not equal pay for equal work. This perception, coupled with a lack of foreign worker integration into unions, which in the 1960s motor plants were mainly representative of French workers, made foreign workers a primary target of extreme Leftist organisational efforts in the wake of the May/June 1968 events. A *grève bouchon* or bottleneck strike at the sprawling Renault-Billancourt factory in 1973 caused consternation (Mehideb, 1973). A shop of some 400 workers succeeded in paralysing production. Similar strikes disrupted the German car industry at roughly the same time and, in Switzerland, Spanish seasonal workers in construction stunned the country with strikes and demonstrations over their housing conditions (Castles, 1989: 28–42; Castles and Kosack, 1973; Miller, 1981).

Prior to 1974, foreign worker employment in the motor car assembly industry was characterised by a high rate of employee turnover. In some factories, such as Citroën, contracts were not renewed so as to ensure a high turnover rate. High turnover rates also stemmed, however, from the transnational nature of foreign labour. Foreign workers would often want to return home after relatively short employment terms to spend time with their families. Many foreign workers would quit their jobs in order to take long vacations and then seek to be rehired in the auto assembly industry upon their return. This pattern, which should also be attributed to the difficult working conditions of many foreign car workers, was profoundly altered by the 1974 recruitment ban. After 1974, foreign car workers without permanent resident alien status who quit their jobs and returned home could no longer legally return to France to seek re-employment. Also the economic recession made it less likely that foreign car workers would find work in other areas of the economy. Hence the foreign worker turnover rate at Renault factories had declined sharply by 1975.

Major consequences of the stabilisation of the foreign workforce in motor manufacturing were the ageing of the foreign workforce, its mounting unionisation and sociopolitical cohesiveness, growing dissatisfaction with assembly line work and resentment of perceived discrimination against foreigners in terms of career opportunities. By the 1980s, most foreign car workers had been employed for at least five years by their company. At the Talbot-Poissy plant by 1982, for example, only one out of the 4400 Moroccan manual workers had worked there less than five years. Some 3200 of the Moroccans had worked there for ten years or more (Croissandeau, 1984: 8–9).

With longer experience of employment came a growing tendency to unionise.[1] Foreign workers often chose to join or to vote for various unions by groups, whether from a specific nationality or from a specific shop. Hence foreign worker support could swing sharply from one union to another, depending on foreign worker views of a union's specific programme on issues of concern to them. The volatility of ties to French unions stemmed in part from the parallel development of cohesive and largely autonomous shop floor organisation among foreign workers. In many cases, shop floor cohesion was based upon national or religious solidarity. By the 1980s, Islamic fundamentalist solidarity groups, whose loci of contact were Muslim prayer-rooms provided by management within the factories, had become an important force. In other instances, underground revolutionary groups affected the form of foreign worker integration into union structures.

In some factories, such as Citroen's Aulnay-sous-Bois plant and Talbot's Poissy plant in the Parisian suburbs, alleged violations of French labour law and other means of management pressure resulted in foreign worker enrollment in so-called house-unions affiliated with the right-wing *Confédération des Syndicats Libres* (CSL). Foreign workers risked losing work and residence permits if they did not support the house union, or they stood to lose company housing and the opportunity to participate in CSL-controlled holiday programmes. It was alleged that factory elections were fraudulent. Foreign workers who openly sympathised with left-wing unions ran the risk of being beaten up and reported to homeland governmental services charged with surveillance and maintenance of foreign worker loyalty. Moroccan sympathisers of left-wing unions, in particular, could be jailed when they returned home on vacation. In several important motor car plants, then, the inferior legal status of foreign labour contributed to the development of labour relations dominated by management interests. This led to an accumulation of foreign worker grievances and bitter antagonism between pro-CSL and anti-CSL employee factions which would explode into violence after the left-wing election victory of 1981.

The extraordinary cohesiveness and sense of collective identity evidenced by foreign auto workers by the 1980s stemmed from the stratification which bound workers of similar ethnic and religious backgrounds together in assembly line and other manual labour jobs. Growing dissatisfaction with dead-end jobs virtually without opportunities for advancement provided an additional dimension of resentment. The striking concentration of foreign workers in unskilled or lowly qualified jobs at Renault-Billancourt was typical of car plants which employed large numbers of foreign workers. Any explanation for the low qualifications or low certified skill levels of most foreign car workers must return to the recruitment process. Citroën, and to a lesser extent other French motor manufacturers, deliberately sought out physically able but poorly educated foreigners to fill manual labour positions. It was felt that their low levels of education and general backwardness made them better suited for monotonous and often physically taxing jobs than Frenchmen. Hence many foreign car workers were illiterate.

At the Aulnay-sous-Bois Citroën factory, for example, 66 per cent of all manual workers, about three-quarters of whom foreigners, were classified as illiterate as late as 1984 (Croissandeau, 1984, 8–9). Despite the availability of worker education programmes, few foreign workers completed them. The arduous working conditions left little time and energy for learning. At the Talbot factory in Poissy, only 213 workers out of a work-force of 9 000 completed literacy courses in

1980. This number declined to 46 in 1981. The fact that many foreign workers were not literate in French and that most had not completed primary education created an enormous barrier to their promotion in the motor manufacturing industry as in other French industries which employ large numbers of foreigners.

Illiterate foreign workers and those lacking in primary education could not compete in written exams which often held the key to professional advancement. Foreign workers frequently possessed skills which were not reflected in their professional rankings because they could not or did not obtain certificates based on examinations and successful completion of courses. A perceived gap developed between actual foreign worker skill levels and the type of jobs they performed and their formal classification as unskilled or lowly skilled. Foreign workers frequently charged that the industry's system of remuneration based on a worker's formal qualifications and job descriptions discriminated against them. The issue remained a bone of contention between French and non-French workers in the industry and strained foreign worker ties to French unions as well.

With few hopes for professional advancement, many foreign car workers grew frustrated with their jobs. Their frustration and the difficulty of their work were reflected in raising absenteeism and generally less disciplined work habits (Willard, 1984). Whereas employers once prized foreign workers for their industry and discipline, they began to complain of their inability to manage foreign labour effectively and resulting production and quality control problems. Employer misgivings over hiring of foreign labour were crystallised by a primarily foreign worker strike wave which plagued the industry in the 1970s before rocking its very foundations in the 1980s. The 1973 Renault-Billancourt strike was portentous.

Foreign car worker unrest was evident by 1978 throughout the industry. However it took the dramatic left-wing coalition electoral victories of 1981 to embolden foreign workers at Talbot and Citroën to strike. The change of government meant that labour laws would be applied at the Talbot and Citroen factories, and that foreign workers would no longer have to fear sanctions if they expressed themselves freely. The announced intention of the new government to strengthen the rights of labour through the Auroux laws buoyed support for anti-CSL forces in works council elections at the two companies. The pro-communist *Confédération Générale du Travail* (CGT) in particular scored impressive gains. The elections were marred by violent confrontations between CGT supporters, most of whom were foreign assembly line workers, and CSL supporters, many if not most of whom were skilled French workers (Ewald, 1983). During and after these employee elections, violence periodically erupted at the two plants. Foreign workers repeatedly struck over a variety of issues. Each strike action seriously disrupted production, with strikers often damaging cars and production equipment.

The strike movements at Talbot-Poissy and Citroën-Aulnay seemed to spark foreign worker dominated strikes at other car companies. Paris-area Renault plants were repeatedly hit by strikes, as were several other manufacturers. In virtually all cases, foreign workers comprised the vast majority of strikers. They generally demanded upgrading of their pay and professional status along with the creation of career opportunities. Many of the strikes were *grèves bouchons* where one or several shops of foreign workers would shut down production and thereby force layoffs of non-striking workers. This situation led to confrontations between strikers and non-strikers, but the violence witnessed at Talbot and Citroën plants was generally avoided elsewhere. Foreign worker strike movements typically began autonomously at the shop level without trade union backing, although left-wing unions would usually seek to represent the strikers. The inability of the established unions to control foreign workers hurt organised labour's credibility within the industry and in French society at large.

The violence of the car workers' strikes, the severe production losses they entailed and the breakdown of management and even union control in the face of a virtual rebellion by foreign car workers had major repercussions upon French politics. The strikes marred a period of national labour tranquillity which resulted from labour support for the left-wing coalition government. As the government's economic policies faltered, leading to an economic crisis, foreign car worker unrest hurt the performance of a key economic sector (Tully, 1983; *Automobile: la France à la traîne*, 1984, no. 589) and seemed to undermine the government's effort to restore confidence in its handling of the economy. Politically the strikes almost certainly contributed to a backlash against official immigration policies, which eroded support for the governmental coalition parties, as witnessed in the 1983 municipal elections (Jarreau, 1983).

The car workers' strikes hastened plans to restructure and modernise the French motor manufacturing industry. Both Peugeot and Renault, the two major automobile firms (Peugeot having acquired Citroen and Chrysler Europe in the late 1970s), announced plans to automate car production through the use of industrial robots. In the summer of 1983, Peugeot announced that it planned to fire 8 000 workers, including almost 3000 workers at its Talbot plant. In December 1983, an agreement between the government and Peugeot was announced that authorised the firing of 1905 workers, most of whom were foreigners. This announcement led to a new strike and a factory occupation, which again was accompanied by a great deal of violence. Over 50 workers were injured before French unions asked the government to send in police forces to restore order. Unrest in French car factories continued sporadically into the early 1990s, but would never again reach dimensions comparable to those of the 1973 to 1983 period. The building industry with its weaker unionisation rate, rampant illegal alien employment, widespread sub-contracting and predominance of small and medium-sized employers, did not experience parallel unrest. However economic restructuring, as seen through the window of these two French industries, had disproportionally affected immigrant employment, with far-reaching political consequences.

The process of labour market segmentation

The French motor manufacture and building industries were typical of the situation of a large proportion of migrant workers in all highly-developed countries, in that they exhibited a pronounced pattern of foreign worker concentration in the least desirable jobs. These jobs were frequently unhealthy, physically taxing, dangerous, monotonous or socially unattractive. There were a multiplicity of factors which shaped this state of affairs. In both industries, recruitment and employment of foreign and colonial workers had already become traditional before the Second World War. In the post-1945 period, both industries faced a serious shortfall of labour, a problem solved by recourse to aliens. The legal foreign worker recruitment system aided employers by making foreign worker employment and residence contingent on employment in a certain firm or industry – usually within one city or region – for a period of several years. Many foreign workers only gradually earned freedom of employment and residential mobility.

The legal recruitment system functioned to funnel foreign workers into less attractive jobs. Employers might have had to improve working conditions and wages if it had not been for the availability of foreign labour. Or they might have been unable to stay in business. Illegal alien employment was widespread in the building industry, but rare in the motor construction industry. The size of firms and the presence of strong unions made illegal alien employment more difficult in the latter. Widespread illegal employment of aliens in the building industry adversely affected wages and working conditions, with the paradoxical effect of making the industry all the more dependent on foreign labour recruitment. As employment in the industry became socially devalued, employers often could find only foreigners to work for them. Similar processes affected female foreign workers, who became highly concentrated in certain sectors of manufacturing, such as clothing and food processing, and in service occupations such as cleaning, catering and unskilled health service work. Undocumented employment of women was even more common than for men, since ideologies about foreign women as mothers and housewives made it easy to conceal their role in the labour force.

There was little direct displacement of French workers by foreigners. In part owing to the prior presence of large numbers of foreign workers, certain types of jobs became socially defined as jobs for foreign labour. Such jobs were increasingly shunned by French workers who, during the long period of post-war expansion, could generally find more attractive employment elsewhere. Indeed massive foreign worker employment enabled the upward mobility of many French workers. This general process prevailed until the late 1970s or early 1980s, when France went into a prolonged recession and unemployment grew. It was at this juncture that displacement of French workers by foreign labour became a significant political issue.

Employee recruitment strategies also contributed to labour market segmentation between French and alien workers. Some building industry employees preferred to hire illegal aliens because they could increase profits, through non-payment of bonuses and payroll taxes for instance, and they ran little risk of legal sanctions until the 1980s. Some motor industry employers deliberately sought to hire poorly educated peasants without industrial experience in order to frustrate left-wing unionisation efforts. This strategy had the effect of making assembly line work even less attractive to French workers. In the

same way, clothing industry employers found it particularly easy to pressure foreign women into undocumented and poorly-paid outwork
    again a situation to be found in virtually all industrial countries (Phizacklea, 1990).

Eventually the pattern of ethnic stratification within French car plants became a major factor in labour unrest. The strategy of divide and rule practised by some employers ultimately boomeranged when foreign car workers struck for dignity in the late 1970s and the early 1980s. The ethnic solidarity produced by the process of labour market segmentation in many French car factories was a key factor in the prolonged unrest. Again parallels can be found in migrant worker movements in other countries (for Australia, for instance, see Lever-Tracy and Quinlan, 1988).

The process of labour market segmentation usually results from a combination of institutional racism and more diffuse attitudinal racism. This applies particularly in countries which recruit 'guest-workers' under legal and administrative rules which restrict foreign workers' rights in a discriminatory way. The legally vulnerable status of many foreign workers in turn fosters resentment against them on the part of citizen workers, who fear that their wages and conditions will be undermined. This may be combined with resentment of foreign workers for social and cultural reasons, leading to a dangerous spiral of racism. Such factors have profoundly affected trade unions and labour relations in most countries which have experienced labour immigration since 1945.

Immigration, minorities and the labour market needs of the future

The plight of laid-off Moroccan car workers in France was emblematic of a host of critical problems facing many industrial democracies. Even in the early 1980s, a Paris-area car plant typically finished painting cars by hand. Teams of immigrant workers generally did the work and, in many cases, it was done by Moroccans. One-fourth of all Moroccans employed in France in 1979 were employed by the car industry alone. The Moroccans were recruited because they were eager to work, recruitment networks were in place and because they were reputed to be physically apt and hardworking people. By 1990, most of the painting teams had been replaced by robots. Many of the workers were unemployed and, owing to their lack of educational background, there was little hope of retraining them to take jobs requiring more advanced educational backgrounds. Their only hope for re-employment lay in finding another relatively low-skilled manual labour job, but such jobs were disappearing.

Throughout Western Europe, unemployment rates of foreign residents had reached alarming proportions by the mid-1980s, well above those for the population as a whole. This was due to the restructuring of the economy which shed so many manual labour jobs and placed a premium on highly-skilled labour. All indications were that there would continue to be an aggregate surplus of manual workers over employment opportunities for the foreseeable future. While blue-collar labour shortages may appear here and there, France, like other industrial democracies, will find it challenging enough in the future to provide employment for its existing manual labour force. Job opportunities will be found primarily in the highly-skilled sector where shortages are already apparent and will continue into the future.

The labour market difficulties of laid-off foreign workers were compounded by several other worrisome trends. Immigrant children comprised a growing share of the school age population but were disproportionally likely to do poorly in school, to be early school leavers or to enter the labour force without the kinds of educational and vocational credentials increasingly required for gainful employment (Castles *et al.*, 1984: Chapter 6). The worst scenario for the French socialists involved the son and daughter of the recently laid-off Moroccan car worker leaving school early or failing in their studies and thereby facing bleak employment prospects on their own. The fear was of a US-style ghetto syndrome in which successive generations of an ethnically distinctive population would become entrapped in a vicious cycle of unemployment – educational failure – socioeconomic discrimination – housing problems.

France, like most industrial democracies, faced an uphill struggle to ensure that the most vulnerable members of its society enjoyed a reasonable measure of equality of opportunity. Immigrants and the immigrant-origin population comprised a disproportionately large share of the at-risk population. This was the major motivation behind Western European efforts to curb illegal immigration. It was generally felt that the population that was the most adversely affected by direct or indirect competition from illegal aliens on labour markets was existing minority and immigrant populations. The overall economic effects of immigration may well be marginally positive. But labour markets effects of international migration, and particularly of illegal immigration, are uneven and spatially concentrated. In the USA, it was thought by some specialists that Afro-Americans and Hispanic citizens were the two groups most affected by illegal migration. These conclusions were disputed, however, and many Hispanic advocacy groups in the USA viewed illegal immigration as a benign, if not positive, inflow, since it provided needed workers and helped in family reunion and community formation processes.

Conclusions

This chapter has argued that the economic restructuring since the 1970s has given rise to new immigration flows and new patterns of immigrant employment. One major result has been increasing diversification of immigrants' work situations and of their effects on labour markets. Patterns of labour market segmentation by ethnic origin and gender which had emerged by the 1970s have generally persisted and, in many ways, have become even more pronounced in the 1990s. However the growth of illegal migration and employment, continuing deficiencies in statistics concerning immigrants (particularly in non-Western settings) and the growing transnational interdependence of which international migration is an integral part make it difficult to generalise about the labour market effects of immigrants. Writing of immigrant women, Morokvasic observed that 'it is probably illusory to make any generalisations based on these findings in different parts of the world . . . They can only be interpreted within the specific socioeconomic and cultural context in which these changes are observed' (Morokvasic, 1984: 895).

There are tremendous variations in immigrant employment patterns according to ethnic and national background, gender, recentness of arrival, legal status, education and training. Varying economic structures, governmental policies, patterns of discrimination and legal traditions further complicate matters. For instance, one important finding in the USA is that immigrants eventually will earn more on average than the Americans of similar age, years of education and other characteristics, despite disadvantage when they first arrived. Typically immigrants who arrived in the 1960s earned less than their American counterparts, but, by the 1980s, the immigrants were earning 10 per cent more (Martin, 1992). However, since the 1970s, Borjas (1990) has discerned a sharp decline in the skills of many immigrants and a rise in immigrant poverty. These findings cast a cloud over the 'American dream' of many immigrants, leading to mounting concern that immigration may be exacerbating social inequalities.

In Western Europe, an authoritative EC study (Commission of the European Communities, 1990) has documented a continuing pattern of employment, educational and housing disadvantages encountered by immigrants. Discrimination endures despite the integration policies of many Western European governments. Disadvantage, therefore, is often intergenerational and this poses a grave challenge to Western European social democratic traditions. In the USA, the passage of time has generally witnessed intergenerational upward mobility for European origin immigrants. The quintessential question asked about immigrants to the USA is: will the Mexican or Dominican immigrants be like the Irish and Italian immigrants of the nineteenth and early twentieth centuries? It seems too early to attempt to answer this question, but the intergenerational mobility evidenced by earlier immigrant waves to the USA created a more optimistic context and expectation than prevails in Western Europe. Much the same could be said for Australia and Canada.

Institutional and informal discrimination have clearly contributed to immigrant disadvantage in employment and socioeconomic status. In Western Europe, the discrimination inherent in the employment and residential restrictions characteristic of guestworker policies funnelled immigrants into specific economic sectors and types of jobs. The analysis of foreign worker employment in the French motor manufacture and building industries demonstrated the disproportionate effects of job losses in the restructuring of the 1970s and early 1980s upon foreign workers. However, in the 1980s, immigrant employment in France grew sharply in the fast-growing tertiary (or services) sector, and legally admitted resident aliens enjoyed more secure legal status and more extensive rights than in the past. The status of legally admitted immigrant workers in industrial democracies compared favourably with that accorded foreign workers in many other parts of the world. Some migrants have developed their own strategies to cope with labour market disadvantages. The growing unionisation of foreign employees in Western Europe and strike movements like those witnessed in the French car industry were forms of adaptation. The proliferation of immigrant entrepreneurs was another.

The general picture which emerges is that labour market segmentation is a central element in the process which leads to formation of ethnic minorities. As discussed in theory in Chapter 2, and as shown through the case studies of Australia and Germany in Chapter 5, labour market segmentation has complex links with other factors that lead to marginalisation of immigrant groups. Low-status work, high unemployment, bad working conditions and lack of opportunities for promotion are both causes and results of the other determinants of minority status: legal disabilities, insecure residency status, residential concentration in disadvantaged areas, poor educational prospects and exposure to racism, crime and other social problems.

Some sociologists argue that, in the 1990s, the conflict between labour and capital is no longer the major social issue in advanced societies. It has been replaced by the problem of *exclusion*: certain groups have been excluded from the mainstream of society. They are economically marginalised through low-status, insecure work and frequent unemployment; socially marginalised through poor education and exposure to crime, addiction and family breakdown; and politically marginalised through lack of power to influence decision making at any level of government. All these factors join to produce a physical marginalisation, that is a concentration in urban and sub-urban ghettoes, where minorities of various kinds are thrown together – virtually cut off from and forgotten by the rest of society (Dubet and Lapeyronnie, 1992). The concept of the 'two-thirds society', which has become current in public debate, carries the same implication. Obviously many immigrant groups have been forced into this situation of exclusion, not only by their disadvantaged labour market position, but also by the gamut of other factors already mentioned. Such immigrants are doubly disadvantaged: they are not only amongst the excluded of post-modern society, but they have also come to be widely seen as the cause of the problems. Thus immigrants experience a rising tide of racism, which isolates them even more. The next chapter will discuss this process of ethnic minority formation in highly-developed countries.

8

New Ethnic Minorities and Society

The migrations of the last half century have led to increasing ethnic diversity in many countries. In Chapter 2 we presented a four-stage model of the migratory process, and suggested that in the fourth stage – that of permanent settlement – immigrants tend to constitute *ethnic groups* in the country of immigration. Such groups are visible not only through the presence of different-looking people speaking their own languages, but also because of the development of ethnic neighbourhoods, the distinctive use of urban space, and the establishment of ethnic associations and institutions. Our argument in this chapter is that new ethnic groups have emerged in all the industrial countries which have had immigration since 1945, but that their character and their position in society varies considerably. In some countries we can speak of the formation of *ethnic communities*, in others of the formation of *ethnic minorities*. In the first case, the immigrants and their descendants are seen as an integral part of a multicultural society which is willing to reshape its culture and identity. In the second, immigrants are excluded and marginalised, so that they live on the fringes of a society which is determined to preserve myths of a static culture and a homogeneous identity. These two extremes may be seen as ideal types; all the societies examined come somewhere in between.

The comparative analysis of the migratory process for Australia and Germany in Chapter 5 provided illustrations for this theory. It suggested that Australia comes fairly close to the ethnic community model and Germany to the ethnic minority model. In this chapter we will broaden the analysis by looking at ethnic diversity in a wider

195

range of highly-developed countries. The topic is a broad one, which really requires detailed description of the situation in each country. That is not possible here for reasons of space. Instead brief summaries of the situation in the USA, Canada, the United Kingdom, France, the Netherlands, Switzerland and Sweden will be presented as 'Exhibits' within the text. The comparative analysis will draw on these, as well as on the detailed accounts of the migratory process in Australia and Germany. Some countries of immigration have had to be omitted altogether. These include Austria, Belgium, Luxemburg, Denmark, Norway, New Zealand and Japan. Nor is there space to discuss the new ethnic minorities in the Southern European countries.

The aim of the chapter is to show similarities and differences in the migratory process in the various countries, and to discuss why ethnic group formation and growing diversity have been relatively easily accepted in some countries, while in others these developments have led to marginalisation and exclusion. We will then go on to examine the consequences of these differences for the ethnic groups concerned and for society in general. The argument in brief is that the migratory process works in a similar way in all countries with respect to chain migration and settlement, and that similar processes of labour market segmentation, residential segregation and ethnic group formation take place. Racism and discrimination are also to be found in all countries, although their intensity towards specific groups varies. The main differences are to be found in state policies on immigration, settlement, citizenship and cultural pluralism. These differences, in turn are linked to different historical experiences of nation-state formation.

Immigration policies and minority formation

Immigration policies have been described in various parts of this book. Three groups of countries emerge. The so-called 'classical countries of immigration' – the USA, Canada and Australia – have encouraged permanent migration and treated most legal immigrants as future citizens, permitting family reunion and granting secure residence status. Sweden, despite its very different historical background, has followed similar policies. The second group includes France, the Netherlands and Britain; these countries have an intermediate position: immigrants from former colonies have received

---

EXHIBIT 8.1

Minorities in the United States of America

US society is a complex ethnic mosaic deriving from five centuries of immigration. The white population is a mixture of the Anglo-Saxon Protestant (WASP) group which achieved supremacy in the colonial period and later immigrants, who came from all parts of Europe between 1850 and 1914.

Native American (or Indian) societies were devastated by white expansion westwards. The survivors, forced into reservations, still have a marginal social situation. Afro-Americans (blacks) were kept in a situation of segregation and powerlessness, even after the abolition of slavery in 1865. After 1914, many migrated from the south to the growing industrial cities of the north and west.

Since 1965, new settlers have come mainly from Latin America and Asia. Hispanics are the descendants of Mexicans absorbed into the USA through Southwest expansion, as well as recent immigrants from Latin American countries. The main Asian countries of origin are the Philippines, China, South Korea, Vietnam and India.

The initial incorporation of Europeans and Afro-Americans into low-skilled industrial jobs led to labour market disadvantage and residential segregation. In the long run, many 'white ethnics' have been able to achieve upward mobility, while Afro-Americans have become increasingly ghettoised. Distinctions between blacks and whites in income, unemployment rates, social conditions and education are still extreme. Members of some recent immigrant groups, especially from Asia, have high educational and occupational levels, while most Latin Americans lack education and are concentrated in unskilled categories.

Incorporation of immigrants into economy and society has been largely left to market forces. The egalitarian character of US society has been seen as providing the best possible chances for immigrant groups to become assimilated into the 'American dream'. Nonetheless government has played a role, by making it easy to obtain US citizenship and through education policies in which the compulsory public school has been used as a way of transmitting the English language and American values.

Legislation and political action following the Civil Rights Movement of the 1950s and 1960s led to an enhanced role for a black middle class, and changes in stereotypes of blacks in the mass media. However commitment to equal opportunities and anti-poverty measures declined during the Reagan Bush era, leading to increased community tension. Racist violence by whites remains a serious problem for Afro-Americans, Hispanics, Asians and other minorities.

The increase in migrant entries in the 1980s caused anxieties about 'alien control' or loss of national identity. One reaction was the 'US English movement', which campaigned for a constitutional amendment to declare English the official language of the country. Such amendments were passed in some states, including California, where a high proportion of the population speak Spanish as their mother tongue.

Sources: Feagin,1989; Portes and Rumbaut, 1990; Coffey, 1987; ADL, 1988.

Population by Race and Hispanic Origin, 1990

	Thousands	Per cent
White	199 686	80.3
Black	29 986	12.1
American Indian, Eskimo or Aleut	1 959	0.8
Asian or Pacific Islander	7 273	2.9
Other race	9 805	3.9
Total population	*248 710*	*100.0*
Hispanic origin (of any race)	22 354	9.0

Source: Bureau of the Census, preliminary figures, 12 June 1991.

preferential treatment and have often been citizens at the time of entry. Permanent immigration has generally been accepted (though with some exceptions) and family reunion has been permitted. Immigrants from other European countries have had a less privileged situation, although family reunion, permanent residence and naturalisation have been permitted to some extent. The third group consists of those countries which have tried to cling to rigid 'guestworker' models – above all Germany and Switzerland. Belgium is similar in many ways. Such countries have tried to prevent family reunion, have been reluctant to grant secure residence status and have highly restrictive naturalisation rules.

The distinctions between these three categories are neither absolute nor static. The openness of the USA, Canada and Australia only applied to certain groups: all three countries had exclusionary policies towards Asians until the 1960s or 1970s. The USA discriminated against Mexican workers by tacitly tolerating illegal farmworker migration and denying such workers rights. Britain's rule on European Voluntary Workers in the 1940s was every bit as repressive as Germany's guestworker system. France had very restrictive rules on family reunion in the 1970s. In response to labour shortages and growing international competition for migrant workers in the late 1960s, Germany and Switzerland improved family reunion rules and residence status. Nor could these countries completely deny the reality of settlement. By the early 1980s, three-quarters of foreign residents in Switzerland had Establishment Permits (*Niederlassungsbewilligungen*), obtainable only after ten years' residence (five for some nationalities). Holders of Establishment Permits cannot be expelled because of unemployment or lack of demand for labour, although they can be deported for serious criminal offences. A far smaller proportion of foreign residents in Germany have Residence Entitlements (*Aufenthaltsberechtigungen*), which confer similar advantages.

One important change has been the erosion of the privileged status of migrants from former colonies in France, the Netherlands and Britain. Making colonised people into subjects of the Dutch or British crown or citizens of France was a way of legitimating colonialism. In the period of European labour shortage it also seemed a convenient way of bringing in low-skilled labour. But citizenship for colonised peoples became a liability when permanent settlement took place and labour demand declined. All three countries have removed citizenship from their former colonies (with a few exceptions such as the French Overseas Departments and Territories) and put their people on a par with foreigners.

There has been a convergence of policies in European countries: the former colonial countries have become more restrictive, while the former guestworker countries have become less so. But this has gone hand-in-hand with a new differentiation: the European Community countries granted a privileged status towards intra-community migrants in 1968. Further improvements are being introduced with the formation of the unified market at the beginning of 1993. At the same time, entry and residence have become far more difficult for non-EC nationals, especially those from outside Europe. Moreover the current emotional debate on the 'refugee influx' from the South and East has had a considerable impact on the situation of non-European groups. Increased racism, restriction of the rights of foreigners, demands for repatriation and the creation of a 'fortress Europa' cannot but worsen the social and political position of existing minorities.

Immigration policies have consequences for most other areas of policy towards immigrants, such as labour market rights, security of residence and naturalisation. If the original immigration policies were designed to keep migrants in the status of temporary mobile workers, then they make it likely that settlement will take place under unsatisfactory and discriminatory conditions. Moreover, official ideologies of temporary migration create expectations within the receiving population. If a temporary sojourn turns into settlement, and the governments concerned refuse to admit this or explain the reasons, then it is the immigrants who are blamed for the resulting problems.

One of the most important effects of immigration policies is on the consciousness of migrants themselves. In countries where permanent immigration is accepted and the settlers are granted secure residence status and most civil rights, a long-term perspective is possible. Secure in the knowledge that they can stay, immigrants are able to plan and build a future for themselves and their families, as part of the receiving society. Where the myth of short-term sojourn is maintained, immigrants' perspectives are inevitably contradictory. Return to the country of origin may be difficult or impossible, but permanence in the immigration country is doubtful. Such immigrants settle and form ethnic groups, but they cannot plan a future as

EXHIBIT 8.2

Minorities in Canada

The table gives figures on Canada's immigrant population by birthplace. According to 1986 data on the 'ethnocultural origins' of Canada's 25 million people, 34 per cent were of British origin, 24 per cent of French origin, 5 per cent British–French combined and 38 per cent of 'other' (mainly immigrant) origin. In 1986 about 6 per cent of the total population were regarded as belonging to 'visible minorities' (that is, non-Europeans), of whom 2 per cent were Native Peoples, 1 per cent South Asian, and 1 per cent black.

In 1971, multiculturalism was proclaimed as Canada's official policy and a Minister of State for Multiculturalism was appointed. There have been two central objectives: maintaining ethnic languages and cultures and combating racism. The Canadian Human Rights Act of 1977 prohibited discrimination based on race, origin or religion. In 1982, equality rights and multiculturalism were enshrined in the Canadian Charter of Rights and Freedoms. The Employment Equity Act of 1986 required all federally regulated employers to assess and report on the composition of their workforces, in order to correct disadvantages faced by women, visible minorities, native people and the disabled. The Multiculturalism Act of 1987 proclaimed multiculturalism as a central feature of Canadian citizenship and laid down principles for cultural pluralism.

Canadian history has been shaped by the struggle between the British and French. After 1945, separatist movements, particularly in French-speaking Quebec, made language and culture into crucial areas of struggle. This led to devolution of power to the provinces and to a policy of bilingualism and two official languages. Conflicts on land rights and the social position of Native People still play an important role in Canadian politics. Recently rights over large tracts of land have been granted to the Inuit peoples of northern Canada.

Despite multicultural policies, community relations appeared to be deteriorating in the 1970s and 1980s. Among the visible signs of conflict were discrimination against Native Canadians and racial assaults against blacks and Asians. The unwillingness of the authorities to respond to racist attacks has been a major cause of politicisation and resistance among visible minorities.

Sources: Breton *et al.*, 1990; Immigration Canada, 1991; Naidoo, 1989; Stasiulis, 1988.

Immigrant Population by Birthplace, Census Figures (thousands)

Country of origin	1981 total	1986 total	1986 females
Europe	2 568	2 435	1 225
of which:			
United Kingdom	879	793	426
Italy	385	367	173
Western Germany	155	158	81
Poland	149	157	78
Portugal	139	140	69
America	582	623	346
of which:			
United States	302	282	161
Caribbean	173	193	108
South & Central America	107	148	77
Asia	541	693	348
of which:			
India	109	130	64
China	52	119	63
Africa	102	114	54
Oceania	33	34	18
Other and not stated	23	8	5
Total	3 848	3 908	1996

Source: OECD SOPEMI, 1992.

part of the wider society. The result is isolation, separatism and emphasis on difference. Thus discriminatory immigration policies cannot stop the completion of the migratory process, but they can be the first step towards the marginalisation of the future settlers.

Labour market position

As Chapter 7 has shown, trends towards labour market segmentation by ethnicity and gender are evident in all the countries examined. Indeed they were intrinsic in the type of labour migration practised until the mid-1970s: obtaining cheaper labour or using increased labour supply to restrain wage growth was a major reason for recruiting immigrant workers. This obviously applied in the guest-worker and colonial migration countries, but even the classical migration countries used migrant labour in this way. Australia, for instance, deliberately steered migrant workers into low-skilled jobs. Institutional discrimination, such as rules against job-changing for migrants, refusal to recognise overseas qualifications or exclusion from public employment, was a major cause of disadvantage. Informal discrimination – the unwillingness of employers to hire or promote immigrant workers – also played a part.

The situation has changed since the 1970s: new migrants are much more diverse in educational and occupational status. There is a trend towards polarisation: highly-skilled personnel are encouraged to enter, either temporarily or permanently, and are seen as an important factor in skill upgrading and technology transfer. Low-skilled migrants are unwelcome as workers, but enter through family reunion, as refugees or illegally. Their contribution to low-skilled occupations, casual work, the informal sector and small business is of great economic importance, but is officially unrecognised.

In any case, trends towards labour market segmentation are part of the migratory process. When people come from poor to rich countries, without local knowledge or networks, lacking proficiency in the language and unfamiliar with local ways of working, then their entry point into the labour market is likely to be at a low level. The question is whether there is a fair chance of later upward mobility. The answer often depends on whether the state encourages the continuation of segmentation through its own discriminatory practices, or whether it takes measures to give immigrants equal

EXHIBIT 8.3

Minorities in the United Kingdom

In 1990, there were 1.9 million foreign citizens in the UK (3.3 per cent of the total population). European Community nationals made up 47 per cent of the foreigners. The largest single group were the 638 000 Irish, followed by Indians (155 000), US citizens (102 000) and Italians (75 000). The 'non-white' population, most of whom are British citizens, totals 2.6 million (4.7 per cent of the population). Most have been born in Britain – they are second or third generation descendants of immigrants. Half of them have their origins in the Indian sub-continent (India, Pakistan and Bangladesh) and about one-fifth in the Caribbean. The overall population of immigrant origin may be estimated at 4.5 million or about 8 per cent of total population. It is above all the Afro-Caribbeans and Asians who constitute ethnic minorities in Britain.

Labour market segmentation developed in the 1950s and 1960s, with Asians and Afro-Caribbeans concentrated in the least desirable jobs. Today black workers still have low average socioeconomic status and high unemployment. In 1986–8, unemployment rates for ethnic minorities averaged 17 per cent, compared with 10 per cent for the white population. Ethnic minorities are heavily concentrated in the most run-down areas of the inner cities.

Commonwealth immigrants who came before 1971 were British subjects, who enjoyed all rights once admitted. This situation was ended by the 1971 Immigration Act and the 1981 British Nationality Act, which put Commonwealth immigrants on a par with foreigners. Irish settlers enjoy virtually all rights, including the right to vote. It is relatively easy for foreigners to obtain citizenship after five years of legal residence in Britain.

Since 1965, a series of Race Relations Acts has been passed, outlawing discrimination in public places, in employment and housing. A Commission for Racial Equality (CRE) was set up, to enforcement anti-discrimination laws and promote good community relations. Despite all this, black people experience institutional discrimination, and black youth allege that they are frequently subjected to police harassment.

Organised racist groups such as the National Front grew rapidly in the 1970s and 1980s. Their electoral success was limited, but they recruited members of violent youth sub-cultures, such as skinheads. Racist violence became a major problem. A Home Office survey in 1981 found that the rate of attacks on Asians was 50 times that for white people, and the rate for blacks was 36 that for white people.

Black youth discontent exploded into riots in inner city areas in 1980–81 and again in 1985–6. In 1991, there was a further series of disturbances, in which so-called 'joy riders' stole cars and publicly raced them to destruction in inner city streets.

Growing racist violence and riots in inner city areas led to government measures to combat youth unemployment, make education more accessible to minorities, improve the conditions in urban areas and to change police practices. Task forces were set up for disadvantaged areas; spending under the Urban Programme was substantially increased and a large scale Youth Training Scheme was introduced.

Sources: Banton, 1985; Beynon, 1986; Home Office 1981; Home Office, 1989; Layton-Henry, 1986; Solomos, 1993; OECD SOPEMI, 1992.

opportunities. This refers not only to formal equality but also to measures to help overcome barriers, such as language instruction, vocational training and anti-discrimination policies.

Again it is possible to discern three groups. Some countries have active policies to improve the labour market position of immigrants and minorities through language courses, basic education, vocational training, equal opportunities and anti-discrimination legislation. These countries include Australia, Canada, Sweden and – to a lesser extent – Britain (see Exhibit 8.3), France and the Netherlands. The USA has a special position: there are equal opportunities, affirmative action and anti-discrimination legislation, but little in the way of language, education and training measures. This fits in with the laissez-faire model of social policy and particularly with the cuts in government intervention in the Reagan–Bush era.

The former guestworker countries – Germany and Switzerland – form a third category. Although there are education and training measures for foreign workers and foreign youth, there are also restrictions on labour market rights. During the period of mass labour recruitment, work permits often bound foreign workers to specific occupations or jobs. Swiss rules on frontier and seasonal workers still maintain such restrictions. Most workers in the two countries now have the right to mobility, but in many cases the rule of primacy for nationals still applies. This means that an employer cannot take on a foreign worker for a job if a national (or an EC citizen in the case of Germany) is available. Foreigners only have the right to compete equally on the labour market if they have long-term residence status, which is, however, becoming increasingly common.

Residential segregation, community formation and the post-modern city

Some degree of residential segregation is to be found in all the immigration countries, though nowhere is it as extreme as in the USA, where in certain areas there is almost complete separation between blacks and whites, and sometimes Asians and Hispanics too. In the other countries there are city neighbourhoods where immigrant groups are highly concentrated, though they rarely form the majority of the population. Their influence is often sufficient to bring about visible changes and to give areas a special character. Causes of residential segregation include low income and lack of local networks, informal and institutional discrimination and the desire of immigrants to group together for cultural maintenance and for protection against racism.

Migrant workers generally start work in low-income jobs and have few savings. Often they have to remit money home. Therefore they tend to seek cheap housing in working-class areas. Proximity to work reinforces this choice of location. Many local people find housing through friends and relations, but such networks are at first not available to migrants. As a group becomes established, the earlier arrivals can assist the newcomers, which strengthens the tendency to ethnic clustering.

Informal discrimination is the result of widespread racism towards immigrants. Many landlords refuse to rent to them or make a business of charging high rents for poor accommodation. Sometimes immigrants become pawns in urban development speculation. In Germany in the 1980s, landlords deliberately crowded migrants into poorly-equipped apartments, in order to make conditions unbearable for long-standing German tenants who could not be legally evicted. When the Germans gave up and left, the foreigners were evicted too, and the block could be demolished to make way for profitable offices or luxury housing. Such practices increased racism towards the immigrants, who became the scapegoats for ruthless urban development practices.[1]

Institutional practices also often encourage residential segregation. Many migrant workers were initially housed by employers or public authorities. There were migrant hostels and camps in Australia, barracks provided by employers in Germany and Switzerland, and hostels managed by the government *Fonds d'Action Sociale* (FAS – Social Action Fund) in France. These generally provided better material conditions than private rented accommodation, and were greatly preferable to the *bidonvilles* (shanty-towns) which developed around French cities in the 1960s (Castles and Kosack, 1973: Chapter 7). But employer or government-provided accommodation led to control and isolation for migrant workers. It also encouraged clustering, for when workers left their initial accommodation, often because their families had come to join them, they tended to seek housing in the vicinity.

Many immigrants wish to move out of initial areas of concentration, because these are generally neighbourhoods with poor housing and social amenities. In countries where racism is relatively weak, immigrants often do move out of the inner city areas to better quality suburbs, as their economic position improves. Sometimes a process of 'ecological succession' takes place,[2] whereby a large proportion of one immigrant group moves out over time, only to be replaced by a newer group. The replacement of Greeks by Vietnamese in Richmond (Melbourne) and Marrickville (Sydney) is a good example. However, where racism is extreme, concentration persists, sometimes leading to virtual segregation – housing estates inhabited mainly by Bengalis in Tower Hamlets (London) are an example.

Residential segregation is a contradictory phenomenon. In terms of the theory of ethnic minority formation set out in Chapter 2, it contains elements of both other-definition and self-definition. It is caused both by discrimination on the part of the majority population and by the desire of immigrants to form their own communities. The relative weight of the two sets of factors varies from country to country and group to group. Immigrants cluster together for economic and social reasons arising from the migratory process, and they are often forced out of certain areas by racism. But they also frequently want to be together, in order to provide mutual support, to rebuild family and neighbourhood networks and to maintain their languages and cultures. Ethnic neighbourhoods allow the establishment of small businesses and agencies which cater for immigrants' needs, as well as the formation of associations of all kinds (see Chapter 5). Residential segregation is thus both a precondition for and a result of community formation.

Interestingly the countries where community formation has been able to take place most easily have been those with open and flexible housing markets, based mainly on owner occupation, such as Australia, Britain and the USA. The continental European pattern of apartment blocks owned by private landlords has not been conducive to community formation, while large publicly owned housing developments have frequently led to isolation and social problems, which are the breeding-ground for racism.

Some members of the majority population perceive residential segregation as a deliberate and threatening attempt to form 'ethnic enclaves' or 'ghettoes'. The result may be citizens' movements which campaign to keep out immigrants. For instance, the Residents' Association of Monterey Park (RAMP) was set up in the mid-1980s to combat the 'Chinese take-over' of a predominantly white suburb of Los Angeles. The group did well in city council elections and was able to get the council to pass a resolution declaring English to be the 'official language' of Monterey Park (Davis, 1990: 207). Such movements may be found in all immigration countries. Sometimes they constitute themselves as formal organisations, working within local political structures; in others they are more diffuse, and their members resort to racial harassment and violence.

Racism is often a self-fulfilling prophecy: it justifies itself by portraying immigrants as alien groups, which will 'take over' the neighbourhood. By forcing immigrants to live together for protection, racism creates the 'ghettoes' it fears. In any case, as already pointed out, many immigrants are forced by powerful social and economic factors into isolated and disadvantaged urban areas, which they share with other marginalised social groups (Dubet and Lapeyronnie, 1992). One official reaction has been dispersal policies, designed to reduce ethnic concentrations. Such policies are discriminatory, even if they are dressed up in the rhetoric of ameliorating housing conditions, because they label immigrants as a problem. Moreover, in the absence of the economic opportunities and political structures needed to overcome the powerful forces of marginalisation, dispersal policies are doomed to failure, as will be discussed below.

Immigration and ethnic minority formation are transforming the post-industrial cities of the highly-developed countries in contradictory ways. The work of Sassen (1988) and others has shown how new forms of global organisation of finance, production and distribution lead to 'global cities'. These attract influxes of immigrants, both for highly-specialised activities and for low-skilled service jobs, which service the high-income life styles of the professional workforce. In turn, this leads to a spatial restructuring of the city, in which interacting factors of socioeconomic status and ethnic background lead to new and rapidly changing forms of differentiation between neighbourhoods. Areas of concentration of specific immigrant groups are often the focus of conflicts with other disadvantaged sections of the population. The mobilisation by the extreme right in Britain, France and elsewhere since the 1970s illustrates this. The 1992 anti-asylum seeker riots in the area of the former German Democratic Republic are amongst the more dramatic cases. But the

---

EXHIBIT 8.4

Minorities in France

Foreign residents made up 6.4 per cent of France's total population in 1990. In addition there were over one million immigrants who had become French citizens, and up to half a million French citizens of African, Caribbean and Pacific island origin from Overseas Departments and Territories.

European community citizens enjoy all basic rights, except the right to vote. Immigrants from Yugoslavia, Poland and other non-EC European countries lack the privileges of EC citizens, and many have an irregular legal situation. People of non-European birth or parentage, whether French citizens or not, constitute the ethnic minorities. These include Algerians, Tunisians and Moroccans, young Franco-Algerians, black Africans, Turks and settlers from the Overseas Departments and Territories.

The *bidonvilles* (shanty-towns) which developed around French cities in the 1960s have disappeared, but there is still residential concentration in inner city areas and in the *grands ensembles* – the public housing areas on the periphery of the cities. The work situation of ethnic minorities is marked by low status, insecure jobs and high unemployment rates. Youth unemployment in the *grands ensembles* is very high.

Citizenship is fairly easy to obtain for immigrants, while children born to foreign residents in France can choose to become citizens at the age of 18. The 1972 Law against Racism prohibited racial incitement and discrimination in public places and employment. There is no special body to enforce the law and the number of prosecutions is small.

Until 1981, deportations of immigrants convicted of even minor offences were common. The socialist government improved residence rights and granted an amnesty to illegals. In the late 1980s, growing racism and serious social problems in the inner cities and *grands ensembles* led to a series of special programmes to improve housing and education and combat youth unemployment.

The position of ethnic minorities in French society has become highly politicised. Immigrants have taken an active role in major strikes, and demanded civil, political and cultural rights. The second generation (known as *beurs*) and the Muslim organisations are emerging political forces. Youth discontent with unemployment and police practices led to riots in Lyon, Paris and other cities in the 1980s.

Immigration is a central issue in party and electoral politics. The extreme-right *Front National* mobilises on issues of immigration and cultural difference. By the early 1990s it had become a major political force.

Sources: Costa-Lascoux, 1989; de Wenden, 1987; Lapeyronnie *et al.*, 1990; Noiriel, 1988; Verbunt, 1985; Weil, 1991a.

Foreign Resident Population, 1990

Country of origin	Thousands	Of which females, thousands
Portugal	646	300
Algeria	620	256
Morocco	585	258
Italy	254	109
Spain	216	104
Tunisia	208	87
Turkey	202	90
Poland	46	28
Yugoslavia	52	24
Other	781	363
Total	3 608	1 619
of which EC	1 309	610

Source: OECD SOPEMI, 1992; Table 9.

areas of immigrant and ethnic minority concentration can also be the site of confrontations with the state and its agencies of social control – particularly the police. Minority youth riots in Britain, France and Belgium are examples, as will be discussed in Chapter 9.

Ethnic clustering and community formation should therefore be seen as necessary products of contemporary forms of migration to the global cities. They may lead to conflicts, but they can also lead to renewal and enrichment of urban life and culture. Gilroy (1987) has taken up Castells' (1983) theory of the emergence of urban social movements, and linked it to the experience of black communities in Britain. Castells argued that such movements were locally based, and that they tended to mobilise around three central goals: (1) collective consumption (that is of goods and services provided by the state), (2) cultural identity and (3) political self-management. Gilroy shows how each of these features can be found in the recent history of Britain's black communities. He emphasises the significance of cultural symbols (such as music) and style in drawing the boundaries of the community.

But specific ethnic groups can never be completely isolated or self-sufficient in modern cities. Cultural and political interaction is negotiated around complex processes of inclusion and exclusion, and of cultural transference. Much of the energy and innovative capacity within the cities lies in the cultural syncretism of the multi-ethnic populations, as Davis (1990) has shown so convincingly in the case of Los Angeles. This syncretism can be seen as a creative linking and development of aspects of different cultures, in a process of community formation, which always has political dimensions. The process is too complex to discuss further here, but it raises questions of burning interest about the way our cities and cultures are likely to develop in the future. Just as there can be no return to mono-ethnic populations (always a myth in any case) so there is no way back to static or homogeneous cultures. The global city with its multicultural population can thus be seen as a powerful laboratory for change.

Social policy

As migrants moved into the inner cities and industrial towns, social conflicts with lower-income groups of the majority population developed. Immigrants were blamed for rising housing costs, declining housing quality and deteriorating social amenities. In response, a whole set of social policies developed in most immigration countries. Sometimes policies designed to reduce ethnic concentrations and ease social tensions achieved the opposite (for Britain, see S. Smith, 1989).

Nowhere were the problems more severe than in France. After 1968, measures were taken to eliminate *bidonvilles* and make public housing more accessible to immigrants. The concept of the *seuil de tolérance* (threshold of tolerance) was introduced in both housing and education, according to which the immigrant presence should be limited to a maximum of 10 or 15 per cent of residents in a housing estate or 25 per cent of students in a class (Verbunt, 1985: 147–55; MacMaster, 1991: 14–28). The implication was that immigrant concentrations presented a problem, and that dispersal was the precondition for assimilation. Subsidies to public housing societies (known as Habitations à loyers modestes – HLMs) were coupled to quotas for immigrants based on the *seuil de tolérance*. The HLM societies used the subsidies to build new estates, where mainly French families were housed. In order to minimise conflicts with the French, immigrant families were concentrated in run-down older estates. The HLM societies could claim that they had adhered to the quotas – on an average of all their dwellings – while in fact creating new ghettoes (Weil, 1991a: 249–58).

By the 1980s, the central social policy issue was therefore the situation of ethnic minorities in the inner city areas and in the great public housing estates constructed around the cities in the 1960s and 1970s. These were rapidly turning into areas of persistent unemployment, social problems and conflicts between ethnic minorities and disadvantaged sections of the French population. Social policies focused on urban youth, for 1.1 million out of the total foreign population of 3.5 million were aged under 20 years in 1985 (Lapeyronnie *et al.*, 1990: 111). The socialist government developed a range of programmes. The three most important were the *zones d'Education prioritaire* (ZEP – educational priority zones) designed to combat social inequality by concentrating educational action on areas of disadvantage; programmes to combat youth unemployment which paid special attention to needs of youth of North African background; and a series of programmes such as the *Développement social des quartiers* (DSQ – neighbourhood social development) aimed at improving housing and social conditions in the most run-down areas. Special measures for immigrants, especially with regard to housing, were co-ordinated by the *Fonds d'Action Sociale* (FAS), with considerable financial resources (1222 million Francs in 1988) (Lapeyronnie *et al.*, 1990: 65–76).

Weil concludes that the social policy measures of the 1980s have failed. They were designed to achieve integration into French society, but in fact they have 'linked all the problems of these towns and neighbourhoods to immigration: schooling, housing, employment or national identity'. Thus social policy has encouraged concentration of minorities, which slows integration, encourages the formation of ethnic communities, and strengthens group religious and cultural affiliations (Weil, 1991a: 176–9).

This is clearly a complex issue which would require careful analysis in each country. Special social policies for immigrants have often reinforced tendencies to segregation. For instance, the 'dual strategy' pursued in German education (see Chapter 5) led to special classes for foreign children, causing both social isolation and poor educational performance. Housing allocation policies in Britain are intended to be non-discriminatory, yet they have sometimes led to the emergence of 'black' and 'white' housing estates. On the other hand, in some countries special policies for immigrants are seen as essential for integration. In Sweden, immigrant children have the right to instruction in mother-tongue classes. The official view is that these do not lead to separation, but encourage 'active bilingualism', which makes it easier for immigrant children to succeed at school and work (Lithman, 1987).

Again it is possible to suggest a rough classification of social policy responses. Australia, Canada, Sweden and the Netherlands have pursued active social policies, linked to broader models of multiculturalism (or minorities policy in the case of the Netherlands). The basic assumption has been that special social policies do not lead to separatism, but, on the contrary, form the precondition for successful integration. This is because the situation of immigrants and ethnic minorities is seen as the result both of cultural and social difference, and of barriers to participation based on institutional and informal discrimination.

A second group of countries are those which reject special social policies for immigrants on principles connected with concepts of citizenship and the role of government. US authorities have opposed special social policies for immigrants because they are seen as

---

EXHIBIT 8.5

Minorities in the Netherlands

Foreign residents made up 4.6 per cent of the total Dutch population of 15 million in 1990 (Exhibit 8.5). However the Dutch government does not regard all foreigners as belonging to minorities, while some Dutch citizens are seen as minority members. The official minorities policy covers Mediterranean workers and their families, people of Surinamese and Antillean origins, Moluccans, refugees (but not asylum-seekers), gypsies and caravan dwellers. These groups were estimated to add up to 876 385 people in 1990, 5.8 per cent of the total population.

The Mediterranean workers and the Surinamese and Antilleans became concentrated in unskilled jobs in manufacturing and the services. In the period of restructuring from the mid-1970s, they bore the brunt of unemployment. In 1989, the unemployment rate among these groups was 37 per cent. The ethnic minority population became overwhelmingly concentrated in the big cities, where they often live in distinct neighbourhoods. In 1990, 38 per cent of Turks, 49 per cent of Moroccans, 52 per cent of Surinamese and 27 per cent of Antilleans lived in the four biggest cities, Amsterdam, Rotterdam, The Hague and Utrecht.

The Minorities Policy, introduced in 1983, accepted the need for specific social policies to integrate minorities, and recognised that is was necessary to deal not just with individuals but with ethnic groups. 'Integration with preservation of cultural identity' became the slogan. The Minorities Policy has been criticised on the grounds that, by labelling specific groups as minorities and focusing social policy on them, it helps to maintain and reinforce distinctions. The 1991 government Action Programme on Minorities Policy pays little attention to the former goal of minority group emancipation and participation, instead emphasising the need for measures to reduce economic and social deprivation, to prevent discrimination and to improve the legal situation for minorities.

The revised Constitution of 1983 introduced municipal voting rights for immigrants. Citizenship is fairly easy to obtain, with a five-year qualification period. There are laws which prohibit racial defamation, incitement to racial hatred, discrimination and violence, and discrimination at work or in public places. Organisations which call for racial discrimination can be forbidden. Nonetheless racism and racist violence are still problems in The Netherlands. The extreme-right *Centrum Partij* (CP) blames unemployment on immigrants and campaigns for repatriation. Its leader, Hans Jaanmat, was elected to parliament in 1989.

Sources: Entzinger, 1985; European Parliament, 1985; Hira, 1991; Muus, 1991; OECD SOPEMI, 1992.

Foreign Resident Population, 1990

Country of origin	Thousands	Of which females, thousands
Turkey	204	93
Morocco	157	70
Germany	44	21
United Kingdom	39	16
Belgium	24	12
Spain	17	7
Italy	17	6
Yugoslavia	13	6
Other	177	80
Total	692	311
Of which EC	168	75

Source: OECD SOPEMI 1992, Table 12.

unnecessary government intervention. Nonetheless equal opportunities, anti-discrimination and affirmative action measures deriving from civil rights laws have benefited immigrants. Special social and educational measures are to be found at the local level. French governments have rejected special social policies on the basis of a different principle – namely that immigrants should become citizens and that any special treatment would hinder that. Yet despite this there have been a number of special social policies, as already described. Britain has also developed a range of social policies in response to the urban crisis and youth riots, despite the ideological rejection of such measures by the Conservative leadership.

The third group of countries is, again, the former guestworker recruiters. Germany has pursued contradictory and changeable polices concerning the access of immigrants to the highly-developed welfare system. In the early period of foreign worker entry, the government delegated the provision of special social services to charitable organisations, linked to the churches and the labour movement. These services were designed to provide advice and help in personal crises. Although foreign workers were guaranteed equal rights to work-related health and pension benefits, they were excluded from some welfare rights. For example, application for social security payments on the grounds of long-term unemployment or disability could lead to deportation (and still can for some categories of foreign residents). Settlement and family reunion have now made it necessary for a whole range of services – family and youth services, education, health, aged care – to take account of the needs of immigrants. In Switzerland, there few special measures for immigrants. Provision of support in emergency situations is left largely to voluntary efforts (Hoffmann-Nowotny, 1985: 224). Anti-racism and anti-discrimination legislation or affirmative action programmes have no place in either Germany or Switzerland, for the state itself openly discriminates against foreign immigrants.

Racism and minorities

Three categories of settlers may be distinguished in the various immigration countries: Firstly, some settlers have merged into the general population (for instance Britons in Australia, French in Switzerland, Austrians in Germany) and cannot be considered to constitute ethnic groups. Secondly, some settlers form ethnic communities: they tend to share a common socioeconomic position, to live in certain neighbourhoods and to maintain their languages and cultures of origin. But these groups are not excluded from citizenship, political participation and opportunities for economic and social mobility. The ethnic community may originally have arisen as the result of discrimination and marginalisation, but the principal reasons for membership today are cultural and psychological. Examples are Italians in Australia, Canada or the USA; the Irish in Britain; European Community citizens of Southern European background in France or the Netherlands. Thirdly, some settlers form ethnic minorities. Like the ethnic communities they tend to share a common socioeconomic position, to live in certain neighbourhoods and to maintain their languages and cultures of origin. But, in addition, they are partially excluded from the wider society by one or more of the following factors: legal disabilities, insecure residence status, refusal of citizenship, denial of political and social rights, restriction of economic and social mobility, ethnic or racial discrimination, racist violence and harassment. Examples are Asian migrants in Australia, Canada or the USA; Latin-Americans in the USA; Afro-Caribbeans and Asians in Britain; North Africans and Turks in most Western European countries; asylum-seekers of non-European background just about everywhere.

All the countries examined have all three categories. The first category generally consists of people whose cultural origins and socioeconomic situation is close to that of the majority population of the receiving country. There is no need to discuss this category further here. The concern is rather with immigrants who form distinct ethnic groups. It is important to examine why some take on the character of ethnic communities, while others become ethnic minorities. It is also important to investigate why a far larger proportion of immigrants take on minority status in some countries than in others. Two groups of factors appear relevant: those connected with characteristics of the settlers themselves, and those connected with the social structures, cultural practices and ideologies of the receiving societies.

If we look at the settlers, it is inescapable that phenotypical difference is the main marker for minority status. For instance, a survey carried out on behalf of the Commission of the European Community in all member countries in 1989 indicated that the trend towards European unity had led to greater acceptance of fellow Europeans. However there were strong feelings of distance and hostility towards non-Europeans, particularly Arabs, Africans and Asians. Overall one European in three believed that there were too many people of another nationality or race in his or her country, with such feelings being most marked in Belgium and Germany (Commission of the European Communities, 1989). This emphasis on phenotypical difference applies even more if non-immigrant minorities, such as aboriginal peoples in the USA, Canada and Australia, or Afro-Americans in the USA, are drawn into the comparison. They, together with black people, Asians, North Africans and Turks, are the most marginalised ethnic groups in all the countries. There are four possible explanations for this: phenotypical difference:

- coincides with recentness of arrival,
- coincides with cultural distance,
- coincides with socioeconomic position,
- is the main target for racism.

The first hypothesis is partly correct: in many cases, black, Asian or Hispanic settlers are among the more recently arrived groups. If we examine the history of settlement in the countries concerned we find racism and discrimination against white settlers or minorities quite as virulent as against non-whites today (see Chapter 3 above). It could be argued that recent arrival makes a group appear stranger and more threatening to the majority population. It could also be that new groups tend to compete more with local low-income groups for entry-level jobs and cheap housing. But recent arrival cannot explain why aboriginal populations are victims of exclusionary practices, nor why Afro-Americans and other long-standing minorities are discriminated against. Nor can it explain why racism against white immigrant groups tends to disappear in time, while that against non-whites continues over generations.

What about cultural distance? Its significance depends partly on our definition of culture. If we stress the distinction between pre-industrial and industrial cultures, it is clear that many non-European settlers come from rural areas with pre-industrial cultures. But the same applied to the majority of Southern European migrants who came to the USA, Canada and Australia, as well as to other

European countries. Today many Asian settlers in North America and Australia are of urban background and highly educated. This does not protect them from racism and discrimination. If culture is defined in terms of language, religion and values, then there is no doubt that some non-European migrants are very different from the receiving populations. The largest non-European groups are often of Islamic background. Fear of Islam and hostility to Muslims has a tradition going back to the mediaeval crusades, and the Turkish siege of Vienna in 1683. In recent years, fears of fundamentalism and loss of modernity and secularity have played a major role. But it could be argued that such fears are based on racist ideologies rather than social realities. The strengthening of Muslim affiliations is often a protective reaction of discriminated groups, so that fundamentalism is something of a self-fulfilling prophecy. In any case, some non-European migrants, such as Afro-Caribbeans in Britain, share the language and many of the cultural values of the immigration countries. Again this has proved no protection from discrimination or racism.

As for the third hypothesis, phenotypical difference does indeed frequently coincide with socioeconomic status. In some cases this is because immigrants from less-developed countries lack the education and vocational training necessary for upward mobility in industrial economies. But many highly-skilled immigrants find that authorities and employers refuse to accept their qualifications. In other cases, immigrants discover that they can only enter the labour market at the bottom, and that it is hard to move upwards from entry-level jobs. Often there is discrimination in hiring and promotion policies. Thus low socioeconomic status is as much a result of processes of marginalisation as it is a cause of minority status.

We may therefore conclude that recentness of arrival is only a partial and temporary explanation of minority status, and that cultural difference and socioeconomic status are not adequate explanations on their own. The most general and significant explanation of minority formation lies in processes of exclusion by the majority populations and the states of the immigration countries. We refer to these processes as *racism*, as discussed above (see Chapter 2). Traditions and cultures of racism are strong in all European countries and former European settler colonies. The increased salience of racism and racist violence in the late 1970s and the 1980s is linked to growing insecurity for many people resulting from rapid economic and social change.

EXHIBIT 8.6

Minorities in Switzerland

In 1990, foreign residents made up 16.3 per cent of the total population of Switzerland – the highest immigrant quota in Europe (except for Luxembourg). Switzerland has few non-Europeans. In recent years there have been growing numbers of asylum-seekers from non-European countries and from Eastern Europe. In 1990, there were 35 836 asylum requests, of which only 571 were granted.

In 1990, there were 669 800 foreign resident workers, as well as 122 000 seasonal workers and 181 366 daily cross-frontier commuters. Workers from the Mediterranean basin have become concentrated in manual employment, while Swiss workers, but also immigrants from Germany, Austria and France, generally have white-collar and supervisory positions. Unemployment for workers from the Mediterranean countries is above the Swiss average of 0.6 per cent, although very low compared with the situation in other countries. Foreign residents have become concentrated in certain housing areas, but there are no areas of extreme social disadvantage.

The Swiss authorities still declare that Switzerland is not a country of immigration, although most immigrants have been in the country for many years. All foreign residents are denied political rights, in particular the right to vote. Foreigners are kept under constant surveillance by the *Fremdenpolizei* (foreigners' police). Employers and landlords have to report changes of job or residence to the authorities. Citizenship is extremely hard to obtain. The waiting period is twelve years, which must have been spent in the same canton, very high fees are charged in some cantons, and the authorities carry out rigorous examinations to ensure that an applicant is 'sufficiently assimilated'. Children of immigrants born in Switzerland have no automatic right to citizenship and can be deported.

In accordance with the Swiss laissez-faire tradition of leaving social issues to market forces and self-regulation, there are no social policies for immigrants. Provision of support in emergency situations is left largely to voluntary efforts. Anti-racist and anti-discrimination legislation or affirmative action programmes have no place in the Swiss model.

Latent racism is widespread, forming the basis for institutional and informal discrimination. One expression of hostility towards immigrants has been a series of referenda, starting in 1965, designed to combat *Überfremdung* (foreign penetration) by limiting immigration and the number of foreign residents. In 1982, a new Aliens Law which would have led to minor improvements in the legal status of foreign residents was narrowly defeated in another referendum.

Sources: Castles *et al.*, 1984; Hoffmann-Nowotny, 1985; OECD SOPEMI, 1992.

Foreign Resident Population, 1990

Country of origin	Thousands	Of which females, thousands
Italy	379	162
Yugoslavia	141	62
Spain	116	52
Portugal	86	40
Germany	83	37
Turkey	64	29
France	50	23
Austria	29	12
Other	152	67
Total	1100	484
of which EC	760	335

Source: OECD SOPEMI, 1992, Table 15.

Racism and racist violence

German reunification was followed by an outburst of racist violence in 1991–2. Neo-Nazi groups attacked refugee hostels and foreigners on the streets – sometimes to the applause of bystanders, especially in the area of the former GDR. Such incidents are not confined to Germany: racist harassment and attacks have become major problems for ethnic minorities in all the countries of immigration.

In Britain, racist violence organised by groups like the National Front and the British Movement became a problem in the 1970s. In London 2 179 racial incidents were reported to the police in 1987, including 270 cases of serious assault, 397 of minor assault, 483 of criminal damage, 47 of arson and 725 of abusive behaviour. A survey in Glasgow found that 49 per cent of Pakistanis and 55 per cent of Indians had experienced damage to their property, 80 per cent of both groups had experienced racial abuse, and that 18 per cent of Pakistanis and 22 per cent of Indians had experienced physical attack (Home Office, 1989). Only a small proportion of attacks ever get reported to the police, partly because of fears of black people, many of whom have experienced racist treatment by the police (Institute of Race Relations, 1987; Gordon, 1986).

In France, there was a series of murders of North Africans in 1973. In the 1980s, the extreme-right *Front National* was able to mobilise resentments caused by unemployment and urban decline, and to crystallise them around the issues of immigration and cultural difference. Although the FN does not openly advocate violence, its calls for immigration control and creates an atmosphere conducive to racist attacks.

The United States has a long history of white violence against Afro-Americans. Despite the anti-racist laws secured by the civil rights movement, the Ku Klux Klan is still a powerful force. Asians, Arabs and other minorities are also frequent targets (ADL, 1988). Police violence against minorities is common. The Los Angeles riots of May 1992 were provoked by police brutality towards a black motorist, which went unpunished by the courts. Aggression was directed not only against whites, but also Koreans and Cubans, who have taken on middleman minority roles in areas where big white-owned companies fear to trade.

Even countries which pride themselves on their tolerance, like Canada, Sweden and the Netherlands, report a growing incidence of

EXHIBIT 8.7

Minorities in Sweden

Until 1945 Sweden was a fairly homogeneous countries, with only a small aboriginal minority the Sami or Lapps (about 10 000 people today). After 1945, labour migration was encouraged. Foreign worker recruitment was stopped in 1972, but family reunion and refugee entries continued. Foreign residents made up 5.6 per cent of the total population in 1990. Many immigrants have become Swedish citizens. In 1986, the total population of immigrant background was calculated to be 920 014, about 11 per cent of the total population. Of these 250 138 had been born in Sweden.

Immigrant workers are overrepresented in manufacturing, and in lower-skilled services occupations. They are underrepresented in agriculture, health care and social work, administrative and clerical work, and commerce. Immigrants have high unemployment rates: in 1986, rates for non-Scandinavians were about twice as high as for Swedes. Immigrants have mainly settled in the cities, and people of the same nationality cluster in certain neighbourhoods, allowing linguistic and cultural maintenance.

The waiting period for naturalisation is two years for Scandinavians and five years for everybody else, while children born to foreign resident parents can obtain Swedish citizenship upon application. In 1975, parliament set out an immigrant policy with three basic objectives: *equality*, which refers to giving immigrants the same living standards as Swedes; *freedom of choice* which means giving members of ethnic minorities a choice between retaining their own cultural identities or assuming Swedish cultural identity; and *partnership*, which implies that minority groups and Swedes benefit from working together. Since 1975, foreign residents have had the right to vote and stand for election in local and regional elections. It was planned to extend such rights to national elections, but it proved impossible to get the parliamentary majority required for a change in the constitution.

In 1986, an Act Against Ethnic Discrimination came into force, and an Ombudsman Against Ethnic Discrimination was appointed. Immigrants have the right to 400 hours of Swedish instruction with financial assistance. Children of immigrants can receive pre-school and school instruction in their own language, within the normal curriculum. Other measures include translator and interpreter services, information services, grants to immigrant organisations and special consultative bodies.

The increase in asylum-seeker entry in the late 1980s led to strains in housing and other areas. The extreme-right *Sverigepartiet* (SP – the Sweden Party) started anti-immigrant campaigns in 1986. In 1988, a referendum in the small town of Sjöbo decided to keep refugees out. This was followed by an increase in racist violence, including arson and bomb attacks on refugee centres. In December 1989, the government decided that the problems connected with refugee reception had become so acute that asylum should henceforth be granted only to applicants meeting the requirements of the UN Refugee Convention.

Sources: Ålund and Schierup, 1991; Hammar, 1985b; Lithman, 1987; Nobel, 1988; Larsson, 1991.

Foreign Resident Population, 1990

Country of origin	Thousands	Of which females, thousands
Finland	120	65
Yugoslavia	41	21
Iran	39	17
Norway	38	19
Denmark	27	12
Turkey	26	13
Chile	20	10
Poland	16	10
Germany	13	6
United Kingdom	10	4
Other	134	61
Total	484	238

Source: OECD SOPEMI, 1992, Table 14.

racist attacks. The European Parliament's Committee of Inquiry into Fascism and Racism in Europe found that 'immigrant communities . . . are daily subject to displays of distrust and hostility, to continuous discrimination . . . and in many cases, to racial violence, including murder' (European Parliament, 1985).

The political implications of anti-immigrant campaigns and of the varying responses by members of ethnic minorities will be discussed in detail in Chapter 9. In the present context it should be noted that racist campaigns, harassment and violence are important factors in the process of ethnic minority formation. By isolating minorities and forcing them into defensive strategies, racism may lead to various types of self-organisation and separatism, and even encourage religious fundamentalism.

Minorities and citizenship

Why do some countries turn most of their settlers into ethnic minorities, while others marginalise only far more limited groups? The answer does not lie primarily in the characteristics of the migrants, but rather in the histories, ideologies and structures of the societies concerned. Varying models of the nation-state lead to different concepts of citizenship (see Chapter 2). Some countries of immigration make it very difficult for immigrants to become citizens, others grant citizenship but only at the price of cultural assimilation, while a third group makes it possible for immigrants to become citizens while maintaining distinct cultural identities. Relative openness to citizenship corresponds closely with other policies concerning immigrants: countries which are unwilling to grant citizenship often deny the reality of settlement, restrict immigrant rights and follow exclusionary social policies. Countries with assimilationist citizenship policies accept permanent settlement, but tend to reject (at least in principle) special social and cultural policies for immigrants. Countries which grant citizenship and accept cultural pluralism generally also see the need for special social policies for immigrants.

Citizenship is more than just formal status, as demonstrated by possession of a passport. It is important to consider the content of citizenship, in terms of civil, political and social rights, as well as the mode of acquisition of citizenship for immigrants and for their children. Immigration policy, residence status and social policy for immigrants are all aspects of citizenship. Moreover possession of citizenship is not an either/or question. With increasing length of residence, immigrants sometime acquire forms of 'quasi-citizenship', which confer some, but not all, rights of citizenship. We will consider some of these issues here.

Naturalisation

Table 8.1 relates the number of naturalisations in various countries to the size of the foreign resident population. This makes it possible to calculate a rough 'naturalisation rate' and to rank countries according to this.

TABLE 8.1

Naturalisations in selected countries

Country	Date of figures	Foreign resident population (thousands)	Number of naturalisations	Naturalisations per thousand foreign resident population
Australia	1988	1 427	81 218	56.9
Belgium	1989	881	1 878	2.1
Canada	1989	na	87 476	na
France	1989	3 752	49 330	13.1
Germany	1988	4 489	16 660	3.7
Britain	1988	2 550	64 600	25.3
Netherlands	1990	642	12 700	19.8
Sweden	1989	456	17 552	38.5
Switzerland	1989	1 040	10 342	9.9
USA	1989	na	233 777	na

Notes: na = not available.

1989 naturalisation figures have not been used for Great Britain and the Netherlands, as the number of naturalisations was unusually high owing to administrative changes. However the foreign resident population for Great Britain is for 1989. The foreign resident population figure for Australia for 1988 is an estimate, made by taking the foreign resident figure from the 1986 Census and adding a factor proportionate to the growth in overall overseas-born population from 1986 to 1988. The foreign resident population figure for France is for 1985, although the naturalisation figure is for 1989. The comparison is not exact, as definitions and categories vary from country to country. It merely has indicative value.

Sources: OECD SOPEMI, 1991; Muus, 1991, Australian Census, 1986.

The rank order of countries according to naturalisations per thousand of foreign resident population is: Australia, Sweden, Britain, Netherlands, France, Switzerland, Germany, Belgium. It has not been possible to calculate rates for the USA and Canada, owing to lack of data on the foreign resident population. However the very large absolute numbers of naturalisations make it reasonable to assume rates of naturalisations somewhere between Australia's and Sweden's. This corresponds closely to what might be expected on the basis of examination of other aspects of policy towards immigrants. Australia, the USA and Canada are countries with policies of permanent immigration, which have always aimed to make settlers into citizens. Sweden does not have a tradition of immigration, but its government has accepted that permanent settlement is taking place and has introduced a policy of multiculturalism. Britain, Netherlands and France all have traditions of granting citizenship to overseas-born people, linked to their colonial histories. Switzerland, Germany and Belgium follow exclusionary policies linked to their perception of immigrants as mainly temporary residents.

Even in countries where naturalisation is easy to obtain, some immigrants are unwilling to give up their original citizenship. This may be due to a refusal to cut symbolic links with the place of birth, but it can also be due to practical reasons connected with military service or land ownership rules in the area of origin. The best solution in such cases is the granting of dual citizenship, especially for the first generation. Dual citizenship is generally rejected by governments, because of fears of 'divided loyalties', yet it is becoming increasingly common, especially for the children of mixed marriages. The issue of political participation for non-citizens is dealt with in Chapter 9.

Status of the second generation

In countries which apply the principle of *ius sanguinis* (that is citizenship by descent from parents who are citizens) such as Germany and Swizerland, children who have been born and grown up in the country are denied not only security of residence, but also a clear national identity. They are formally citizens of a country they may have never seen, and can even be deported there in certain circumstances. In countries with *ius soli* (that is citizenship through birth on the territory) such as Australia, Canada, the USA and Britain, second generation settlers still generally have multiple cultural identities, but they have a secure legal basis on which to make decisions about their life perspectives. Intermediate forms, such as choice of citizenship at the age of 18 (as in France or Sweden) seem reasonably satisfactory. Again dual citizenship seems the best solution, as it would avoid decisions which can be extremely difficult for many individuals.

Linguistic and cultural rights

Maintenance of language and culture is seen as a need and a right by most settler groups. Many of the associations set up in the processes of ethnic community formation are concerned with language and culture: they teach the mother tongue to the second generation, organise festivals and carry out rituals. Language and culture not only serve as means of communication, but take on a symbolic meaning which is central to ethnic group cohesion. In most cases, language maintenance applies in the first two to three generations, after which there is a rapid decline. The significance of cultural symbols and rituals may last much longer.

Many members of the majority see cultural difference as a threat to a supposed cultural homogeneity and to national identity. Migrant languages and cultures become symbols of otherness and markers for discrimination. Giving them up is seen as essential for success and integration in the country of immigration. Failure to do so is regarded as indicative of a desire for separatism. Hostility to different languages and cultures is rationalised with the assertion that the official language is essential for economic success, and that migrant cultures are inadequate for a modern secular society. The alternative view is that migrant communities need their own languages and cultures to develop identity and self-esteem. Cultural maintenance helps create a secure basis which assists group integration into the wider society, while bilingualism brings benefits in learning and intellectual development.

Policies and attitudes on cultural and linguistic maintenance vary considerably. Some countries have histories of multilingualism. Canada's policy of bilingualism is based on two 'official languages', English and French. Multicultural policies have led to limited recognition of and support for immigrant languages, but they have hardly penetrated into mainstream contexts, such as broadcasting. Switzerland has a multilingual policy for its founding languages, but does not recognise immigrant languages, nor does it provide much in the way of language services (Belgium is similar). Australia and Sweden both accept the principle of linguistic and cultural maintenance. They provide a wide range of language services (interpreting, translating, mother-tongue classes) and support for ethnic community cultural organisations. Both countries have multicultural education policies. Australia has a 'national policy on languages', concerned with both community languages and languages of economic significance. Multicultural radio and television are funded by the government.

In the USA, language has become a contentious issue. The tradition of monolingualism is being eroded by the growth of the Hispanic community. This has led to a backlash, in the form of 'the US English movement' which has called for a constitutional amendment to declare English the official language. Despite official rejection of linguistic pluralism, it has proved essential to establish a range of multilingual services. Monolingualism is also the basic principle in France, Britain, Germany and the Netherlands. Nonetheless all these countries have been forced to introduce language services to take account of migrant needs in communicating with courts, bureaucracies and health services. The multilingual character of inner city school classes has also led to special measures for integration of immigrant children, and to a gradual shift towards multicultural education policies in some areas.

Minorities and nation

On the basis of the preceding comparisons, it is possible to roughly divide the immigration countries into three categories.

The exclusionary model

Countries in which the dominant definition of the nation is that of a community of birth and descent (referred to as the 'folk or ethnic model' in Chapter 2) are unwilling to accept immigrants and their children as members of the nation. This unwillingness is expressed through exclusionary immigration policies (especially limitation of family reunion and refusal to grant secure residence status), restrictive naturalisation rules and the ideology of not being countries of immigration. Countries like Switzerland and Belgium have developed as nations with more than one 'founding group'. The historical arrangements developed to deal with this have led to delicate balances that make it hard to incorporate new groups. As for Germany, the long and chequered history of border struggles, unification, division and reunification helps to explain – though not to justify – present attitudes. In such countries, settlers are members of civil society (as workers, tax-payers, parents and so on) but it is very hard for them to become members of the nation or to participate in the state.

The republican model

In this second category, which refers to community based on political participation and culture, it seems necessary to conflate what we referred to as the 'imperial model' and the 'republican model' in Chapter 2. This is because the countries concerned, France, Britain and the Netherlands, all have aspects of both models, albeit in different respects. All three have been imperial powers, which turned colonial subjects into citizens. France moved to the model of citizenship as a political community after the 1789 revolution, yet its policies towards colonised peoples have maintained elements of the 'imperial model'. Britain and The Netherlands have moved away from the 'imperial model' as their empires have crumbled in the post-1945 period. Introduction of a more modern form of citizenship, based on membership of the political community, has often meant depriving former colonial subjects of citizenship and rights. The ambiguity of the situation of minorities in these countries reflects the contradictory and transitional nature of these post-imperial states. Essentially the current citizenship model permits people who have become members of civil society to join the nation and to participate in the state – at the price of some degree of cultural assimilation.

A closer look at the republican model in France shows some of its contradictions. Many of its proponents now link it with a demand for cultural assimilation, which seems to contradict its basic principle. The essence of the republican model is to be found in the first report of the official *Haut Conseil à l'Intégration* (High Council for Integration) which was established in 1990:

> French conceptions of integration should obey a logic of equality and not a logic of minorities. The principles of identity and

equality which go back to the Revolution and the Declaration of Rights of Man and of Citizens impregnate our conception, thus founded on the equality of individuals before the law, whatever their origin, race, religion . . . to the exclusion of an institutional recognition of minorities. (HCI, 1991: 10, quoted here from Lloyd, 1991: 65)

The central idea is that immigrants can (and should) become integrated into the political community as French citizens, and that this will bring about cultural integration. There is therefore no room for long-term cultural or ethnic diversity. Exponents of the model see France as temporarily multi-ethnic, but not as permanently multi-cultural. The emphasis on citizenship as the main instrument of integration was one reason why attempts by the centre–right government of 1986–8 to change the *Code de Nationalité* to make it harder to become a French citizen were rejected.

According to Weil, citizenship is essentially a political relationship, most simply expressed by the statement: '*Celui qui vote est français et citoyen*' 'he who votes is French and a citizen'. Any granting of rights (such as local voting rights) to non-citizens means watering down this principle, and could lead to new identifications, not only by migrants but also by French people, on the basis of 'origins, blood, race or culture'. In this view, rights for minorities lead directly to racism. Despite the emphasis on political integration, the implication of cultural homogenisation is very strong. Weil argues that naturalisation presupposes a form of 'socialisation' leading to 'a collection of social roles based on cultural dispositions adequate to permit an understanding for the state and of civic matters'. He goes on to lament that the 'great Republican institutions' have become too weak to carry out this socialisation function and to produce national identity (Weil, 1991a: 300–2).

It is obvious that the republican model is unlike the German model of citizenship based on ethnicity. But, with regard to integration of immigrants, it is also quite distinct from the US model, in which nation building has been based on immigration. France embodies a paradox: on the one hand it represents the model of the 'completed nation'[3] (on the basis of antiquity of its formation, the homogeneity of its population, the rigidity of its political frameworks) but, on the other hand, it has been obliged to resort to massive immigration, which has transformed the composition of its original population

(Noiriel, 1988: 334–6). This implies a certain instability in the French model, since it is based on the absurdity of believing that immigrants who become French citizens lose their distinct ethnic or cultural characteristics by virtue of this fact.

The relationship between citizenship and cultural difference has become an area of struggle. In the 1980s, ethnic minority organisations called for municipal voting rights, which were seen as a form of quasi-citizenship, to take account of the transitional position of immigrants. The demand was rejected by the state, because it was seen as a threat to the supposedly unitary and egalitarian nature of citizenship (compare Costa-Lascoux, 1989: 115–44). By the end of the 1980s, ethnic minority groups had moved on to demand full citizenship, but in a new form. Their critique of the republican model had two aspects. Firstly, going back to origins of the concept of *citoyen* after the revolution, they pointed out that it was based purely on residence on French territory, had nothing to do with culture and was granted even to non-nationals (Bouamama, 1988; compare also de Wenden, 1987: 44). *Citoyenneté* and *nationalite* were almost antithetical concepts.[4] Citizenship should therefore be automatically granted to all permanent immigrants, who should also be permitted to maintain the citizenship of the country of origin. Secondly, they pointed out that the ideal of equality of rights embodied in citizenship is a dead letter for people who are socioeconomically marginalised and victims of racism. It is absurd to expect members of ethnic minorities to become culturally assimilated, when they need their communities for protection and to struggle for rights. The demand has thus become one for both citizenship and cultural rights (Bouamama, 1988).

The multicultural model

The final category is the 'multicultural model' of membership of the nation on the basis of residence and acceptance of core political values, which applies mainly to Australia, Canada and Sweden, and to a lesser extent to the USA. In these four countries, membership of civil society, initiated through permission to immigrate, leads to participation in the state and the chance of becoming a member of the nation. The Netherlands has an intermediate position, for its minority policy also has some elements of multiculturalism.

It is easy to see why the 'classical countries of immigration' (Australia, Canada and the USA) have moved towards this model. It appears as the best way of incorporating large groups of immigrants with diverse backgrounds in a relatively short period. Moreover the imperative of making immigrants into citizens reinforces the pressure for a multicultural policy: by making immigrants into voters, ethnic groups can gain political clout. Nonetheless it would be wrong to think that the adoption of this model has been automatic – there have been strong exclusionary and assimilationist movements in all three countries and multicultural models remain controversial. The USA differs from the other two 'classical immigration countries' mainly in the lower degree of state intervention in ethnic affairs. Laissez-faire policies in an expanding society seem to have had similar effects to state intervention in favour of ethnic groups in the other countries.

Sweden appears as an anomaly: it is a society which was unusually homogeneous until recently. Yet it has had large-scale settlement, and adopted multicultural policies very close to those of Australia and Canada. The reason seems to lie in the strongly state interventionist model of Swedish social democracy, which has used the same approaches to integrating immigrants into civil society and the state as were used earlier to integrate the working class and reduce class conflict. A closer look at current debates in Sweden helps illustrate some of the dilemmas of the multicultural model.

As mentioned above, in 1975 the Swedish parliament unanimously passed a resolution setting out guidelines for immigrant policy. The model was based on the expectation of long-term integration into Swedish society and culture, even though this might take some generations. Public policies towards immigrants fall into two categories: indirect policies, concerned with guaranteeing access to general social programmes, and direct policies, which relate to immigrants' special needs. Indirect policies include measures to ensure that immigrants have equal rights to employment, social services, housing and education. This can involve use of anti-discrimination regulations, or the provision of interpreter and translator services where necessary. Direct policies include voting rights for resident non-citizens, mother-tongue classes at school, information services for immigrants, a system of state grants to immigrant central organisations, participation in official consultative bodies such as the Immigrants' Council, and multilingual services provided by trade unions.

Despite the rhetoric of free choice and cultural rights, the Swedish model involves a high degree of social control. For example, non-Scandinavian citizens require work permits and residence permits, and can only obtain social benefits if they are registered with the authorities. The system of grants to immigrant associations allows government to select bodies worthy of funding, and thus to influence their activities. Schierup (1991: 140) speaks of 'the Swedish experience of "prescribed multiculturalism", whereby immigrant and ethnic organisations are co-opted into the corporatist state where they end up politically marginalised'. Moreover the relatively liberal policies towards settlers are based on strict control of new immigration (Hammar, 1985b: 28–32).

There are signs that the Swedish model is running into difficulties. In December 1989, the government decided to tighten up rules on recognition of refugees (OECD SOPEMI, 1991: 67). Alund and Schierup (1991) argue that Sweden is being influenced by the current development of a 'fortress Europe' mentality, in which there are strong fears of economic influxes — disguised as political refugees — from the impoverished South. Islam is increasingly being seen as a threat to Swedish culture and values. A preference is emerging for using Eastern Europe as a future labour reserve, and reorienting refugee policy away from purely humanitarian criteria towards considerations of economic usefulness. Alund and Schierup conclude.

> The moral compact on which Swedish immigrant policy is built is gradually disintegrating, giving way to a culturalist construction of new discriminatory boundaries . . . The hidden logic of a new commonsense cultural racism . . . finds . . . its way into the language and practices of public servants, professionals and into the everyday commonsense discourses of ordinary people. (1991: 10)

Similar conflicts on immigration and pluralism exist in other countries with multicultural policies. The pluralist minority policies in The Netherlands is currently under attack. In Australia and Canada, multiculturalism is a constant topic of heated debate, but the model continues to evolve and gain acceptance. Debates on multicultural policies play an increasing role in virtually all immigration countries, as the difficulties of exclusionary and assimilationist models become apparent.

Conclusion

The comparison of the situation in various immigration countries can be summed up by saying that ethnic group formation takes place everywhere, but the conditions under which this happens vary considerably. This leads to different outcomes: in some countries ethnic groups become marginalised and excluded minorities, in others they take the form of ethnic communities which are accepted as part of a pluralist society. Exclusion is most severe in the former guestworker countries, Germany and Switzerland. Multicultural models are to be found in countries with explicit policies of permanent settlement and pluralism: above all Australia, Canada and Sweden. The USA, as a permanent settlement country without multicultural policies, comes close to the pluralist model, but without its explicit political goals. The Netherlands also comes close to the multicultural model, though in a weaker form. Between the extremes of exclusion or multiculturalism are countries like France and Britain, which recognise the reality of permanent settlement, but are unwilling to accept long-term pluralism. However there are important differences between France and Britain, particularly with regard to the role of the state in managing cultural difference.

The reality in each country is much more complex and contradictory than our brief account can show. Nonetheless these general trends are significant, and can be applied to other immigration countries. There is no space here to discuss the situation in countries as diverse as Austria, Norway, Italy or Japan, but there are some clear lessons. The first is that policies of temporary migrant labour recruitment are almost certain to lead to permanent settlement and formation of ethnic groups. The second is that the character of these future ethnic groups will, to a large measure, be determined by what the state does in the early stages of migration. Policies which try to deny the reality of immigration by tacitly tolerating large-scale illegal movements — and this is the case for both Italy and Japan — lead to social marginalisation, minority formation and racism. A third lesson is that ethnic groups arising from immigration need their own associations and social networks, as well as their own languages and cultures. Policies which deny legitimacy to these lead to isolation and separatism. A fourth lesson is that the best way to prevent marginalisation and social conflicts is to grant permanent immigrants full rights in all social spheres. This means making citizenship easily available, even if this leads to dual citizenship.

This last conclusion has far-reaching consequences: removing the link between citizenship and ethnic origin means changing the defining principle of the nation-state. This applies particularly to nations based on the ethnic model, such as Germany. The rapid shift away from ideas of ethnic homogeneity in Sweden shows that such changes can be carried out fairly smoothly. The principles of citizenship also need redefining in countries with post-imperialist or republican models, such as France, Britain and The Netherlands. The classical countries of immigration – Australia, Canada and the USA – have already moved towards citizenship based on territoriality and are capable of incorporating newcomers of varying origins.

Migration to developed countries is likely to continue, and even accelerate, in the years ahead, so the presence of ethnic communities will be an inescapable part of society. The most direct impact will be felt in the expanding 'global cities' like Los Angeles, Paris, Berlin and Sydney. The formation of ethnic groups and the spatial restructuring of the city which this helps to bring about is a powerful force for change. It may give rise to conflicts and violence, but it can also be a great source of energy and innovation.

In this situation, exclusionary models of immigrant rights and nationhood are questionable, because they lead to divided societies. Similarly assimilationist models are not likely to succeed, because they fail to take account of the cultural and social situation of settlers. Policies and ideologies which lead to the emergence of ethnic minorities denied full participation in political, economic, social and cultural life must be destabilising for state and society. The multicultural model is a combination of a set of social policies to respond to the needs of settlers, and a statement about the openness of the nation to cultural diversity. It appears to be the most viable solution to the problem of defining membership of the nation-state in an increasingly mobile world.

9

Immigrant Politics

As international migration reshapes societies, it inevitably and often profoundly affects political life, yet, paradoxically, international migration is frequently viewed as a socioeconomic phenomenon largely devoid of political significance. This viewpoint is part and parcel of the temporary worker idea examined earlier. During the initial stages of an international migration, it may well be that most migrants are apolitical and their presence may be viewed as posing no political problem. Relatively few Western Europeans foresaw that the decision to recruit foreign labour in the wake of the Second World War would one day affect the political landscape of Western Europe. But post-war migration did lead to a significantly altered political environment: one that now includes Islamic fundamentalist parties and political movements comprised mainly of immigrants, as well as extreme-right anti-immigrant parties.

In the end, the most lasting significance of international migration may be its effects upon politics. This is not inevitably the case. Much depends on how immigrants are treated by governments, and on the origins, timing, nature and context of a particular migratory flow. It makes a difference whether migrants were legally admitted and permitted to naturalise or whether their entry (legal or illegal) was seen as merely temporary but they then stayed on permanently. On the one hand, immigrants can quickly become citizens without a discernible political effect, save for the addition of additional voters who may or may not exercise their franchise. On the other hand, international migration may lead to an accretion of politically disenfranchised persons whose political marginality is compounded by various socioeconomic problems.

231

The universe of possible political effects of international migration is vast and characteristically intertwines the political systems of two states, the homeland and the host or receiving society. The political significance of international migration can be active or passive. Immigrants can become political actors in their own right or manifest apoliticism, which itself can be extremely important to maintenance of a political status quo. On the other hand, immigrants often become the object of politics – political allies for some and foes for others. This chapter cannot hope to do justice to all the facets of immigration-related politics. Only a few themes can be considered. The emphasis is on newly emergent political forces and issues that have rendered politics within and between states more complex and volatile.

Immigrants as political actors: participation, representation and mobilisation in Western Europe

By 1970, the immigrant population of Western Europe had become so sizable that scholars and governments began to ask what were the political ramifications of this massive presence. The answer was not clear-cut. The fact that large numbers of immigrant workers and their families were not entitled to vote in Western European elections because of their alien status probably helped conservative parties, as working-class voters often support parties of the left. However not all immigrants necessarily support left-wing parties. Within Germany's Turkish community, for example, there was considerable support for right-wing Turkish parties. Many immigrants were uninterested in the politics of Western Europe. Their principal political concern continued to be politics in their homelands. Political extremism in Turkish politics spilled over to Turkish communities in Western Europe which, at times, became veritable battlegrounds. German governmental statistics on known political extremists included large numbers of aliens, both left-wing and right-wing (Miller, 1981).

That immigrant communities in Western Europe would become key areas for, say, Algerian or Turkish politics is scarcely surprising. After all, it is not unusual for 10 per cent of some emigration countries' populations to reside abroad. Immigrants are often freer to express themselves politically as aliens in Western European democracies than they were back home. Immigrant communities in Western Europe became the object of competition – occasionally violent – between pro-status quo and anti-status quo homeland political forces. Governments of emigration countries were acutely aware of the stakes involved and characteristically sought to influence the 'hearts and minds' of their citizens or subjects abroad through the nurturing of pro-governmental organisations amongst immigrants and through diplomatic and consular services.

The *Amicale des Algeriens en Europe* (AAE) epitomised such efforts by homelands. The AAE was the overseas branch of the ruling National Liberation Front in Algeria. The head of the AAE was usually simultaneously a high-ranking official of the National Liberation Front and of the Algerian government. The AAE enjoyed a quasi-diplomatic status in France and it served as a channel for emigrant participation in Algerian politics. The AAE also represented the interests of Algerian emigrants in Algerian governmental policy-making circles as well as *vis-à-vis* the French government.

Throughout the 1960s and 1970s, the AAE virtually monopolised representation of Algerians in France, although it was opposed by rival groups. Opponents like the outlawed Movement of Arab Workers, a revolutionary communist organisation with ties to radical Palestinian factions, played a key role in organising large street demonstrations and strikes to protest against attacks on Algerians and other North Africans in 1973 (Miller, 1981: 89–104). It was no wonder that the AAE opposed the French governmental decision in 1981 granting aliens the right to form associations (Weil, 1991a: 99–114). Prior to 1981, associations of foreigners required government authorisation in order to operate, which condemned anti-Algerian regime parties to clandestinity. The 1981 reform undercut the virtual AAE monopoly by making it easier for organisations not controlled by the government to operate. Open opposition to the Algerian regime soon flourished.

The Algerian government was particularly concerned by the ability of Muslim fundamentalist groups, such as the Islamic Salvation Front, to operate openly in France, which they could not do across the Mediterranean. This concern was shared with several other non-Islamic governments in predominantly Muslim societies such as Turkey and Tunisia. The political dissidence expressed on French soil presaged the fundamentalist electoral victory in the December 1991 elections, although many Algerians who voted for the Islamic Salvation Front were not so much voting for an Islamic republic as protesting against National Liberation Front rule. The influence of French policies with regard to aliens' associations illustrates how international migration binds together the politics of two societies. Host societies can greatly influence politics in the homelands through their policies towards emigrants and vice versa.

Foreign workers and their dependants in Western Europe benefited from diplomatic representation and bilateral labour agreements regulated most major foreign labour flows to Western Europe. These agreements, along with international instruments pertinent to migrant labour, had some influence on Western European policies towards migrants. Generally, however, diplomatic representation of migrant interests was insufficient. Homeland governments did not want to appear to be meddling in the sovereign affairs of other states. Moreover their stake in a continuing homeward flow of foreign worker remittances often made them reluctant to criticise treatment of their citizens abroad. The asymmetrical power of homelands and immigrant-receiving states was clearly demonstrated when one Western European state after the other abruptly and unilaterally curbed foreign worker recruitment in the 1970s.

The Algerian decision to suspend labour emigration in 1973, in the face of mounting attacks on Algerians in France, constituted a significant exception to the general pattern. Still Western European governments found it much harder to force out unwanted migrants through administrative means that they had in the 1930s (Ponty: 1988). The French government did not want to renew the permits of several hundred thousand Algerians in the second half of the 1970s. But a combination of legal constraints and pro-immigrant political pressure forced the government to accept the principle of voluntary repatriation. In other words, the French government could not force out legally admitted foreign residents against their will (Weil, 1991a).

The inadequacy of diplomatic representation of foreign workers and their dependants in Western Europe was one reason behind the emergence of distinctive channels of alien participation and representation in Western European politics despite their lack of citizenship. The key difference between most Western European countries and the classic lands of immigration like the USA, Canada and Australia was the difficulty of naturalisation and acquisition of citizenship in the former (Brubaker, 1989). Most foreign workers admitted to Western Europe were not expected to stay on and to become citizens. The classic immigration lands expect immigrant admission to lead eventually to naturalisation. Political participation by the new citizens in their adopted lands is viewed as legitimate. By contrast, many Western Europeans do not view immigrant participation in politics as fully legitimate, yet participate immigrants do, both as non-citizens and, increasingly, as citizens.

Indeed there is reason to believe that nascent immigrant participation in Western European politics contributed to the decisions to curb foreign worker recruitment. By the early 1970s, supposedly politically quiescent aliens had become involved in a number of significant industrial strikes and protest movements. In some instances, extreme leftist groups succeeded in mobilising foreigners. Largely foreign worker strikes in French and German car plants demonstrated the disruptive potential of foreign labour and constrained trade unions to do more to represent foreign workers. Generally speaking, foreigners were poorly integrated into unions in 1970. By 1980, significant strides had been made towards integration. This was reflected in growing unionisation rates among foreign workers and the election of foreign workers to works councils and union leadership positions. Still foreign worker-related issues continued to pose novel issues for many unions.

Immigrants also increasingly sought participation and representation in local government. In several countries advisory councils were instituted which were designed to give immigrants a voice in local government affairs. Experiences with these advisory councils varied and some were discontinued. Political controversy often accompanied their creation: some contested them as efforts to co-opt aliens, while others saw them as illegitimate interference by aliens in the politics of the host society. In other Western European states, aliens were accorded a right to vote in local and regional election. Sweden was the pacesetter in this regard, but alien participation in Swedish local and regional elections declined over time. The Netherlands was the second country to accord qualified aliens voting rights. However the results of alien voting there have also been somewhat disappointing (Rath, 1988: 25–35). This has not prevented the granting of voting rights to aliens from becoming a significant political issue in many Western European countries.

Successive French governments have argued that it would be unconstitutional to accord aliens local voting rights. The German Federal Constitutional Court reached a similar conclusion in 1990, when the state government of Schleswig-Holstein sought to grant foreign residents voting rights. Nonetheless the French Socialist Party included the grant of municipal voting rights to foreign resident among the 110 planks of the party platform when it won the presidential and legislative elections of 1981. The Socialist Foreign Minister, Claude Cheysson, endorsed the concept during a visit to Algiers in 1982, only to find that his endorsement precipitated a storm of criticism both within and outside the Socialist Party. By 1983, the government of Prime Minister Mauroy had printed pamphlets explaining why resident aliens should be allowed to vote in municipal elections, but these pamphlets were never distributed for fear that they would increase support for the nascent *Front National* (FN), already a rapidly growing anti-immigrant political party.

When the French socialists emerged from the 1988 presidential and legislative elections with a diminished but still government-forming plurality, President Mitterrand once again pledged to back the granting of municipal voting rights to certain resident aliens. By June of 1990, however, the minority government of Prime Minister Michel Rocard felt constrained to renounce support for alien municipal voting rights as a precondition for the traditional opposition parties joining in a national dialogue over immigration (Sole, 1990: 8). As if to mark his distance from Prime Minister Rocard, President Mitterrand would continue to speak in support of municipal voting rights after June of 1990.

The question of the granting of municipal voting rights to resident aliens illustrates well how questions of migrant rights came to the forefront of politics in many Western European states in the 1980s. Aliens could participate in politics through a variety of channels, ranging from membership in trade unions, to voting for representatives on alien parliaments, to joining political parties and demonstrating in the streets. Despite these avenues of influence, their status as long-term resident aliens living in a democracy remained anomalous. Even in countries with liberal naturalisation policies, such as Sweden, many immigrants did not naturalise. The granting of local and regional voting rights to them was therefore something that enriched Swedish democracy.

By the 1980s, the stakes involved in the granting of voting rights to resident aliens were quite high in many Western democracies. Aliens were spatially concentrated in major cities and certain neighbourhoods. Enfranchising them would dramatically affect political outcomes in many local elections. Supporters of the granting of municipal voting rights generally regarded it as a way to foster integration and as a counterweight to the growing influence of parties like the FN in France. However many immigrants were politically enfranchised, particularly in the United Kingdom, where the vast majority of them enjoyed citizenship rights. This did not prevent the eruption of riots involving immigrants and their British-born children in the mid-1980s. The granting of local voting rights to resident aliens, was thus not in itself a panacea for the severe problems facing immigrants in Western Europe.

Since the 1970s, immigrants have increasingly articulated political concerns, participated in politics and sought representation. Much of this political activity was non-institutionalised and included strikes, protests and riots. Immigrant protest movements became part of the tapestry of Western European politics and frequently affected policies towards immigrants. Persistent hunger strikes by immigrants and their supporters, for example, brought pressure to bear on French and Dutch authorities to liberalise rules regarding legalisation. There was great variation in patterns of alien political participation and representation from country to country, with some countries, like Sweden, succeeding in institutionalising much of it.

Mobilisation of immigrants and ethnic minorities outside the normal channels of political representation is often linked to experience of exclusion from the system, either through racist violence or institutional discrimination. For instance, members of ethnic minorities often feel that the police are more concerned with social control than with protecting them from racist violence. In Britain, Afro-Caribbean and Asian youth have organised self-protection groups against racist attacks. Sub-cultures of resistance developed around reggae music and rastafarianism for the West Indians, and Islam and other religions for the Asians (Gilroy, 1987). The reaction by government and the media was to see ethnic minority youth as a problem of public order – a 'social time bomb' on the verge of explosion. There was widespread moral panic about the alleged high rates of street crime ('mugging') by black youth and a tendency to see black people as an 'enemy within', who threatened British society (CCCS, 1982).

Black youth discontent exploded into uprisings in many inner city areas in 1981 and 1985 (Sivanandan, 1982; Beynon, 1986). In 1991, there were new disturbances, in which 'joy riders' stole cars and publicly raced them to destruction in inner city streets – to the acclaim of crowds of onlookers. After both the 1981 and the 1985 riots, the initial official response was to insist that the central issue was one of crime and to lament the breakdown of parental control (Solomos, 1988). Newspapers blamed the problems on 'crazed Left-wing extremists' and 'streetfighting experts trained in Moscow and Libya'. The disturbances were generally labelled as 'black youth riots'. But, in fact, there was a high degree of white youth involvement (Beynon, 1986) .

The riots were caused by a number of interrelated factors. Deteriorating community relations and lack of political leadership against racism were major causes of alienation of black youth. There were concentrations of disadvantaged people (both white and black) in inner city areas, marked by high unemployment, poor housing, environmental decay, high crime rates, drug abuse and racist attacks. As Beynon (1986: 268) points out, the areas where riots took place were politically disadvantaged: they lacked the institutions, opportunities and resources for putting pressure on those with political power. Finally these areas had suffered repressive forms of policing, experienced by young people as racism and deliberate harassment. The riots may be seen as defensive movements of minority youth, connected with protection of their communities as well as assertion of identity and culture (Gilroy, 1987; Gilroy and Lawrence, 1988).

Similar urban uprisings have taken place in France, where a second generation has emerged of young people of mainly Arab descent who feel French, but find themselves excluded by discrimination and racism. In the 1981 'hot summer' of Lyons, youth riots in public housing estates protested against heavy-handed policing, racism and unemployment (Lapeyronnie *et al.*, 1990: 65). They were to be repeated in Lyons, Paris and elsewhere in the following years (Weil, 1991a: 262–3; Lloyd, 1991: 63).

Fear of further unrest has led to a multifaceted response by governments. Some of the French measures were mentioned in Chapter 8. In Britain programmes have been introduced to combat youth unemployment, make education more accessible and appropriate to minorities, improve conditions in urban areas and to change police practices. Task forces were set up for disadvantaged areas; spending to improve conditions in the inner cities was substantially increased and a large scale Youth Training Scheme was introduced (Layton-Henry 1986: 87–91). Police forces, local authorities and social services departments devised strategies to deal with racial violence and harassment. However it is doubtful whether such policies can combat the powerful economic, social and political forces which marginalise ethnic minority youth.

New issues and new political forces: the emergence of Islam in Western Europe

By 1970, Islam was the second religion of France. By 1990, it was the second religion of the French. There were perhaps six million Muslims in Western Europe by 1990, including over three million in France alone, and virtually this entire presence could be attributed to post-1945 immigration. While France has long had a significant Islamic minority – indeed France regarded itself as an Islamic power during the Third Republic – the number of Muslims in metropolitan France grew enormously after 1947. Nonetheless, as late as 1970, Islam was largely invisible in France. According to Kepel and Leveau, the affirmation of Islam in France after 1970 was part and parcel of the settlement of foreign workers, the progression of the migratory chain (Kepel and Leveau, 1987). It was manifested primarily through construction of mosques and prayer-rooms and through formation of Islamic associations. All these grew rapidly in number between 1970 and 1990.

This affirmation of Islam profoundly affected French politics. In turn, the reaction to Islamic affirmation, manifested above all by the emergence of the FN, undermined governmental integration policies. By 1990, immigration had clearly become the key political issue in France and the politicisation of immigration issues at times appeared to threaten the stability of French democratic institutions. The paradox was that this was largely unforeseen.

The politicisation of immigration issues in France became apparent around 1970 (de Wenden, 1988: 209–19). In that year, extreme-right student groups began to demonstrate against *immigration sauvage* – illegal migration. These demonstrations were usually matched by counterdemonstrations, and violence erupted. By 1972, the extremist groups principally involved in this violence – the Trotskyist Communist League and the neo-fascist New Order – were banned. Leftist and extreme leftist groups continued to mobilise immigrants into various kinds of frequently highly publicised immigrant struggles such as the long rent strike in the SONACOTRA housing for foreign workers (Miller, 1978). Elements of the extreme right, however, began to mobilise on anti-immigration themes. Françoise Gaspard has related how the FN began to campaign in local elections in the Dreux area near Paris by the mid-1970s (Gaspard, 1990). The FN slowly increased its share of the vote before scoring a dramatic breakthrough in a 1983 election in Dreux, when it obtained 16.7 per cent of the vote. By 1989, a FN candidate in the second round of a by-election in Dreux won a seat in the Chamber of Deputies, with 61.3 per cent of the vote. In the space of 11 years, the number of FN voters increased from 307 to 4716 (Gaspard, 1990: 205). Something fundamental had changed and the emergence of Islam had much to do with it.

The French reaction to Islam was both irrational and grounded in concrete immigration-related problems. The irrational dimension stemmed from the trauma of the Algerian war and the association of Islam and terrorism. In 1982, following a series of crippling strikes in major car plants in the Paris region which principally involved North African workers, French Prime Minister Mauroy insinuated that Iran was trying to destabilise French politics by backing Islamic fundamentalist groups involved in the strike (*Le Monde*, 1 February 1983). While no evidence of an Iranian involvement was produced, it was clear to all that Islamic groups were heavily involved in the strikes, with the French Communist Party and its trade union affiliate, the CGT, desperately trying to regain control of the strike movement (Miller, 1986: 361–82). Islam was seen by many French as incompatible with democracy because no distinction was made between church and state in Islam. Moreover France's Muslims were portrayed as heavily influenced by Islamic fundamentalism when, in fact, only a small minority of France's Muslims consider themselves fundamentalists and they are divided into multiple and often competitive organisations (Kepel and Leveau, 1987).

The integration problems affecting France's Islamic minority were perhaps more central to the politicisation of immigration issues. Gaspard (1990) recounts how tensions over housing exacerbated French–immigrant relations in the Dreux area. Immigrants, and particularly North African-origin immigrants, disproportionally live in inadequate housing. As settlement and family reunification proceeded, more and more immigrants applied for subsidised governmental housing, causing severe friction when numbers of immigrants grew while non–immigrant residents diminished. Before long, entire buildings came to be viewed as immigrants' quarters. The physical isolation of many immigrants in sub-standard housing, along with the educational problems faced by disproportionally high numbers of immigrant children, contributed to a malaise on which the FN fed. By the 1980s, primarily North African Muslim-origin youths, most of whom probably were French citizens, became conspicuously involved in urban unrest that was deeply unsettling to the French.

The French Socialist Party sought to galvanise support by appealing to North African-origin voters. The pro-immigrant *SOS-racisme* organisation was largely an initiative of the Socialist Party. The party clearly appealed to voters as a bulwark against the National Front. Yet support for the socialists had plunged dramatically by 1992 and they were booed at pro-immigrant rallies. The socialist message of integration of resident aliens and curbing illegal immigration was viewed as pro-immigrant by the extreme right and as anti-immigrant by the extreme left. The diminished credibility and appeal of the socialists was due to a variety of factors, including persistent campaign-financing scandals, but its decline appeared to be setting the stage for heightened conflict over immigration in which the role of Islam was certain to figure prominently.

Illustrative of the broader issue was the question of the *foulards* or Islamic headscarves worn by some young girls to school in the late 1980s. In a country where the tradition of the separation of church and state is deeply rooted and politically salient, wearing of the headscarves appeared to many French as incompatible with the very principles of the French Republic: French republican tradition prohibited the wearing of religious articles, and no exception should be made for Muslims. On the other side of the debate was the claim that the choice of wearing a headscarf was an individual's prerogative, a private matter of no consequence to public authorities. In the end, French authorities ruled in favour of the girls, but not before the question had become a *cause célébre*. Should school cafeterias serve *halal* food, that is food prepared in accordance with Islamic ritual prescriptions? Should Muslims be granted representation in French politics-as Roman Catholics are through governmental consultations with the bishops and French Jews are through the consistory? Should factories honour Islamic holidays in addition to Catholic feast days? As Islam was affirmed, a host of long latent issues came to the fore, with major consequences for the French political system.

Paradoxically the French government had encouraged the creation of Islamic mosques and prayer-rooms back in the 1960s and 1970s. Islam was seen by some businesses and public authorities as a means of social control. Prayer-rooms were constructed in factories in the hope that North African workers would be less likely to join left-wing trade unions. Moreover supporting Islam was part of a policy of cultural maintenance, designed to encourage the eventual repatriation of migrant workers and their families. Saudi Arabia and Libya financed the construction of mosques across Western Europe, hoping to influence thereby the emerging Islam of Western Europe (Kepel and Leveau, 1987).

Despite the separation of church and state in France, many French local governments supported the construction of mosques as part of integration policy. The building of mosques was often violently opposed, and several were bombed. Other Western European governments also fostered Islam through policies which brought Islamic teachers to Western Europe. These policies usually stemmed from provisions of bilateral labour agreements which granted homeland governments a role in educating migrant children in Western Europe. Many so-called Koran schools in Germany, for example, were controlled by Islamic fundamentalists. Such institutionalisation of Islam in Western Europe has probably progressed the furthest in Belgium.

Most of Western Europe's Muslims saw their religion as a private matter. The Rushdie Affair made Islamic identity more of a political problem than, say, Roman Catholicism or Protestantism. Salman Rushdie is an Indian-born Muslim citizen of the UK, who scandalised many Muslims with his book *The Satanic Verses* and was condemned to death by Iran's Ayatollah Khomeini. Much-publicised anti-Rushdie demonstrations by Muslims in England, France and Belgium confirmed the incompatibility of Islam with Western institutions in the eyes of some critics of the Islamic presence in Western Europe.

The onset of the crisis over the Iraqi occupation of Kuwait in 1990 also prompted fear of Islamic subversion, particularly in France. Muslims in France were more supportive of Iraq than was French society as a whole (Perotti and Thepaut, 1991: 76–9). But many French Muslims opposed the Iraqi invasion, and the Gulf War did not produce the political terrorism and mass unrest in Western Europe that some had predicted. Nonetheless it was clear that French governmental support for the war effort alienated it from France's Islamic community. Tensions between Muslims and non-Muslims reached new heights during the Gulf crisis, prompting rumours of thousands of Tunisians in the South of France returning home out of a feeling of insecurity (Perotti and Thepaut, 1991: 70–1). Similarly in Australia, incidents of abuse and harassment against Muslims, particularly women, increased during the Gulf Crisis, prompting government action to improve community relations.

While the vast majority of Western Europe's Muslims eschewed fundamentalism, Western Europe certainly was affected by the upsurge in fundamentalism and religious piety that swept the Muslim world in the 1980s. Islamic fundamentalism often had the greatest appeal in areas beset by high unemployment, poverty, educational failure and social marginalisation. The integration problems facing Western Europe's immigrants in general were most deeply felt in Islamic communities. The depth of these long-term problems virtually ensured that Islam would remain a key Western European political concern for a long time to come.

In The Netherlands, unemployment among overwhelmingly Muslim Turks and Moroccans grew sharply in the late 1970s. Their disproportionally high unemployment rate was due to inadequate educational backgrounds and lack of skills, as well as to the concentration of Turkish and Moroccan workers in the industries most adversely affected by the recession. When unemployment of Dutch workers declined, by the mid-1980s, the unemployment rates of Turks and Moroccans continued to increase.

Across Western Europe, Muslims are affected by disproportionally high unemployment rates. In areas where unemployment problems are compounded by educational and housing problems, and these underlying socioeconomic tensions are overlain with highly politicised religious identity issues, the ingredients for socio-political explosions are strong. All it takes is an incident, usually a violent encounter between a Muslim youth and the police, for violence to erupt. This was the pattern behind urban unrest in France in the 1980s and 1990s. One of the great questions on the European horizon is whether far more severe social explosions can be averted through reforms (Layton-Henry, 1990). The profound problems facing Western Europe's Muslims are one reason that integration will remain the top immigration policy priority for Western European governments and for the EC for the foreseeable future (Commission of European Communities, 1990).

Immigrants as the objects of politics: the growth of anti-immigrant extremism

The French were not alone in finding it politically difficult to come to grips with the emergent Islamic reality in their midst. Belgium became the scene of urban unrest in 1991, when largely Moroccan-origin youths clashed with police following a rumour that an anti-immigrant political party, the Flemish *Vlaams Blok*, was going to organise a political rally in an area heavily populated with immigrants (*The Bulletin*, 1991: 20). Partly as a result of this violence, support for the *Vlaams Blok* increased sharply in the 1991 Belgian elections.

Similarly, in the 1991 municipal and regional elections, the Austrian anti-immigrant Freedom party scored an important break-through by increasing its share of the vote to almost one-quarter. In Italy, the anti-immigrant Leagues did surprisingly well in regional elections, although it was unclear precisely how much of this new-found strength was due to anti-immigrant sentiment (Perotti and Thepaut, 1990: 49–77). Some explained the Leagues' success as primarily a protest vote directed against wastage of governmental funds in the South of Italy (Miller, 1991). Certainly the vote for anti-immigrant parties like the FN in France involved an element of protest voting as well. While 15 per cent of the French electorate planned to vote for the FN and one-third of all French voters agreed with FN positions on immigration (Weil, 1991b: 82), it also was clear that the FN was picking up part of the protest vote traditionally received by the French Communist Party. FN opposition to the Single European Market was also a major point of attraction to some of its electorate.

The conclusion was inescapable, nonetheless, that anti-immigrant political movements had developed virtually across Western Europe by the 1990s. Many of these movements had historical precedents. Part of the hardcore support for the French National Front, for example, came from quarters traditionally identified with the anti-republican right. These political forces had been discredited by the

Second World War and their programs and policies were generally viewed as illegitimate until the anti-immigrant reaction of the 1980s. Immigration issues have served as an entrée for extreme right-wing parties into mainstream politics across Western Europe.

It would be mistaken to dismiss the upsurge in voting for anti-immigrant parties as simply an expression of racism and intolerance. As pointed out in Chapter 2, support for extreme-right groups is often the result of bewilderment in the face of rapid economic and social change. The erosion in organisational and ideological strength of labour organisations due to changes in occupational structures is important as well. Extreme-right parties also attract support as a result of public dissatisfaction with certain policies, such as those concerning asylum-seekers and illegal immigration. Other extremist parties have fared less well. The National Front in the United Kingdom, for example, appeared to be gaining strength in the mid-1970s before the Conservative Party under Margaret Thatcher preempted it by adopting key parts of its programme (Layton-Henry and Rich, 1986: 74–5).

Some scholars have suggested that the emergence of right-wing parties has had anti-immigrant effects across the political spectrum (Messina, 1989). It has been argued, for example, that French socialist stands on immigration shifted to the right as support for the FN increased. However it is difficult to reconcile the Socialist Party's celebration of its anti-racism with such a thesis. As Patrick Weil observed, '...immigration can appear as the ideal arena for differentiating politics of the Left from the Right. The Socialist Party, first and foremost François Mitterrand, has found in immigration and antiracism a privileged domain for political intervention' (Weil, 1991b: 95).

The French Communist Party has been accused of exploiting anti-immigrant feelings for electoral ends. There were cases in the 1980s of communist mayors leading bulldozers in to demolish housing illegally constructed by immigrants. Much of the frustration that led to such widely-publicised incidents was rooted in efforts by communist municipal governments to get housing for immigrants constructed elsewhere in addition to the communist suburbs. When confronted by often illegal housing, they sometimes took ill-considered steps to dramatise their opposition to the immigrant housing situation, which were roundly criticised by friend and foe alike. The French Communist Party was consistently critical of governmental laissez-faire immigration policies in the 1950s and 1960s, but it has staunchly supported equal rights for immigrants and militantly opposed racism. The electoral collapse of the French Communist Party in the 1980s, from 20 per cent of the electorate to less than 10 per cent, created a void which the FN deftly filled.

In addition to immigrants becoming the object of political party programmes, they have also become the object of violence in Western Europe, some of which is politically inspired. Anti-immigrant violence in the Eastern part of reunited Germany since 1990 has already been discussed. This usually involved attacks by skinheads and extreme rightists against immigrant housing. Guestworkers from Vietnam and Mozambique were victimised, as were more recently arrived aliens, including asylum-seekers from the Middle East and Eastern Europe. But far deadlier violence against immigrants has long been the pattern on the other side of the Rhine. The roots of anti-immigrant violence in France can be traced back to the nineteenth century (Lequin,1988: 389–410). During the latter stages of the Algerian war there was horrific violence against Algerian Muslims residing on the mainland (Belloula, 1965: 84–102). In 1973, there was a new explosion of anti-North African violence following the killing of a Marseilles bus driver by a mentally deranged Algerian. The toll in lives and injuries to immigrants as a result of racial attacks has been high and steady since the early 1970s (Bernard and Chemin, 1991).

In 1970, few political parties in Western Europe gave any thought to immigration issues. By 1990, many parties had hired immigration specialists for advice and had detailed immigration programmes. The FN in France issued a 50-point immigration programme which it pledged to implement if it came into power (Sole, 1991). That programme was largely seen as confirming the worst fears about the National Front. Critics denounced it as racist and as seeking to establish apartheid *à la française*. The essence of the FN programme was to turn back the clock on immigrant rights, much as the French extreme right in the 1930s wanted to turn the clock back on the rights acquired by Jews since 1789. Indeed there is much that is anachronistic in the new politics of immigration in Western Europe in the 1980s and 1990s. Although FN spokesmen attempted to play down the radicalness of the 50 propositions and to emphasise their similarity to the position of the traditional conservative parties in France, it was no exaggeration to regard them as incompatible with the founding principles of the French Republic. Clearly further growth in support for the FN would endanger French political stability.

Immigrants and ethnic voting blocs: a factor of growing importance in electoral outcomes?

The most extreme example of international migration transforming politics undoubtedly is to be found in the case of Palestine/Israel. Immigration significantly increased the Jewish presence in the British mandate of Palestine. The goal of the mainstream Zionists was the creation of a Jewish homeland, which did not necessarily connote the creation of a Jewish state in Palestine. A minority Zionist current – the so-called Revisionists, led by Vladimir Jabotinsky – proclaimed the creation of a Jewish state on all the territory of what they saw as the Palestine Mandate, which included the East Bank of the Jordan, as the goal of Zionism (Laqueur, 1972). During the Holocaust and the Second World War, the Zionist movement was radicalised and the creation of a Jewish state in Palestine became the immediate and paramount goal of the movement. Palestinians and other Arabs had long opposed the Zionist project because they feared it would displace the Palestinian Arabs or reduce them from majority to minority status. Fighting broke out in 1947 and the worst fears of the Arabs were realised.

The politics of the Jewish state of Israel, created in 1948, remain heavily influenced by immigration. As a result of the inflow of so-called Oriental or Sephardic Jews primarily from largely Muslim societies during the 1950s and 1960s, the Sephardic-origin Jewish population of Israel surpassed that of European-origin Ashkenazi Jews in the mid-1970s. This demographic shift benefited the modern-day followers of Jabotinsky and the Revisionists – the Likud bloc led by Menachem Begin, who was elected prime minister of Israel in 1977 with the support of Sephardic-origin Jews. In 1990, a new wave of Soviet Jewish immigration began. Some 400 000 Soviet Jews arrived in Israel in the space of two years. As Jewish immigrants quickly became Israeli citizens according to the Law of Return, one of the key questions during the Israeli general election of 1992 concerned the voting patterns of recent Soviet immigrants who comprised about one tenth of the electorate. The Israeli case illustrated in the extreme the potential impact of an immigrant voting bloc upon electoral outcomes. Given the rough parity between the two principal Israeli political parties – Labour and the Likud – Russian immigrant votes were vied for by all Israeli parties and a strong showing by one of the principal parties among Russian immigrants could conceivably enable that party to win.

Immigrants generally are not such an important factor as they are in Israeli elections and immigrants do not necessarily vote in ethnic blocs. It was not at all clear that Soviet Jews would give a large majority of their vote to a single party. Yet immigration clearly is affecting electoral politics across Western democracies as growing numbers of aliens naturalise and as immigrant-origin populations are mobilised to vote.

The growing mass of immigrant voters has made many political parties and their leaders more sensitive to multicultural concerns and issues. In some instances, immigration policy debates have been influenced by electoral calculations. In general, political parties on the left side of the political spectrum appear to take the lead in appealing to immigrant voters and are rewarded for their efforts. Conservative parties often benefit electorally from anti-immigrant backlash. And a number of conservative parties have begun to compete in earnest for the immigrant-origin electorate, particularly in Great Britain and the United States. The endorsement of multiculturalism by the conservative coalition which was in power in Australia from 1975–82 also seemed to be connected with concern about the 'ethnic vote' (Castles *et al.*, 1990). In several countries, new ethnic voting blocs have come into existence. This is seen as normal in some democracies, but as a problem in others.

The history of American parties vying for immigrant votes is well known. While anti-immigrant sentiment was a boon to the Know-Nothing party in the 1840s and 1850s, the Democratic Party benefited from the support of immigrant groups like the Irish whose overwhelming identification with the Democratic Party remains one of the fixtures of American politics. In the 1920s, anti-immigrant sentiment was a factor in fairly widespread support for the Ku Klux Klan which was a significant political force in many states. Indeed, at the apogee of the Ku Klux Klan's influence, it controlled state governments even in quite populous non-Southern states like Indiana. It was during the 1920s and 1930s that the enduring identification of recent immigrant groups such as the Italians and

Poles with the Democratic Party was forged (Archdeacon, 1983). Voting blocs based on ethnicity became part of the fabric of American politics, especially in major urban areas, where party tickets were often tailored to maximise appeal to ethnic voters.

Immigrant ethnicity largely concerned European-origin ethnic voters until the 1965 amendments to the Immigration and Natur-alisation Act. These amendments had the unintended effect of opening the door to immigration from around the world, a trend that was reinforced by subsequent reforms of immigration law until the Immigration Act of 1990 which, in part, sought to redress the ethnic balance by admitting more European-origin groups.

The seemingly inevitable outcome of the changed composition of legal immigration to the USA has been the emergence of new constituencies appealed to, in part, on an ethnic basis. Much attention has focused on the Hispanic and Asian voters, whose numbers increased sharply in the 1980s. Indeed European-origin Americans already have been or shortly will be outnumbered by so-called minorities in a number of key states, including California, and in several major cities, including New York City. Obviously not all persons enumerated as minorities are of recent immigrant origin. The ancestors of most Afro-Americans and many Hispanics were established on the territory of the present-day United States long before the ancestors of many European-origin Americans migrated to the New World. Nonetheless the largely immigration-driven evolu-tion of the American population may profoundly affect the future of American politics. The question is: will the current wave of immigrants, the Mexicans and the Filipinos, be like the waves that preceded them? For áll the alarm raised by the mass arrival of Irish Catholics in the nineteenth century, they ended up becoming Americans. The tendency is to believe that the outcome will be the same for immigrants of Latin American and Asian origin, but such results are not foreordained and the emerging debate over multi-culturalism may affect the ultimate outcome.

Immigrants from various countries and regions evidence quite variable rates of naturalisation, with key Hispanic nationalities like the Mexicans lagging far behind the average rate for all foreign born. Harry Pachon has pointed out that the issue of Hispanic naturalisa-tion dates from the cession of nearly a third of Mexico to the United States after the US victory in the war of 1848, a war precipitated by a revolt by white settlers in Texas. The treaty ending the war gave US citizenship to Mexicans in the territory lost by Mexico, but access to US citizenship by post-1848 immigrants was unclear. Federal law restricted naturalisation to 'free white aliens' before extending it to 'aliens of African nativity or descent' in 1870. An 1897 court case concluded that Mexican immigrants were eligible to naturalise on the basis of the 1848 treaty. But it was not until 1940 that Congress formally extended naturalisation rights to aliens indigenous to the western hemisphere (Pachon, 1987: 299–310).

This historical background may help account for the lagging Hispanic naturalisation rate in the USA, but other factors have also been cited – proximity of such countries as Mexico and various provisions of immigration law with regard to family entry. Immigrants in other Western democracies also have variable rates of naturalisation (see Chapter 8). Nationality groups comprising large numbers of refugees, however, almost always evidence the highest rates of naturalisation, presumably because of the circumstances leading to their dislocation. Vietnamese and Cubans in the USA, for example, have high rates of naturalisation, as do Vietnamese and Eastern European-origin nationality groups in Western Europe and Australia.

Many immigrants who become naturalised do not exercise their voting rights. Abstention rates among Asian–American and Hispanic American voters are very high despite voter registration and participation drives specifically at them. Only 350 000 of the estimated 2.9 million Asian–Americans living in California, for instance, were registered to vote (Choo, 1992). Abstention rates are also high for French citizens of North African origin. In Sweden, participation by non-citizens in local and regional elections has declined since it was first introduced in 1975.

Still the immigration trends of the last several decades have significantly affected electoral politics in many Western democracies. In the United States, Hispanics and Asian–Americans have emerged as significant ethnic voting blocs since the 1970s. Hispanic voters, in particular, have become a focus of inter-party competition as Democrats and Republicans attempt to woo them. The inroads made by the conservative Republic Party into an ethnic clientele traditionally viewed as predisposed towards the Democrats have affected electoral outcomes in several areas with large concentrations of Hispanic voters. A large segment of the Hispanic community of Florida, for instance, is comprised of Cubans to whom the

Republicans appeal through a stridently anti-communist, anti-Castro rhetoric. Homeland politics are of concern for virtually all immigrant voters, a factor that interjects political issues pertaining to US foreign policy towards their homelands into campaigns. While the foreign policy concerns of immigrant voters generally are not enough to alter the traditional focus of US electoral campaigns on domestic issues, candidates often adopt foreign policy positions favoured by immigrant groups in the quest for campaign donations and the electoral support of the group.

Immigrant groups can also have some influence on domestic issues. Perhaps the best illustration of the growing significance of Hispanic voters in the USA came during the 1984 campaign for the Democratic nomination for the presidency. All three of the major Democratic candidates voiced their opposition to pending legislation that would enact sanctions against illegal employment of aliens. Their stated reason for opposing employer sanctions was the fear that such sanctions would cause additional employment discrimination against minorities. However such principled positions were probably influenced by a perception that Hispanics were strongly opposed to enactment of employer sanctions. The most strident opposition to employer sanctions came from Hispanic groups like the Mexican–American Legal Defense Fund. Nationally, however, Hispanics were about evenly split on the wisdom of employer sanctions, whereas the general US population was strongly supportive of the concept.

The size of the Asian–American community in the United States roughly doubled over the 1980s to number over seven million by 1990. Asian–Americans have been less successful than the far more numerous Hispanic–Americans in winning public office. But their growing propensity to donate money to candidates has become a factor of some influence (Choo, 1992). A 1992 report by the Federal Civil Rights Commission found that Asian–Americans faced extensive discrimination and that 'there has been a widespread failure of government at all levels and of the nation's public schools to provide for the needs of immigrant Asian–Americans' (Dagger, 1992). The extent to which issues of concern to Asian–American and Hispanic voters influenced the agendas and platforms of the two major political parties was unclear. The 1992 presidential primary, for instance, was marked by 'Japan bashing' that perhaps contributed to an upsurge in attacks on Asians. Such campaign rhetoric did not endear several candidates to Asian–Americans.

The ability of legal immigrants to naturalise, and eventually to vote, constitutes a major concern for any democracy. That immigrant political participation is viewed as legitimate and as an anticipated outcome demarcates the USA, Australian and Canadian experiences from those of many Western European nations. Political exclusion is inherent in the concept of temporary worker policy. That is one reason why it is commonplace in authoritarian and undemocratic settings, such as in the Arab monarchies of the Gulf. Post-Second World War Western European guestworker policies created a conundrum when unplanned, unforeseen mass settlement occurred. The guestworkers and their families could not be excluded from Western European democracies without grievous damage to the fabric of democracy.

The United Kingdom constitutes an exception to the Western European pattern in that most post-1945 immigrants – those from the Commonwealth up to 1971, and the Irish – entered with citizenship and voting rights. However, as previously suggested, this seemed to have little effect upon the socioeconomic role of post-war immigration which was quite similar to that of guestworkers on the continent. Immigration became an object of political debate in the United Kingdom as early as 1958 when there were race riots in Notting Hill in London and other areas. In 1962, British immigration law was tightened up, setting a precedent for even more restrictive measures in the future. In the late 1960s, right-wing politicians such as Enoch Powell warned of looming racial conflict, of 'rivers of blood' on the horizon. Immigration became increasingly politicised in the mid-1970s. The National Front, a descendant of Sir Oswald Mosley's British Union of Fascists of the 1930s, played a key role in provoking immigration-related violence (Reed, 1977). British neo-fascists and leftists battled over immigration in much the same way that French neo-fascists and left-wing, pro-immigrant groups had confronted one another several years earlier (Reed, 1977).

The much-publicised and frequently quite violent clashes, which then were regarded as so uncharacteristic of normally civil British politics, combined with the mounting numbers of immigrants to make immigration a key issue in the 1979 general election. Margaret Thatcher, the Conservative leader, adroitly capitalised on the backlash over the immigration issue to deflate growing support for the National Front and to score a victory over the Labour Party, which was supported by most immigrant voters. A 1975 pamphlet published by the Community Relations Commission underscored the growing electoral significance of immigrant ethnic minorities, and even the Conservative Party began efforts to recruit ethnic minority members as a result (Layton-Henry, 1981).

In the 1983 and 1987 general elections and in local elections, black and Asian Briton participation in electoral politics became more conspicuous. In 1987, four black Britons were elected to parliament and three of them joined a black member of the House of Lords to form a black parliamentary caucus styled upon the 24 member strong US Congressional black caucus. Hundreds of black and Asian Britons were elected to positions in local government. In the industrial city of Birmingham, for example, the first Muslim municipal councillor, like most immigrant-origin elected officials a Labourite, was elected in 1982. In 1983, two more Muslim Labourites were elected. By January 1987, there were 14 municipal councillors of immigrant origin, including six Muslims. Within the Birmingham Labour Party, in the Sparkbrook area, 600 of the 800 local party members were Muslims (Joly, 1988: 177–8).

Britons of immigrant origin, therefore, fairly erupted into British electoral and extra-parliamentary politics in the 1980s, but, Studlar and Layton-Henry argue, this growing participation and representation in British politics generally has not resulted in greater attention being paid to immigrant issues, problems and grievances:

> Aside from a small number of race-conscious liberal politicians and activists, the discovery of non-white problems has never really generated optimism about the capacity of the British polity to cope with them. Both political decision makers and the public have more commonly simply wanted the problems to go away without government or public commitment to alter them. Serious and active consideration of race-related problems is rare and is even harder to maintain. (Studlar and Layton-Henry, 1990: 288)

Part of the difficulty faced by immigrants in getting their concerns on the Labour Party agenda stems from the necessity of defining group issues in terms of class. However formation of an alternative immigrants' party is not a viable option. Hence, even in a Western European country where most immigrants are enfranchised, their participation and representation remains problematic. Immigrant-origin voters can significantly affect electoral outcomes in 30–60 of

Great Britain's 650 parliamentary constituencies. These are located in cities.

The weight of immigrant voters is generally far less on the continent. Sweden, France and Austria have significant foreign-born or immigrant-origin citizen populations, but an immigrant vote appears to be openly counted only in France, where the Socialist Party has appealed with mixed results to the growing electorate of North and Sub-Saharan African background. US-style ethnic voter campaigning, however, would violate the Jacobin rules of the game that govern French politics and tend to exacerbate a political backlash against immigrants manifest in the growing electoral appeal of the FN headed by Jean-Marie Le Pen.

Even in the United States, politicians and parties had to weigh the expected benefits of appealing to immigrant voters, say Hispanics or Asian–Americans, against possible backlash. The right-wing Republican presidential hopeful Patrick Buchanan, as well as the Louisiana gubernatorial and later US presidential candidate David Duke (who was a Ku Klux Klan leader) both made anti-immigrant themes key elements of their electoral campaigns in 1991 and 1992.

In Australia, there has been considerable debate on the impact of postwar migration on politics. Most observers argue that postwar immigration has had little effect. For instance Jupp *et al.* write that, 'Australians of non-English-speaking background are marginal to the exercise of political power and influence in Australia' (1989: 51). McAllister states that post-war immigration 'has not resulted in any discernible change in the overall pattern of voting behaviour. Despite large-scale immigration, social class, not birthplace, has remained the basis for divisions between political parties' (1988: 919). A recent study of the role of Italo-Australians in political life found that they did not have a high profile, and argued that this was typical for immigrants in Australia (Castles *et al.*, 1992). Italians have not established their own political parties or trade unions, nor have they gained significant representation in parliaments. On the other hand, there are a large number of local councillors and some mayors of Italian origin. Yet even at this level of government Italo-Australians are underrepresented in comparison to their share in the population. Despite this, the 'ethnic vote' appears to be an issue which influences the behaviour of Australian political leaders. Not only do they make efforts to approach Italian (and other ethnic) associations to mobilise electoral support, they also make concessions to ethnic needs and interests in their policies.

The explanation for this combination of a low political profile with fairly successful interest articulation seems to lie in the relative openness of the Australian political system for immigrant groups, at least at a superficial level. As a reaction to mass immigration since 1947, governments and trade unions have combined to guarantee orderly industrial relations, which would not threaten the conditions of local workers. The policy of assimilation from the 1940s to the early 1970s was discriminatory in its rejection of cultural maintenance for migrants, but, by providing civil rights and citizenship, it did lay the groundwork for political integration. Recent multicultural policies have accepted the legitimacy of representation of special interests through migrant or ethnic community associations. Their leaderships have been granted a recognised, if limited, political role in government consultative bodies.

Thus Italo-Australians and other immigrant groups have obtained some political influence in ethnic affairs and welfare policies, and have been able to develop their own leaderships within the context of the Australian political system, but they are still far from having any measure of control in central political and economic areas. The question is whether this situation will change as the mainly poorly educated migrant generation leaves the centre stage and is replaced by a new self-confident second generation, which has passed through the Australian educational system (Castles *et al.*, 1992: 125–39).

An example of a multicultural issue: the politics of naturalisation

Immigration can affect politics by transforming electorates, creating new issues and affecting the ways that issues, candidates, parties – practically the entire warp and woof of politics in a country – are perceived. Or it may scarcely affect politics at all.

It was noted above that Hispanic, and particularly Mexican-origin, immigrants to the USA had much lower rates of naturalisation than did other immigrants to the USA. This is not exceptional. As seen in Chapter 8, only a small percentage of resident alien populations in Western democracies naturalise each year. And most

Western democracies have large populations of resident aliens who are eligible for naturalisation but do not naturalise. In 1988, the Australian government proclaimed 'a year of citizenship' to encourage the estimated one million resident aliens who were eligible to naturalise to do so.

One result of recent immigration to Western democracies has been growing concern over naturalisation requirements and procedures. In many instances, they are seen as too strict and cumbersome. For instance, foreign residents in Germany have to wait ten years before becoming eligible for naturalisation and then their applications are subject to stringent criteria. The administrator reviewing the request can deny it on many grounds. The high cost of the application and the requirement that applicants show evidence of integration into German life are widely seen as discouraging many potential applicants. Germany is a signatory of the European convention suppressing dual nationality. Many Turks do not want to relinquish their original nationality, both for psychological reasons and because they would lose the right to own land in their area of origin. Other Turks formally seek to renounce their citizenship but are unable to do so. An estimated one-quarter of all successful Turkish applicants for German citizenship in the late 1980s actually remained Turkish citizens, becoming dual nationals. German authorities granted them citizenship despite their being unable to relinquish their citizenship.

Many Western democracies, including Germany and the United States in 1990, have revised their naturalisation laws and procedures in order to facilitate naturalisation. In 1986, the qualification period for naturalisation in Australia was reduced to two years of residence. The United States eligibility requirement – five years of continuous residence – is quite liberal but many of its administrative requirements were viewed as cumbersome. The US Immigration Act of 1990 was expected to streamline and expedite naturalisation. Most recent reforms of naturalisation have gone in this direction as democracies seek to reduce the anomaly of possessing large disenfranchised resident alien populations. Some specialists, like Tomas Hammar, have advocated dual nationality as a solution to this problem posed to contemporary democracies (Hammar, 1990).

In France, however, liberal naturalisation requirements have come under attack. By 1986, during the period of so-called cohabitation, the government of Jacques Chirac sought to discontinue automatic acquisition of French nationality by certain groups of aliens. The proposed reform of the nationality code, however, was dropped in the face of massive protests by French students. The protests centred upon proposed reforms of the French educational system. The government wanted to create a more American-style university system in which universities would have greater autonomy, including a greater capacity to select students. A growing part of the French student body is comprised of students of immigrant origin – both resident aliens and citizens. Students of immigrant background were very much involved in the protests against proposals that were seen as creating a less egalitarian university system. As students of immigrant origin already encountered manifold problems in the French educational system, it was likely that they would have been the most adversely affected by the proposed reforms.

The unexpectedly massive protests against the proposed educational reform, in classically French fashion, quickly created an atmosphere of crisis. The minister of education resigned and the reform proposal was dropped by the government. But another casualty was the Chirac government's proposed reform of the nationality code. While this was distinct from the educational issue, it was affected by the student demonstrations and prudently dropped. Nonetheless elements from the conservative side of the French political spectrum have continued to press for reform of French nationality and citizenship laws in a restrictive sense. The FN, in particular, wants to greatly restrict access to French citizenship.

The debate over access to French citizenship led to the creation of a governmental commission to study the issue and make recommendations. Its creation exemplified the politicisation of immigration-related issues in France and underscored the way immigration had spawned complex, new issues for political systems. The issues included dual nationality, military service requirements for citizens of immigrant background, and legal issues concerning such matters as divorce and the definition of the family. Much of the complexity and saliency of these issues derived from their transnational nature. For instance, the French government permitted Franco-Algerian dual nationals of military age to elect to accomplish their military service in Algeria despite the individual's residency in France. A 1992 recommendation by the French High Committee on Integration sought to discontinue this option.

Conclusion

International migration has played a major role in fostering multi-cultural politics. Migration can dramatically affect electorates, as witnessed in the Israeli case, and immigrants can influence politics through non-electoral means as well. Immigrants have fostered transnational politics linking homeland and host society political systems in fundamental ways. Migrants and minorities are both subjects and objects of politics. Anti-immigrant backlash has strengthened the appeal of right-wing parties in Western Europe. One way in which migration has fundamentally altered the Western European political landscape is through the constitution of increasingly vocal Islamic organisations, which present a dilemma for democratic political systems: refusal to accept their role would violate democratic principles, yet many people see their aims and methods as intrinsically anti-democratic. International migration has fostered new constituencies, new parties and new issues. Many of Western Europe's newly emerging political parties, such as the FN in France, feature anti-immigrant themes. Violence against immigrants has also grown everywhere, and is a factor in ethnic minority formation and political mobilisation.

In the USA, Canada and Australia immigrant political participation and representation is less of a problem, partly because of the preponderance of family-based legal immigration. However virtually everywhere international migration renders politics more complex. Ethnic mobilisation and the ethnic vote are becoming important issues in many countries. Another new issue may be seen in the politics of naturalisation. One or two decades ago, virtually no one knew naturalisation law or considered it important. The changing nature of international migration and its politicisation has changed that. Most democracies now face a long-term problem stemming from growing populations of resident aliens who do not choose to naturalise. Hence a heightened concern over dual nationality.

Immigrant politics are in a continual state of flux, because of the rapid changes in migratory flows as well as the broader transformations in political patterns which are taking place in many Western societies. As migratory movements mature – moving through the stages of immigration, settlement and minority formation – the character of political mobilisation and participation changes. There is a shift from concern with homeland politics to mobilisation around the interests of ethnic groups in the immigration country. If political participation is denied through refusal of citizenship and failure to provide channels of representation, immigrant politics is likely to take on militant forms. This applies particularly to the children of immigrants born in the countries of immigration. If they are excluded from political life through non-citizenship, social marginalisation or racism, they are likely to present a major challenge to existing political structures in the future.

10

Conclusion: Migration in the New World Disorder

This book has argued that international migration is a constant, not an aberration, in human history. Population movements have always accompanied demographic growth, technological change, political conflict and warfare. Over the last five centuries mass migrations have played a major role in colonialism, industrialisation, the emergence of nation-states and the development of the capitalist world market. However international migration has never been as pervasive, nor as socioeconomically and politically significant, as it is today. Never before have statesmen accorded such priority to migration concerns. Never before has international migration seemed so pertinent to national security and so connected to conflict and disorder on a global scale.

The hallmark of the age of migration is the global character of international migration: the way it affects more and more countries and regions, and its linkages with complex processes affecting the entire world. This book has endeavoured to elucidate the principal causes, processes and effects of international migration. Contemporary patterns, as discussed in Chapters 4 and 6, are rooted in historical relationships and shaped by a multitude of political, demographic, socioeconomic, geographical and cultural factors. These flows virtually everywhere result in greater ethnic diversity and deepening transnational linkages between sovereign states and societies. International migrations are greatly affected by governmental policies and may, in fact, be started by decisions to recruit foreign workers or to admit refugees.

Yet international migrations may also possess a relative autonomy and be more or less impervious to governmental policies. People as well as governments shape international migration. Despite the growth in migratory movements, and the strength of the factors which cause them, resistance to migration is also of growing importance. Large sections of the populations of receiving countries may oppose immigration. Governments sometimes react by adopting strategies of denial – hoping that the problems will go away if they are ignored.

In Chapter 2 we provided some theoretical perspectives on the reasons international migrations take place and discussed how they almost inevitably lead to permanent settlement and the formation of distinct ethnic groups in the receiving societies. We suggested that the migratory process needs to be understood in its totality as a complex system of social interactions with a wide range of institutional structures and informal networks in both sending and receiving countries, and at the international level. In subsequent chapters it was shown that the model of a four-stage migratory process, put forward in Chapter 2, fits better in some cases than others. In a democratic setting, however, legal admission of migrants almost always will result in some settlement, even when migrants are admitted temporarily.

The comparison of two very different immigration countries – Australia and Germany – in Chapter 5 showed how the migratory process takes on its own dynamics, sometimes leading to consequences unforeseen and unwanted by policy-makers. Acceptance of the seeming inevitability of permanent settlement and formation of ethnic groups is the necessary starting-point for any meaningful consideration of desirable public policies. Serious discussion requires an elementary measure of realism, something not found, for instance, in the time-worn slogan that 'Germany is not a country of immigration'. The key to adaptive policy making in this realm as in others is understanding of the causes and dynamics of international migration. Policies based on misunderstanding or mere wishful thinking are virtually condemned to fail. Hence, if governments decide to admit foreign workers, they should from the outset make provision for the legal settlement of that proportion of the entrants that is sure to remain permanently – a consideration that needs to be taken to heart by the governments of countries as diverse as Japan, Malaysia, Italy and Greece at present.

Today the governments and peoples of immigration countries have to face up to some very serious dilemmas. The answers they choose will help shape the future of their societies, as well as their relations with the poorer countries of the South. Central issues include:

- regulating legal immigration and integrating settlers;
- policies to cope with illegal migration;
- finding 'durable solutions' to emigration pressure through improved international relations; and
- the role of ethnic diversity in social and cultural change, and the consequences for the nation-state.

Legal migration and integration

Virtually all democratic states, and many not so democratic states as well, have growing foreign populations. As shown in Chapters 4, 5 and 6, the presence of these immigrants is generally due to conscious labour recruitment or immigration policies, or to the existence of various linkages between sending and receiving countries. In some cases (notably the USA, Canada and Australia) policies of large-scale immigration still exist. Invariably they are selective: economic migrants, family members and refugees are admitted according to certain quotas which are politically determined. In other countries (particularly in Western Europe), past labour recruitment policies have been suspended, and governments try to limit entries of workers, family members or refugees. Nonetheless most countries welcome one group of migrants – highly-skilled temporary workers – and have policies which allow at least some entries on humanitarian grounds. Finally countries with labour shortages admit workers, either in an overt and controlled way (as in the Arab oil countries or Singapore) or by tacitly permitting illegal entries (as in Italy and Japan).

There is considerable evidence that planned and controlled entries are conducive to acceptable social conditions for migrants as well as to relative social peace between migrants and local people. Countries with immigration quota systems generally decide on them through political processes which permit public discussion and the balancing of the interests of different social groups. Participation in decision making increases the acceptability of immigration programmes. At the same time this approach facilitates the introduction of measures to prevent discrimination and exploitation of immigrants, and to provide social services to support successful settlement. There is therefore a strong case for advocating that all countries which actually continue to have immigration should move towards planned immigration policies. This would apply to most of Western Europe.

As Chapter 8 showed, governmental obligations towards immigrant populations are shaped by the nature of the political system in the host society, as well as the mode of entry of the newcomers. Governments possess an internationally recognised right to regulate entry of aliens, a right that may be voluntarily limited through governmental signature of bilateral or multilateral agreements, for example in the case of refugees. Clearly it makes a difference whether an alien has arrived on a territory through legal means of entry or not. In principle, the proper course for action with regard to legally admitted foreign residents in a democracy is straightforward. They should be rapidly afforded equality of socioeconomic rights and a large measure of political freedom, for their status would otherwise diminish the quality of democratic life in the society. However this principle is frequently ignored in practice.

Guestworker policy-style restrictions on the employment and residential mobility of legally admitted aliens appear anachronistic and, in the long run, administratively unfeasible. They are difficult to reconcile with prevailing market principles, to say nothing of democratic norms. The same goes for restrictions on political rights. Freedom of speech, association and assembly should be unquestionable. Under normal circumstances of international co-operation, there is no reason to restrict recent immigrants' ability to participate in their homeland's political system. The only restriction on the rights of legally admitted aliens which seems compatible with democratic principles is the reservation of the right to vote and to stand for public office to citizens. This is only justifiable if resident aliens are given the real opportunity of naturalisation, without daunting procedures or high fees. But, even then, some foreign residents are likely to decide not to become citizens, for various reasons. A democratic system needs to secure their political participation too. This can mean setting up special representative bodies for resident non-citizens, or extending voting rights to non-citizens who fulfil certain criteria of length of stay (as in Sweden and the Netherlands).

The global character of international migration results in the intermingling and cohabitation of people from increasingly different physical and cultural settings. The severity of immigration-related integration problems is highly variable. In some instances, public authorities may regard it as unnecessary to devise specific policies to facilitate integration. In most cases, however, specific, selective measures are necessary in order to forestall the development of socioeconomic, cultural or political cleavages which can be conflictual. Here the multicultural models developed in Australia, Sweden and Canada deserve careful scrutiny. Their common thread is an acceptance of the cultural diversity and social changes wrought by immigration. Immigrants are not forced to conform to a dominant cultural or linguistic model but rather can maintain their native languages and cultural life if they choose to do so. The diversity produced by immigration is seen as an enrichment rather than as a threat to the predominant culture.

A multicultural approach enhances democratic life in that it allows for choice. It can mean a redefinition of citizenship to include cultural rights, along with the widely accepted civil, political and social rights. With the passage of time, it is expected that most immigrants and their offspring will reconcile their cultural heritage with the prevailing culture, and the latter will be somewhat altered, and most likely richer, for that. Conflict will have been minimised. Nonetheless multicultural models have their contradictions and are often the subject of heated debate and renegotiation. For instance, multiculturalism may proclaim the right to use of an immigrant's mother tongue, but those who do not learn the dominant language can find themselves disadvantaged in the labour market. Maintenance of some cultural norms may be a form of discriminatory social control, particularly for women and youth. The dividing line between real participation of ethnic leaderships in decision making and their co-option through the patronage of government agencies can be very thin.

Many people argue that an explicitly multicultural approach to immigrant integration may not be appropriate for all societies. This applies particularly in states like the USA and France, with established traditions of immigrant incorporation and assimilation. In these countries it is believed that political integration through citizenship provides the essential precondition for social and cultural integration. Special cultural or social policies for immigrants are thought to perpetuate distinctions and lead to formation of ghettoes and separatist groups. Thus the basic principle of the US model is a policy of benign (but not unthinking) neglect in the public sphere and a reliance on the integrative potential of the private sphere: families, neighbourhoods, ethnic solidarity organisations and the like. Yet the formation of racial or ethnic ghettoes in the USA and the growth of ethnic conflict in France present a challenge to such approaches at the present time.

However, whether the choice is made for benign neglect or for more explicitly multicultural policies, certain preconditions must be met if marginalisation and isolation of minorities are to be avoided. The state needs to take measures to ensure that there is no long-term link between ethnic origin and socioeconomic disadvantage. This requires legal measures to combat discrimination, social policies to alleviate existing disadvantage and educational measures to ensure equal opportunities and to provide the chance of upward mobility. The state also has the task of eliminating racism, combating racial violence and above all of dealing with organised racist groups. As pointed out in Chapter 8, racist discrimination and violence are major factors leading to formation of ethnic minorities in all the countries of immigration examined. There is clearly a great need for action in this area.

What seem counterproductive to the long-range goal of integration are policies that assume cultural conformity or that seek to impose it. Former 'guestworker' countries like Germany or Switzerland are beginning to move away from their previous exclusionary policies, which were based on the illusion that immigrants were just temporary foreign workers. But often the price they demand of immigrants in return for the right to settle is complete assimilation. As other countries of immigration have learnt, processes of adaptation and integration take time, and complete assimilation requires many generations. Policies requiring conformity of immigrants do not take this into account and thereby can increase the risk of conflict latent in immigration.

Regulating 'unwanted' immigration

Prospects are slim for significantly increased legal immigration flows to Western democracies over the short to medium term. Some increases might be warranted on demographic grounds or because of persistent labour shortages, but immigration cannot appreciably alter the demographic ageing of most Western societies unless it is substantially increased. Political constraints will not permit this. There will be some room for highly skilled labour, family reunification and refugees, but not for a resumption of massive recruitment of foreign labour for low-level jobs. Most industrial democracies will have to struggle to provide adequate employment for existing populations of low-skilled citizen and resident alien workers. The generally adverse labour market situation will make any recruitment of foreign labour politically controversial.

One of the most pressing challenges for highly-developed countries today is therefore to find ways of coping with 'unwanted' migratory flows. 'Unwanted immigration' is a somewhat vague blanket term, which embraces:

- illegal border-crossers,
- legal entrants who overstay their entry visas or who work without permission,
- family members of migrant workers, prevented from entering legally by restrictions on family reunion,
- asylum-seekers not regarded as genuine refugees.

Most such migrants come from poor countries and seek employment, but generally lack work qualifications. They compete with disadvantaged local people for unskilled jobs, and for housing and social amenities. Western European countries have had an enormous increase in such 'unwanted immigration' in the last ten years or so, but North America, Australia and other regions are also affected. Of course, the migration is not always as 'unwanted' as is made out – employers often benefit from cheap workers who lack rights, and some governments tacitly permit such movements. 'Unwanted immigration' is often seen as being at the bottom of public fears of mass influxes. It is therefore a catalyst for racism and is at the centre of extreme-right agitation.

Stopping 'unwanted immigration' is increasingly regarded by governments as essential for safeguarding social peace. In Western Europe, the result has been a series of agreements designed to secure international co-operation in stopping illegal entries, and to speed up the processing of applications for asylum (see Chapter 4). But the European experience is that such agreements are hard to introduce –

some of the agreements have still not been ratified by member governments years after the initial signing – and even harder to implement. There is no real indication that governmental and intergovernmental control measures are effective. In the USA, Canada and Australia, measures have also been taken to improve border control and to speed up refugee determination. This has not prevented a steady increase in the number of entrants who do not fit into official quotas. The USA, in particular, has moved towards sanctions against employers who employ undocumented workers. Again the success of the policy appears to be very limited.

The reasons for the present insufficiency of control measures are not difficult to understand. They contradict the powerful forces which are leading towards greater economic and cultural interchange. In an increasingly international economy, it is difficult to open borders for movements of information, commodities and capital and yet close them to people. Global circulation of investment and knowhow always means movements of people too. Moreover, as shown in Chapter 6, flows of highly-skilled personnel tend to encourage flows of less-skilled workers too. The instruments of border surveillance cannot be sufficiently fine-tuned to let through all those whose presence is wanted, but to stop all those who are not.

The matter is further complicated by a number of factors: the eagerness of employers to hire foreign workers (whether documented or not) for menial jobs, when nationals are unwilling to take such positions; the difficulty of adjudicating asylum claims and of distinguishing economically motivated migrants from those deserving of refugee status; and the inadequacies or insufficiencies of immigration law. The weakening of organised labour and declining trade union membership in many Western democracies has also tended to increase unauthorised foreign employment. Similarly policies aimed at reducing labour market rigidities and enhancing competitiveness may result in expanded employer hiring of unauthorised foreign workers. Social welfare policies also have unintended consequences, making employment of unauthorised alien workers more propitious.

Thus, despite the claimed desire of Western governments to stop illegal migration, many of the causes are to be found in the political and social structures of the immigration countries, and their relations with the less-developed world. This has led to the call for 'durable solutions' to address the root causes of mass migration (see below).

But such measures are not likely to bring a quick reduction in 'unwanted immigration'. There is every reason to expect the number of individuals worldwide desiring to emigrate to Western democracies to continue to expand in coming decades, perhaps exponentially. In the current political climate there is no doubt that the highly-developed states will continue to regulate migration and attempt to curb and deter illegal immigration. This will require investing more manpower and budgetary resources into enforcement of employer sanctions and adjudication of asylum claims than in the past. Enforcement of immigration laws will probably be accorded higher priority in the future, if only because of growing apprehension over the possible political consequences of continuing illegal migration. How successful such measures can be remains to be seen.

Durable solutions and international relations

Clearly international migration is not the solution to the North–South gap. Migration will not resolve North Africa's unemployment problem, nor appreciably reduce the income and wage gap between the USA and Mexico, nor make a significant impact on rural poverty in India. The only realistic long-term hope for reduction of international migration is broad-based, sustainable development in the less-developed countries, enabling economic growth to keep pace with growth in the population and labour force. Growing realisation in the highly-developed countries that border control alone cannot stop 'unwanted immigration' has led to a discussion on 'durable solutions', to achieve a long-term reduction of migration pressures. Such measures are wide-ranging and closely linked to the debate on development strategies for the countries of the South. They include trade policy, development assistance, regional integration and international relations.

Reform of trade policies could help encourage economic growth in the less-developed countries. The most important issue is the level of prices for primary commodities as compared with industrial products. This is linked to constraints on world trade through tariffs and subsidies. If successful, the GATT round could make a major contribution to improving the perspectives of many less-developed countries, as could a reform in the European Common Agricultural Policy. But trade policies generally operate within tight political constraints: few politicians are willing to confront their own farmers, workers or industrialists, particularly in times of economic recession. Reforms favourable to the economies of the less-developed countries will only come gradually, if at all.

Development assistance is a second strategy which might help to reduce 'unwanted' international migration over the long term. Some states have good records in this respect, but international assistance generally has not been at a level sufficient to make a real impression on problems of underdevelopment. Indeed the balance of nearly four decades of development policies is not a positive one. Although some countries (the oil countries and the NICs) have managed to achieve substantial growth, in general the gap between the poor and rich countries has grown. Income distribution within the countries of the South has also become more inequitable, increasing the gulf between the wealthy elites and the impoverished masses. The problems of rapid demographic growth, economic stagnation, ecological degradation, weak states and abuse of human rights still affect most countries of Africa, Asia and Latin America. In many cases, development assistance became a political instrument in the Cold War, leading to 'aid' in the form of weapons, and the fighting of surrogate wars on behalf of the great powers. The result was political instability, increased poverty and outflows of refugees. Moreover control of world finance by bodies such as the International Monetary Fund and the World Bank led to credit policies which made many countries of the South even more dependent and unstable than before.

Regional integration – the creation of free-trade areas and regional political communities – is sometimes seen as a way of diminishing 'unwanted' international migration by reducing trade barriers and spurring economic growth, as well as by legalising international movement of labour. But regional integration usually takes place between states which share political and cultural values and which resemble one another economically. Italy's membership in the EC has contributed to the dramatic lessening of Italian emigration and it is becoming a significant country of immigration. However a more pertinent reference is to Turkey's application to join the EC. In this case, EC apprehension over increased Turkish immigration if Turkey were to be accorded full membership played a decisive role in the decision to deny that country membership. Another example is North American Free Trade Agreement negotiations between Mexico and the USA. In the NAFTA negotiations, labour mobility has been specifically excluded from the free-trade agreement (although many people believe that NAFTA will lead to increased Mexican migration, at least in the short run). Generally the development gap is too profound to enable extension of freedom of labour mobility between developed and less-developed societies to be viewed as desirable.

Policies designed to limit immigration are likely to play a growing role in international relations. This has already been shown in the case of intra-European discussions on co-operation to control migration. Some of the first co-operative agreements between Western Europe and the new states of Eastern Europe have concerned arrangements for limiting migration. There are many conceivable situations in which bold and imaginative foreign policy holds out a genuine prospect for substantial reduction in refugee flows and economic migrant movement. In this respect, the United Nations decision to intervene in Iraq's Kurdish area in 1991, to prevent a further outflow of refugees to Turkey and to enable their repatriation, set a significant precedent.

Perhaps the end of the Cold War could provide the resources, and the current fear of migrant influxes could provide the motivation, to achieve real change through international co-operation. This would mean restricting the international weapons trade, altering the terms of trade between the North and the South, and changing world financial systems so that they encourage a real transfer of resources from the rich to the poor countries, rather than the other way round, as at present. It would also mean basing development assistance programmes on criteria of human rights, environmental protection, ecological sustainability and social equity. Worker migration could be linked to development policies through training and investment measures, designed to help returning migrants contribute to growth in their home countries.

Yet however successful such policies might be – and sadly they seem fairly utopian in the light of the current world disorder – they will not bring about substantial reductions of international migration in the short term. As shown in Chapters 2 and 6, the initial effect of development and integration into the world market is to increase migration from less-developed countries. This is because the early stages of development lead to rural–urban migration, and to acquisition by many people of the financial and cultural resources needed for international migration. Neither restrictive measures nor development strategies can totally curb international migration, at least in the short term, because there are such powerful forces stimulating population movement. These include the increasing pervasiveness of a global culture and the growth of cross-border movements of ideas, capital, commodities and people. The world community will have to learn to live with mass population movements for the foreseeable future.

Ethnic diversity, social change and the nation-state

The age of migration has already changed the world and many of its societies. Most highly-developed countries and many less-developed ones have become far more culturally diverse than they were even a generation ago. A large proportion, indeed the majority, of nation-states must face up to the reality of ethnic pluralism. In fact few modern nations have ever been ethnically homogeneous. However the nationalism of the last two centuries strove to create myths of homogeneity. In its extreme forms, it even tried to bring about such homogeneity through expulsion of minorities and genocide. The appalling spectacle of 'ethnic cleansing' in the ruins of former Yugoslavia shows that such tendencies still exist. But the reality for most countries today is that they have to contend with a new type of pluralism, and that – even if migration were to stop tomorrow – this will affect their societies for generations. Moreover, as this book has documented, migration shows no signs of ceasing and is indeed more likely to grow in volume as we move into the twenty-first century.

One reason why immigration and the emergence of new ethnic groups have had such an impact in most highly-developed countries is that they have coincided with the crisis of modernity and the transition to post-industrial societies. The labour migration of the pre-1973 period appeared at the time to be reinforcing the economic dominance of the old industrial nations. Today we can interpret it as part of a process of capital accumulation which preceded a seminal change in the world economy. Growing international mobility of capital, the electronic revolution, the decline of old industrial areas and the rise of new ones are all factors which have led to rapid economic change in Western Europe, North America and Australia. The erosion of the old blue-collar working class, and the increased polarisation of the labour force, have led to a social crisis, in which immigrants find themselves doubly at risk: many of them suffer unemployment and social marginalisation, yet at the same time they are often portrayed as the cause of the problems. That is why the emergence of the 'two-thirds society' is everywhere accompanied by ghettoisation of the disadvantaged and the rise of racism.

Nowhere is this more evident than in the global cities of the late twentieth century. Los Angeles, Toronto, Paris, London, Berlin and Sydney – to name just a few – are crucibles of social change, political conflict and cultural innovation. They are marked by enormous gulfs: between the corporate elite and the informal sector workers who service them, between rich, well-guarded suburbs and decaying and crime-ridden inner cities, between citizens of democratic states and illegal non-citizens, between dominant cultures and minority cultures. The gulf may be summed up in that between inclusion and exclusion. The included are those who fit into the self-image of a prosperous, technologically innovative and democratic society. The excluded are the shadow side: those who are necessary for the reproduction of society, but who do not fit into the ideology of the model.

Both groups include nationals and immigrants, though the immigrants are more likely to belong to the excluded. But the groups are more closely bound together than they might like to think: the corporate elite need the illegal immigrants, the prosperous suburbanites need the slum-dwellers they find so threatening. It is out of this contradictory and multi-layered character of the post-modern city that its enormous energy, its cultural dynamism and its innovative capability emerge. But these co-exist with potential for social breakdown, conflict, repression and violence. It is here that the complex social and cultural interaction between different ethnic groups may in future give birth to new peoples and provide the basis for new forms of society.

The new ethnic diversity affects societies in many ways. Amongst the most important are issues of political participation, cultural pluralism and national identity. As Chapter 9 showed, immigration and formation of ethnic groups have already had major effects on politics in most developed countries. These effects are potentially destabilising. The only resolution appears to lie in broadening political participation to embrace immigrant groups, which in turn may mean rethinking the form and content of citizenship, and decoupling it from ideas of ethnic homogeneity or cultural assimil-ation.

This leads on to the issue of cultural pluralism. Processes of marginalisation and isolation of ethnic groups have gone so far in many countries that culture has become a marker for exclusion on the part of some sections of the majority population, and a mechanism of resistance by the minorities. Even if serious attempts were made to end all forms of discrimination and racism, cultural and linguistic difference will persist for generations – especially if new immigration takes place. That means that majority populations will have to learn to live with cultural pluralism, even if it means modifying their own expectations of acceptable standards of behaviour and social conformity.

This move towards cultural pluralism corresponds with the emergence of a global culture, which is fed by travel, mass media and commodification of cultural symbols, as well as by migration. This global culture is anything but homogeneous, but the universe of variations which it permits have a new meaning compared with traditional ethnic cultures: difference need no longer be a marker for strangeness and separation, but rather an opportunity for informed choice among a myriad of possibilities. The new global culture is therefore passionately syncretistic, permitting endless combinations of elements with diverse origins and meanings. The major obstacle to the spread of the global culture is that it coincides with a political, economic and social crisis in many regions. Where change is fast and threatening, narrow traditional cultures seem to offer a measure of defence. Hence the resurgence of exclusionary nationalism in areas like the former Soviet Union and Yugoslavia which have been cut off so long from global influences that change, now that it has come, is experienced as a cataclysm. And hence the resurgence of racism in highly-developed societies amongst those groups who find themselves the main victims of economic and social restructuring.

Clearly trends towards political inclusion of minorities and cultural pluralism can threaten national identity, especially in countries in which it has been constructed in exclusionary forms. If ideas of belonging to a nation have been based on myths of ethnic purity or of cultural superiority, then they really are threatened by the growth of ethnic diversity. Whether the community of the nation has been based on belonging to a '*Volk*' (as in Germany) or on a unitary culture (as in France), ethnic diversity inevitably requires major political and psychological adjustments. The shift is far smaller for countries that have seen themselves as nations of immigrants, for their political structures and models of citizenship are geared to incorporating newcomers. However these countries too have historical traditions of racial exclusion and cultural homogenisation which still need to be worked through. Assimilation of immigrants, as epitomised in the American Dream, seems less viable in view of continuing population movements and strong trends towards cultural and linguistic maintenance by ethnic communities.

That means that all countries of immigration are going to have to re-examine their understanding of what it means to belong to their societies. Monocultural and assimilationist models of national identity may no longer be adequate for the new situation. Immigrants may be able to make a special contribution to the development of new forms of identity. It is part of the migrant condition to develop multiple identities, which are linked to the cultures both of the homeland and of the country of origin. Such personal identities possess complex new transcultural elements.

Immigrants are not unique in this – multiple identities are becoming an almost general characteristic of the people of post-modern societies. But it is above all migrants who are compelled by their situation to have multi-layered sociocultural identities, which are constantly in a state of transition and renegotiation. Moreover migrants frequently develop a consciousness of their transcultural position, which is reflected not only in their artistic and cultural work, but also in social and political action. Despite current conflicts about the effects of ethnic diversity on national cultures and identity, immigration does offer perspectives for change. The hope must be that new principles of identity can emerge, which will be neither exclusionary nor discriminatory, and which will provide the basis for better inter-group co-operation.

Inevitably this will affect our fundamental political structures. The nation-state is a fairly young political form, which came into being with the American and French revolutions and achieved global dominance in the nineteenth century. It is characterised by principles on the relationship between people and government which are mediated through the institution of citizenship. The nation-state was an innovative and progressive force at its birth, because it defined the citizens as free political subjects, linked together through democratic structures. But the nationalism of the nineteenth and twentieth centuries turned citizenship on its head by equating it with membership of a dominant ethnic group, defined on biological or cultural lines. In many cases the nation-state became an instrument of exclusion and repression.

National states, for better or worse, are likely to endure. But global economic and cultural integration and the establishment of regional agreements on economic and political co-operation are undermining the exclusiveness of national loyalties. The age of migration could be marked by the erosion of nationalism and the weakening of divisions between peoples. Admittedly there are countervailing tendencies, such as racism, the 'fortress Europe' mentality, or the resurgence of nationalism in certain areas. The decline of national divisions is likely to be uneven, and setbacks are possible, especially in the event of economic or political crises. But the inescapable central trends are the increasing ethnic and cultural diversity of most countries, the emergence of transnational networks which link the societies of emigration and immigration countries and the growth of cultural interchange. The globalisation of migration provides grounds for optimism, because it does give some hope of increased unity in dealing with the pressing problems which beset our small planet.

Notes

2 The Migratory Process and the Formation of Ethnic Minorities

1. Migration can even transcend death: members of some migrant groups have been known to pay money into burial societies, which, after death, transport their bodies back for burial in their native soil.
2. This definition is adapted from that quoted in Castles *et al.* (1984: 96–7). The original source was Taifel (1982: 217). See also Feagin (1989: 10).
3. The visible markers of a phenotype (skin colour, features, hair colour, and so on) correspond to what is popularly understood as 'race'. We avoid using the term 'race' as far as possible, since there is increasing agreement among biologists and social scientists that there are no measurable characteristics among human populations that allow classification into 'races'. Genetic variance within any one population is greater than alleged differences between different populations. 'Race' is thus a social construction produced by the process we refer to as racism.
4. We lay no claim to originality with regard to this definition and discussion of racism. It is oriented towards current sociological debates, which have generated a large body of literature. See, for example, CCCS, 1982; Miles, 1989; Rex and Mason, 1986; Cohen and Bains, 1988; Solomos, 1993; Wieviorka, 1991, 1992. There is no unanimity among social scientists about the correct definition and explanations of racism, but we have no space for a more detailed discussion of these matters here.

4 Migration to Highly-developed Countries since 1945

1. A detailed review of the literature is not possible here. For Europe the account is based mainly on our own works: Castles and Kosack, 1973; Castles *et al.*, 1984; Castles, 1986; Castles, 1989; Miller, 1981. For the USA, see Briggs, 1984; Portes and Rumbaut, 1990. For Australia, see Collins, 1990. For useful overviews, see *International Migration Review*, 1989; Kritz *et al.*, 1983; and Cohen, 1987. Precise references will only be given where absolutely necessary.

2. Post-1945 refugee movements were most significant in the case of Germany, as will be discussed in Chapter 5.
3. Another case worth mentioning is that of Italy, in which migration from the underdeveloped south was crucial to the economic take-off of the northern industrial triangle between Milan, Turin and Genoa in the 1960s: this was internal migration, but very similar in its economic and social character to foreign worker movements in other European countries.
4. Including Pakistan, which subsequently left the Commonwealth.
5. The exception is the roughly 32 000 Moluccans, who wanted to return to their homeland if it could achieve independence from Indonesia. They remained segregated in camps, and rejected integration into Dutch society. In the late 1970s, their disaffection led to several violent incidents.
6. For more detail and sources on Australia, see Castles *et al.*, 1990; Collins, 1991.
7. See Castles and Kosack (1973: Chapter 9) and Castles *et al.* (1984: Chapter 2) for more discussion of these issues.
8. The use of the terms South–North and East–West is Eurocentric, but will be retained here because it has become part of general usage. It is important to understand that these concepts refer not primarily to geographical locations but to economic, social and cultural divisions.
9. The total fertility rate is the average number of births per woman during her lifetime, assuming constant fertility. The rate needed to maintain a constant population is just over two children per woman.

5 The Migratory Process: A Comparison of Australia and Germany

1. For convenience we use the name 'Germany' to refer to the Federal Republic of Germany (FRG) in this text. Where confusion with the late and unlamented German Democratic Republic (GDR) is possible, we will use the full names or their abbreviations.
2. Kreuzberg was a backwater with low property values because it was cut off from Berlin's old centre by the Wall. After the demolition of the Wall in 1989, prices soared, and minority groups were displaced, though not without resistance.
3. That is why we have to use *birthplace figures* to show the immigrant population in Australia, while we use *foreign resident* figures for Germany, where few immigrants have obtained citizenship.
4. For a definition of racism, see Chapter 2.

6 The Next Waves: The Globalisation of International Migration

1. We use the term 'the Arab region' to include not only the Arab countries of North Africa and Western Asia, but also the non-Arab states of

Turkey, Iran and Israel. The term refers to a geographical, rather than a political or ethnic, area. The term 'the Arab region' is not entirely satisfactory, but seems better than the possible alternatives: the term 'Middle East' is Eurocentric, and excludes North Africa; the term 'Western Asia' also excludes North Africa.

2. The situation of Algerians in France is discussed in more detail in Chapters 7, 8 and 9.

3. Strictly speaking, Asia includes the Middle East and Turkey. However these countries have already been dealt with, so that this section will be concerned mainly with South Asia (the Indian sub-continent) East Asia and South-east Asia.

4. One exception to this was the recruitment of 400 000 Korean workers by Japan between 1921 and 1941. Many settled, to form a permanently discriminated minority. Japan also made extensive use of forced labour during the Second World War.

5. There were also some smaller movements, as of people from Goa, Macau and East Timor to Portugal.

6. A further movement which will not be discussed here for reasons of space, was that of Vietnamese workers to the Soviet Union and the German Democratic Republic. Although often disguised as trainees, these migrants shared many of the characteristics of other contract workers.

7. These figures are worldwide remittances, but the largest component is remittances from the Middle East.

8. In addition, about ten million Bengalis sought asylum in India at the time of the Bangladesh independence struggle in 1971. They were able to return home the following year (UNHCR, 1991).

7   Migrants and Minorities in the Labour Force

1. France does not have unions organised on the basis of a single union for each industry or trade. Rather there are a number of competing trade union federations, which try to organise in each industry. The federations have different political and ideological characters. The most important are the communist *Confédération Générale du Travail* (CGT), the militant–reformist *Confédération Française Démocratique du Travail* (CFDT), the more moderate *Force Ouvriére* (FO) and the employer-dominated *Confédération des Syndicats Libres* (CSL). For accounts of the policy of the different unions towards foreign workers see Gani, 1972; Castles and Kosack, 1973; Miller, 1981.

8   New Ethnic Minorities and Society

1. This passage is based on one of the authors' personal experience as a member of a community group in Frankfurt in the early 1980s.

2. This phrase was coined by the 'Chicago school' of sociology in the early part of this century.

3. Noiriel's phrase is *le modèle achevé de la nation*.

4. The British and Americans use citizenship and nationality as almost identical terms. For the French they have almost opposite meanings: *citoyenneté* refers to political belonging to the nation-state, *nationalité* refers to belonging to a cultural community, which could be called the nation or indeed the ethnic group. The French generally refer to *groupes ethniques* only in an ethnological context. The term *communitaire* is not to be confused with the English term 'community'. It refers to affiliations on the basis of a relatively closed group, and should be translated as 'ethnic', in sociological usage as 'Gemeinschaft'. *Mouvement communitaire* (local community or ethnic community-based movement) is often used as the opposite of *mouvement social* (class-based or interest group-based movement).

Further Reading

1 Introduction

Important information on all aspects of international migration is provided by a large number of specialised journals, of which only a few can be mentioned here. *International Migration Review* (published by the Centre for Migration Studies, New York) was established in 1964 and provides excellent comparative information. Particularly valuable are the special issues:

- *Women in Migration*, 1984, 18:4
- *Civil Rights and the Sociopolitical Participation of Migrants*, 1985, 19:3
- *Temporary Worker Programs*, 1986, 20:4
- *Migration and Health*, 1987, 21:3
- *International Migration: An Assessment for the '90s*, 1989, 23:3
- *The New Europe and International Migration*, 1992, 26:2

International Migration, published by the International Organisation for Migration, Geneva, is also a valuable comparative source. Journals with a European focus include *Migration* (Berlin: Edition Parabolis, in English and German) and the *Revue Européenne des Migrations Internationales* (Paris, in French and English). In Britain there are three main journals: *Race and Class* (London: Institute for Race Relations), *Ethnic and Racial Studies* (Routledge) and *New Community* (Commission for Racial Equality). In Australia there is the *Journal of Intercultural Studies* (Melbourne: Monash University). The recently started *Asian and Pacific Migration Journal* (Quezon City, Philippines: Scalabrini Migration Center) provides information on movements in the world's most populous region.

Several international organisations provide comparative information on migrations. The most useful is the OECD's annual *Trends in International Migration* (Paris: OECD), which until 1991 was known OECD SOPEMI *Continuous Reporting System on Migration*. This provides comprehensive statistics on most OECD countries of immigration, as well as some data on countries of emigration.

2 The Migratory Process and the Formation of Ethnic Minorities

Zolberg (1989) provides a useful overview of theories of migration, while Boyd (1989) is good on migration networks. Several other articles in the same special issue of *International Migration Review* (1989, 23:3) are also valuable. Morokvasic (1984) and Phizacklea (1983) have edited collections on the relationship between migration and gender. Sassen (1988) gives an original perspective on the political economy of migration, while Borjas (1990) presents the neo-classical view. Rex and Mason (1986) is a very useful collection of theoretical approaches to 'race' and ethnic relations. Mosse (1985), Miles (1989) and Cohen and Bains (1988) are good on racism. For those who can read French, Wieviorka (1991 and 1992) has carried out important work. Anderson (1983) and Gellner (1983) provides stimulating analyses of nationalism, while A. D. Smith (1986) discusses the relationship between ethnicity and nation. Bauböck (1991) gives a useful summary of citizenship issues.

3 International Migration before 1945

Cohen (1987) provides a valuable overview of migrant labour in the international division of labour, while Potts (1980) presents a history of migration which leads from slavery and indentured labour up to modern guestworker systems. Blackburn (1988) and Fox-Genovese and Genovese (1983) analyse slavery and its role in capitalist development. Archdeacon (1983) examines immigration in US history, showing how successive waves of entrants have 'become American'. For German readers, Dohse (1981) gives an interesting historical analysis of the role of the state in controlling migrant labour in Germany. Cross gives a detailed account of the role of migrant workers in French industrialisation, de Lepervanche shows how ethnic divisions played a central role in the formation of the Australian working class, while Homze (1967) describes the extreme exploitation of migrant labour practised by the Nazi war machine.

4 Migration to Highly-developed Countries since 1945

Castles and Kosack (1973 and 1985) is a comparative study of immigrant workers in France, Germany, Switzerland and Britain during the phase of mass labour recruitment from 1945 to 1973. Castles *et al.* – (1984) continues the story for the period following the ending of recruitment in 1973–4. Portes and Rumbaut (1990) gives a detailed analysis of recent immigrant settlement in the USA, while Collins (1991) provides a valuable account for Australia. Hammar (1985a) provides a comparative study of the position of immigrants in Western European countries. The *International Migration Review* Special Issues 23:3 (1989) and 26:2 (1992) also provide comparative material. The OECD reports (mentioned in further reading for Chapter 1) gives useful data on migratory movements and immigrant populations. Zolberg *et al.* (1989) examine global refugee movements.

5   The Migratory Problem: A Comparison of Australia and Germany

Details of migration and ethnic group formation in Australia are to be found in Wilton and Bosworth (1984), Collins (1991), Lever-Tracy and Quinlan (1988), Castles *et al.* (1990) and Castles *et al.* (1992) For Germany see Martin (1991), Castles and Kosack (1973 and 1985) and Castles *et al.* (1984). German readers will also find Hoffmann (1990), Leggewie (1990), Tichy (1990), Funcke (1991) and Nirumand (1992) useful.

6   The Next Waves: The Globalisation of International Migration

Appleyard (1988 and 1991), Stahl (1988) and Stichter (1985) provide global perspectives on international migrations. The *International Migration Review* Special Issue 26:2 (1992) give an overview of East–West movements within Europe. Kerr and Yassin (1982) and Moshe and Lewin-Epstein (1987) provide information on labour migrations concerning Arab countries and Israel. Ricca (1990) gives an overview of international migration in Africa. Fawcett and Cariño (1987) and the *Asian and Pacific Migration Journal* I:1 (1992) examine migratory patterns within and from Asia.

7   Migrants and Minorities in the Labour Force

Böhning (1984) and OECD (1987) provides comparative perspectives on migrants in the labour market. Sassen's work (1988) is significant for this topic too. Borjas (1990) and Portes and Rumbaut (1990) examine the US situation. Piore's earlier work (1979) is still useful. Collins (1991) and Lever-Tracy and Quinlan give good analyses for Australia. Waldinger *et al.* (1990) is excellent on ethnic small business, while Phizacklea (1990) looks at the links between gender, racism and class, through a case study of the fashion industry.

8   New Ethnic Minorities and Society

Feagin (1989) gives a good overview of ethnic relations, with special emphasis on the USA. Breton *et al.* (1990) present a thorough empirical study on ethnic identity and class in Canada. Solomos (1993), Cohen and Bains (1988) and Layton-Henry and Rich (1986) describe and analyse racism and political reactions to it in Britain. Gilroy's work (1987) has led to considerable debate on the significance of culture and community, especially for second generation migrants. Hammar's comparative study (1985a) is valuable here too. Ålund and Schierup (1991) provide a sceptical account of Swedish multiculturalism, with important theoretical insights. Davis's, (1990) book on Los Angeles is a fascinating case study of the 'post-modern' city and the role of minorities within it. For those who read French, the books of de Wenden

(1988), Noiriel (1988), Weil (1991a) and Dubet and Lapeyronnie (1992) are highly recommended.

9 Immigrant Politics

Miller (1981) provides one of the first comparative studies on the political role of migrant workers. Layton-Henry (1991) looks at the political rights of migrants workers in Western Europe. The *International Migration Review* Special Issue 19:3 (1985) gives information on the political situation in several countries. The comparative studies on citizenship by Hammar (1990) and Brubaker (1989) are of great value. Solomos and Wrench (1993) examine racism and migration in several European counties, while Layton-Henry and Rich (1986) focuses on Britain. Shain (1989) looks at the consequences of refugee movements for the nation-state.

Bibliography

'Automobile: la France à la traîne' (1984) *Le Point*, no. 589, 2 January.

ABS (Australian Bureau of Statistics) (1989) *Overseas Born Australians: A Statistical Profile* (Canberra: Australian Government Publishing Service).

ADL (1988) *Hate Groups in America* (New York: Anti-Defamation League of B'nai B'rith).

Alcorso, C., Popoli, C. and Rando, G. (1992) 'Community networks and institutions', in S., Castles, C., Alcorso, G. Rando, and E. Vasta, (eds), *Australia's Italians: Culture and Community in a Changing Society* (Sydney: Allen and Unwin).

Ålund, A. and Schierup, C.-U. (1991) *Paradoxes of Multiculturalism* (Aldershot: Avebury).

Andepoju, A. (1988) 'Links between internal and international migration: the African situation' in Stahl, C (ed.) *International Migration Today*, vol. 2, (UNESCO/University of Western Australia).

Anderson, B. (1983) *Imagined Communities* (London: Verso).

Anthias, F. and Yuval-Davis, N. (1989) 'Introduction', in N. Yuval-Davis, and F. Anthias, (eds), *Woman–Nation–State* (Basingstoke and London: Macmillan).

Appleyard, R. T. (ed.) (1988) *International Migration Today: Trends and Prospects* (Paris: UNESCO).

Appleyard, R. T. (1989) 'International migration and developing countries' in R. T. Appleyard, (ed.) *The Impact of International Migration on Developing Countries* (Paris: OECD).

Appleyard, R. T. (1991) *International Migration: Challenge for the Nineties* (Geneva: International Organisation for Migration).

Archdeacon, T. (1983) *Becoming American: An Ethnic History* (New York: The Free Press).

Arnold, F., Minocha, U. and Fawcett, J. T. (1987) 'The changing face of Asian immigration to the United States', in J. T. Fawcett, and B.V. Cariño, (eds), *Pacific Bridges: the New Immigration from Asia and the Pacific Islands* (New York: Center for Migration Studies).

Aronson, G. (1990a) 'Soviet Jewish Emigration, the United States and the Occupied Territories', *Journal of Palestine Studies*, 19:4.

284

Aronson, G. (1990b) *Israel, Palestinians and the Intifada: Creating Facts on the West Bank* (Washington, DC: Institute for Palestine Studies).

Asian and Pacific Migration Journal (1992) 1:1.

Banton, M. (1985) *Promoting Racial Harmony* (Cambridge University Press).

Barlán, J. (1988) *A System Approach for Understanding International Population Movement: The Role of Policies and Migrant Community in the Southern Cone*, IUSSP Seminar, Genting Highlands, Malaysia, September.

Bauböck, R. (1991) 'Migration and citizenship', in New Community, 18:1.

Bell, D. (1975) 'Ethnicity and socal change', in N. Glazer, and D. P. Moynihan, (eds), *Ethnicity - Theory and Experience* (Cambridge, Mass.: Harvard University Press).

Belloula, T. (1965) *Les Algériens en France* Algiers: Editions nationales algériennes.

Bernard, P. and Chemin, A. (1991) 'Les faux-semblants de la délinquance étrangére' *Le Monde*, 6 December.

Beynon, J. (1986) 'Spiral of decline: race and policing', in Z. Layton-Henry, and P. B. Rich, (eds), *Race, Government and Politics in Britain* (London: Macmillan).

Binur, Y. (1990) *My Enemy, Myself*, (New York: Penguin).

BIR (Bureau of Immigration Research) (1991) *Immigration Update June Quarter* (Melbourne: BIR).

Birks J. S., Sinclair, C. A. and Seccombe, I. J. (1986) 'Migrant Workers in the Arab Gulf: The Impact of Declining Oil Revenues', *International Migration Review*, 20:4.

Blackburn, R. (1988) *The Overthrow of Colonial Slavery 1776–1848* (London and New York: Verso).

Böhning, W. R. (1984) *Studies in International Labour Migration* (London: Macmillan, New York: St. Martin's).

Böhning, W. R. (1991a) 'Integration and immigration pressures in western Europe' *International Labour Review*.

Böhning, W. R. (1991b) 'International Migration to Western Europe: What to Do?', paper presented to the *Seminar on International Security* (Geneva: Graduate Institute of International Studies) 15–20 July.

Borjas, G. J. (1989) 'Economic theory and international migration', *International Migration Review*, Special Silver Anniversary Issue, 23:3.

Borjas, G. J. (1990) *Friends or Strangers: The Impact of Immigration on the US Economy* (New York: Basic Books).

Bouamama, S. (1988) 'De l'anti-racisme à la citoyenneté', IM'média 8.

Boudahrain, A. (1985) *Nouvel ordre social international et migrations* (Paris: L'Harmattan/CIEM).

Boyd, M. (1989) 'Family and Personal Networks in Migration', *International Migration Review*, Special Silver Anniversary Issue, 23:3.

Breton, R., Isajiw, W. W., Kalbach, W. E. and Reitz, J. G. (1990) *Ethnic Identity and Equality* (Toronto: University of Toronto Press).

Briggs, V. M. Jr. (1984) *Immigration Policy and the American Labor Force* (Baltimore and London: Johns Hopkins University Press).

Brubaker, W. R. (ed.) (1989) *Immigration and the Politics of Citizenship in Europe and North America* (Lanham, MD: University Press of America).

Bureau of the Census (1991) 'Census Bureau Releases 1990 Census Counts on Specific Racial Groups', *Commerce News* (Washington, DC: US Department of Commerce) 12 June.

Callovi, G. (1992) 'Regulation of immigration in 1993. Pieces of the European Community Jig-Saw Puzzle', *International Migration Review*, Special Issue on the New Europe and International Migration, 26:2.

Castells, M. (1983) *The City and the Grassroots* (London: Edward Arnold).

Castles, S. (1985) 'The guests who stayed – the debate on "foreigners policy" in the German Federal Republic', *International Migration Review*, 19:3.

Castles, S. (1986) 'The guest-worker in western Europe: an obituary', *International Migration Review*, 20:4.

Castles, S. (1989) *Migrant Workers and the Transformation of Western Societies* (Ithaca: Cornell University).

Castles, S. and Kosack, G. (1973 and 1985) *Immigrant Workers and Class Structure in Western Europe* (London: Oxford University Press).

Castles, S., Alcorso, C., Rando, G. and Vasta, E. (eds) (1992) *Australia's Italians: Culture and Community in a Changing Society* (Sydney: Allen and Unwin).

Castles, S., Booth, H. and Wallace, T. (1984) *Here for Good: Western Europe's New Ethnic Minorities* (London: Pluto Press.

Castles, S., Rando, G and Vasta, E. (1992) 'Italo-Australians and Politics', in S. Castles, C. Alcorso, G. Rando, and E. Vasta (eds), *Australia's Italians: Culture and Community in a Changing Society* (Sydney: Allen and Unwin).

Castles, S., Cope, B., Kalantzis, M. and Morrissey, M. (1990) *Mistaken Identity – Multiculturalism and the Demise of Nationalism in Australia*, second edition (Sydney: Pluto Press).

Castles, S., Collins, J., Gibson, K., Tait, D. and Alcorso, C. (1991) *The Global Milkbar and the Local Sweatshop: Ethnic Small Business and the Restructuring of Sydney* (Wollongong: Centre for Multicultural Studies for the Office of Multicultural Affairs, Working Papers on Multiculturalism).

CCCS (Centre for Contemporary Cultural Studies) (1982) *The Empire Strikes Back* (London: Hutchinson).

Choo, A. L. (1992) 'Asian–American political clout grows stronger', *Wall Street Journal*, 21 February.

Cinanni, P. (1968) *Emigrazione e Imperialismo* (Rome: Riuniti).

Coffey, J. F. (1987) 'Race training in the United States: an overview', in J. W. Shaw, R. M. Nordlie, and M. Shapiro, (eds), *Strategies for Improving Race Relations: The Anglo-American Experience* (Manchester University Press).

Cohen, P. and Bains, H. S. (eds), (1988) *Multi-Racist Britain* (Basingstoke and London: Macmillan).

Cohen, R. (1987) *The New Helots: Migrants in the International Division of Labour* (Aldershot: Avebury).

Cohen, R. (1991) 'East–West and European migration in a global context', in *New Community* 18:1.

Collins. J. (1978) 'Fragmentation of the working class', in E. L. Wheelwright, and K. Buckley, (eds), *Essays in the Political Economy of Australian Capitalism 3*, (Sydney: ANZ Books).

Collins, J. (1991) *Migrant Hands in a Distant Land: Australia's Post-War Immigration* second edition, (Sydney: Pluto Press).

Collins, J. and Castles, S. (1991) 'Restructuring, migrant labour markets and small business in Australia', *Migration*, 10.

Commission of the European Communities (1989) *Eurobarometer: Public Opinion in the European Community, Special: Racism and Xenophobia* (Brussels: Commission of the European Community).

Commission of the European Communities (1990) *Policies on Immigration and the Social Integration of Migrants in the European Community* (Brussels: Commission of the European Community).

Costa-Lascoux, J. (1983) 'L'immigration algérienne en France et la nationalite des enfants algériens', in Larbi Talha (ed.) *Maghrebins en France: Emigrés ou immigrés* (Paris: Edition du CNRS).

Costa-Lascoux, J. (1989) *De l'Immigré au Citoyen* (Paris: La Documentation Francaise).

Croissandeau (1984) 'La formation alternative au chomage?', *Le Monde de l'Education*, February.

Cross, G. S. (1983) *Immigrant Workers in Industrial France: The Making of a New Laboring Class* (Philadelphia: Temple University Press).

CSIMCED (The Commission for the Study of International Migration and Cooperative Economic Development) (1990) *Unauthorized Migration: An Economic Development Response* (Washington, DC: US Government Printing Office).

Dagger, C. W. (1992) 'Study says Asian-Americans face widespread discrimination', *New York Times*, 29 February.

Davis, M. (1990) *City of Quartz: Excavating the Future in Los Angeles* (London: Verso).

de Lepervanche, M. (1975) 'Australian immigrants 1788–1940', in E. L. Wheelwright and K. Buckley, (eds), *Essays in the Political Economy of Australian Capitalism, Vol. 1.* (Sydney: ANZ Books Company).

de Wenden, C. (1987) *Citoyenneté, Nationalité et Immigration* (Paris: Arcantère Editions).

de Wenden, C. (1988) *Les Immigrés et la Politique* (Paris: Presses de la Fondation Nationale des Sciences Politiques).

Decloîtres, R. (1967) *The Foreign Worker* (Paris: OECD).

Dohse, K. (1981) *Ausländische Arbeiter und bürgerliche Staat* (Konistein/Taunus: Hain).

Dubet, F. and Lapeyronnie, D. (1992) *Les Quartiers d'Exil* (Paris: Seuil).

Engels, F. (1962) *The Condition of the Working Class in England*, in Marx, *Engels on Britain* (Moscow: Foreign Languages Publishing House).

Entzinger, H. B. (1985) 'The Netherlands', in T. Hammar, (ed.) *European Immigration Policy: a Comparative Study* (Cambridge University Press).

European Parliament (1985) *Committee of Inquiry into the Rise of Fascism and Racism in Europe: Report on the Findings of the Inquiry* (Strasbourg: European Parliament).

Ewald, (1983) *L'Ecole des Esclaves* (Paris: Editions de la Table Ronde).

Fadil, M. A. (1985) 'Les effets de l'émigration de main d'oeuvre sur la distribution des revenus et les modèles de consommation dans l'économie égyptienne', *Revue Tiers Monde*, 26:103.

Fawcett, J. T. (1989) 'Networks, linkages, and migration systems', *International Migration Review*, Special Silver Anniversary Issue, 23:3.

Fawcett, J. T. and Arnold, F. (1987) 'Explaining diversity: Asian and Pacific immigration systems' in J. T. Fawcett, and B. V. Cariño, (eds), *Pacific Bridges: the New Immigration from Asia and the Pacific Islands* (New York: Center for Migration Studies).

Fawcett, J. T. and B. V. Cariño, (eds), (1987) *Pacific Bridges: the New Immigration from Asia and the Pacific Islands* (New York: Center for Migration Studies).

Feagin, J. R. (1989) *Racial and Ethnic Relations* (Englewood Cliffs, NJ: Prentice-Hall).

Fergany, N. (1985) 'Migrations inter-arabes et développement', *Revue Tiers Monde*, 26:103.

Fishman, J. A. (1985) *The Rise and Fall of the Ethnic Revival: Perspectives on Language and Ethnicity* (Berlin, New York, Amsterdam: Mouton Publishers).

Foot, P. (1965) *Immigration and Race in British Politics* (Harmondsworth: Penguin).

Fox-Genovese, E. and Genovese, E. D. (1983) *Fruits of Merchant Capital: Slavery and Bourgeois Property in the Rise and Expansion of Capitalism* (New York and Oxford: Oxford University Press).

French, H. W. (1990) 'Sugar Harvest's Bitter Side: Some Call It Slavery', *New York Times*, 27 April.

French, H. W. (1991) 'Haitians Expelled by Santo Domingo' *New York Times*, 11 August.

Fritscher, F. (1989) 'Sauve-qui-peut au Sahel', *Le Monde*, 3 May.

Funcke, L. (1991) *Bericht der Beauftragten der Bundesregierung für die Integration der ausländischen Arbeitnehmer und ihrer familienangehörigen* (Bonn: German Government).

Gallagher D. and Diller, J. M. (1990) 'At the crossroads between uprooted people and development in Central America', *Commission for the Study of International Migration and Cooperative Economic Development*, working paper no. 27, Washington DC.

Gani, L. (1972) *Syndicats et Travailleurs Immigrés* (Paris: Éditions Sociales).

Gardner, R. W. (1992) 'Asian immigration: the view from the United States', *Asian and Pacific Migration Journal*, 1:1.

Garrard, J. A. (1971) *The English and Immigration: A Comparative Study of the Jewish Influx 1880–1910* (London: Oxford University Press).

Gaspard, F. (1990) *Une Petite Ville en France* (Paris: Gallimard).

Geertz, C. (1963) *Old Societies and New States – the Quest for Modernity in Asia and Africa* (Glencoe, Ill.: Free Press).

Gellner, E. (1983) *Nations and Nationalism* (Oxford: Blackwell).

Gilroy, P. (1987) *There Ain't no Black in the Union Jack* (London: Hutchinson).

Gilroy, P. and Lawrence, E. (1988) 'Two-tone Britain: white and black youth and the politics of anti-racism', in P. Cohen, and H. S. Bains, (eds), *Multi-Racist Britain* (Basingstoke and London: Macmillan).

Glazer, N. and Moynihan, D. P. (1975) 'Introduction', in N. Glazer, and D. P. Moynihan (eds), *Ethnicity: Theory and Experience* (Cambridge Mass.: Harvard University Press).

Gordon, M. (1978) *Human Nature, Class, and Ethnicity* (New York: Oxford University Press).

Gordon, P. (1986) *Racial Violence and Harassment* (London: Runnymede Trust).

Halliday, F. (1985) 'Migrations de main d'oeuvre dans le monde arabe: l'envers du nouvel ordre économique', *Revue Tiers Monde*, 26:103.

Hammar, T. (ed.) (1985a) *European Immigration Policy: a Comparative Study* (Cambridge University Press).

Hammar, T. (1985b) 'Sweden', in T. Hammar, (ed.) *European Immigration Policy: a Comparative Study* (Cambridge University Press).

Hammar, T. (1990) *Democracy and the Nation-State: Aliens, Denizens and Citizens in a World of International Migration* (Aldershot: Avebury).

HCI (Haut Conseil à l'Intégration) (1991) *Journal Officiel, Assemblée Nationale* (Paris: French Government) 7 June.

Hira, S. (1991) 'Holland: the bare facts', *Race and Class*, 32:3).

Hoffmann, L. (1990) *Die unvollendete Republik* (Cologne: Pappy Rossa Verlag).

Hoffmann-Nowotny, H.-J. (1985) 'Switzerland' in T. Hammar, (ed.) *European Immigration Policy: a Comparative Study* (Cambridge University Press).

Home Office (1981) *Racial Attacks: Report of a Home Office Study* (London: Home Office).

Home Office (1989) *The Response to Racial Attacks and Harassment: Guidance for the Statutory Authorities – Report of the Inter-Departmental Racial Attacks Group* (London: Home Office).

Homze, E. L. (1967) *Foreign Labor in Nazi Germany* (New Jersey: Princeton University Press).

Houstoun, M. F., Kramer, R. G. and Barrett, J. M. (1984) 'Female Predominance in Immigration to the United States Since 1930: A First Look', *International Migration Review*, 18:4.

HREOC (Human Rights and Equal Opportunity Commission) (1991) *Racist Violence: Report of the National Inquiry into Racist Violence in Australia* (Canberra: Australian Government Publishing Service).

Hugo, G. (1986) *Australia's Changing Population: Trends and Implications* (Melbourne: Oxford University Press).

Hugo, G. (1990) 'Recent international migration trends in Asia', *paper presented to the Fifth Conference of the Australian Population Association* (Melbourne).

ILO (International Labour Organisation) (1991) *Report of the Director-General: Third Supplementary Report* (Geneva: ILO).

Immigration Canada (1991) *Annual Report to Parliament: Immigration Plan for 1991–1995 Year Two* (Ottawa: Canadian Government).

Institute of Race Relations (1987) *Policing Against Black People* (London: Institute of Race Relations).

Interagency Task Force on Immigration Policy (1979) *Staff Report* (Washington DC: Department of Justice, Labour and State).

International Migration Review (1984) Special Issue on Women in Migration 18:3.

International Migration Review (1985) Special Issue on Civil Rights and the Sociopolitical Participation of Migrants, 19:3.

International Migration Review (1989) Special Silver Anniversary Issue 23:3.

International Migration and the New Europe *International Migration Review* (1992) Special Issue 26:2.

IOM (1990) 'Background Document' presented at the *IOM Seminar on Migration* Geneva.

Jackson, J. A. (1963) *The Irish in Britain* (London: Routledge and Kegan Paul).

Jackson, J. A. (ed.) (1969) *Migration* (Cambridge University Press).

Jakubowicz, A.(1989) 'The state and the welfare of immigrants in Australia', *Ethnic and Racial Studies*, 12:1.

Jarreau, P. (1983) 'Cher Mustapha', *Le Monde*, 13–14 March.

Joly, D. (1988) 'Les musulmans à Birmingham', in R. Leveau, and G. Kepel, (eds), *Les Musulmans dans la Société Française* (Paris: Presse de la Fondation Nationale des Sciences Politiques).

Jupp, J., York, B. and McRobbie, A. (1989) *The Political Participation of Ethnic Minorities in Australia* (Canberra: AGPS).

Kepel, G. and Leveau, R. (1987) *Les Banlieues d'Islam* (Paris: Seuil).

Kerr, M. amd Uassin, E. S. (1982) *Rich and Poor States in the Middle East: Egypt and the New Arab Order* (Boulder: Westview Press).

Kindleberger, C. P. (1967) *Europe's Postwar Growth – the Role of Labor Supply* (Cambridge, Mass.: Harvard University Press).

Kritz, M. M., Keely, C. B. and Tomasi, S. M. (eds), (1983) *Global Trends in Migration* (New York: Center for Migration Studies).

Kubat, D. (1987) 'Asian Immigrants to Canada', in J. T. Fawcett, and B. V. Cariño, (eds), *Pacific Bridges: the new Immigration from Asia and the Pacific Islands* (New York: Center for Migration Studies).

Kwong, P. (1992) 'The first multicultural riots', *Voice* New York, 9 June.

Lapeyronnie, D., Frybes, M., Couper, K. and Joly, D. (1990) *L'Intégration des Minorités Immigrées, Étude Comparative: France – Grande Bretagne* (Paris: Agence pour le Développement des Relations Interculturelles).

Laqueur, W. (1972) *A History of Zionism* (New York: Holt, Rinehart and Winston).

Larsson, S. (1991) 'Swedish racism: the democratic way', *Race and Class*, 32:3.

Lattes, A. and de Lattes, Z. (1991) 'International migration in Latin America: patterns, implications and policies', *Informal Expert Group Meeting on International Migration* (Geneva: UN Economic Commission for Europe/ UNPF paper).

Layton-Henry, Z. (1981) *A Report on British Immigration Policy Since 1945* (Coventry: University of Warwick).

Layton-Henry, Z. (1986) 'Race and the Thatcher Government', in Z. Layton-Henry, and P. B. Rich, (eds), *Race, Government and Politics in Britain* (London: Macmillan).

Layton-Henry, Z. (ed.) (1990) *The Political Rights of Migrant Workers in Western Europe* (London: Sage).

Layton-Henry, Z. and Rich, P. B. (eds), (1986) *Race, Government and Politics in Britain* (London: Macmillan).

Le Monde Dossiers et Documents (1983) 102.

Leggewie, C. (1990) *Multi Kulti: Spielregeln für die Vielvölkerrepublik* (Berlin: Rotbuch).

Lequin, Y. (ed.) (1988) *La Mosaïque France* (Paris: Larousse).

Leveau, R. and Kepel, G. (eds), (1988) *Les Musulmans dans la Société Française* (Paris: Presse de la Fondation Nationale des Sciences Politiques).

Lever-Tracy, C. and Quinlan, M. (1988) *A Divided Working Class* (London: Routledge).

Light, I., and Bonacich, E. (1988) *Immigrant Entrepreneurs* (Berkeley: University of California Press).

Lithman, E. L. (1987) *Immigration and Immigrant Policy in Sweden* (Stockholm: Swedish Institute).

Lloyd, C. (1991) 'Concepts, models and anti-racist strategies in Britain and France' *New Community*, 18:1.

Lohrmann, R. (1987) 'Irregular Migration: A Rising Issue in Developing Countries' *International Migration*, 25:3.

Loutete-Dangui, N. (1988) 'L'immigration étrangère au Congo,' in Association Internationale des Démographes de Langue Française, *Les Migrations Internationales* (Paris: Edition de l'INED).

MacMaster, N. (1991) 'The "seuil de tolérance": the uses of a "scientific" racist concept', in M. Silverman, (ed.) *Race, Discourse and Power in France* (Aldershot: Avebury).

Manfrass, K. (1992) 'Süd-Nord oder Ost–West Wanderung', *International Migration Review*, Special Issue on the New Europe and International Migration, 26:2.

Mann, J. A. (1979) 'For Millions in Colombia, Venezuela is El Dorado', 23 December.

Marshall, T. H. (1964) 'Citizenship and Social Class', in *Class, Citizenship and Social Development: Essays by T. H. Marshall* (New York: Anchor Books).

Martin, P. L. (1991a) *The Unfinished Story: Turkish Labour Migration to Western Europe* (Geneva: International Labour Office).

Martin, P. L. (1991b) 'Labor migration in Asia: conference report', *International Migration Review*, 25:1.

Martin, P. L. (1992) 'Trade, Aid and Migration', *International Migration Review*, 26:1.

Martinez, J. N. (1989) 'Social Effects of Labour Migration: The Colombian Experience', *International Migration* 27:2.

McAllister, I. (1988) 'Political attitudes and electoral behaviour', in J. Jupp, (ed.) *The Australian People: an Encyclopedia of the Nation, its People and their Origins* (Sydney: Angus and Robertson).

Mehideb, J. (1973) 'Usines Renault Billancourt: le tiers monde à l'usine' *Croissance des Jeunes Nations*, June.

Meissner, D., Papademetriou, D. and North, D (1987) *Legalization of Undocumented Aliens: Lessons from Other Countries* (Washington, DC: Carnegie Endowment for International Peace).

Merckling, O (1987) 'Nouvelles politiques d'emploi et substitution de la main d'oeuvre immigrée dans les entreprises françaises', *Revue Européenne des Migrations Internationales*, 3:1–2.

Messina, A. M. (1989) 'Anti-immigrant illiberalism and the "new" ethnic and racial minorities in Western Europe', *Patterns of Prejudice* 23:3.

Miles, R. (1989) *Racism* (London: Routledge).

Miller, J. (1985) 'Wave of Arab Migration Ending with Oil Boom', *New York Times*, 6 October.

Miller, J. (1991) 'Egyptians now replace other Arabs in Saudi jobs', *New York Times*, 4 February.

Miller, M. J. (1978) *The Problem of Foreign Worker Participation and Representation in France, Switzerland and the Federal Republic of Germany* (Madison: University of Wisconsin).

Miller, M. J. (1979) 'Reluctant Partnership: Foreign Workers in Franco-Algerian Relations, 1962–1979' in Robert E. Matthews *et al.* (eds), *International Conflict and Conflict Management* (Scarborough, Canada: Prentice-Hall).

Miller, M. J. (1981) *Foreign Workers in Western Europe: an Emerging Political Force* (New York: Praeger).

Miller, M. J. (1984) 'Industrial policy and the rights of labor: the case of foreign workers in the French automobile assembly industry', *Michigan Yearbook of International Legal Studies*, vol. vi.

Miller, M. J. (1986) 'Policy ad-hocracy: The Paucity of Coordinated Perspectives and Policies', *Annals* 485.

Miller, M. J. (1991A) 'La nouvelle loi américaine sur l'immigration: vers un modèle d'aprés-guerre froide', *Revue Européenne des Migrations Internationales*, 7:3

Mitchell, C. (1989) 'International migration, international relations and foreign policy', *International Migration Review*, Special Silver Anniversary Issue, 23:3.

Morokvasic, M. (1984) 'Birds of passage are also women', *International Migration Review*, 18:4.

Mosse, G. C. (1985) *Towards the Final Solution* (University of Wisconsin Press).

Muus, P. J. (1991) *Migration, Minorities and Policy in the Netherlands: Recent Trends and Developments – Report for SOPEMI* (Amsterdam: University of Amsterdam, Department of Human Geography).

Naidoo, J. C. (1989) *Canada's Response to Racism: Visible Minorities in Ontario*, background paper, Third International Symposium on the World Refugee Crisis, Oxford.

Nirumand, B. (ed.) (1992) *Angst vor den Deutschen: Terror gegen Ausländer und der Zerfall des Rechtsstaates* (Reinbek bei Hamburg: Rowohlt).

Nobel, P. (1988) *Human Rights of Aliens – Experience and Practice of the Ombudsman* (Stockholm: Ombudsman Against Ethnic Discrimination).

Noble, K. B. (1991) 'Congo Expelling Zairian Citizens', *New York Times*, 11 December.

Noiriel, G. (1988) *Le creuset français: Histoire de l'immigration XIXe–XXe siècles* (Paris: Seuil).

NPC (National Population Council) (1991) *Refugee Review* (Canberra: National Population Council).

OECD (1987) *The Future of Migration* (Paris: OECD).

OECD SOPEMI (1990) *OECD Continuous Reporting System on Migration, Report 1989* (Paris: OECD).

OECD SOPEMI (1991) *OECD Continuous Reporting System on Migration, Report 1990* (Paris: OECD).

OECD SOPEMI (1992) *Trends in International Migration* (Paris: OECD).

Office National d'Immigration (1981) *Statistiques de L'immigration* (Paris: ONI).

Pachon, H. P. (1987) 'An overview of citizenship in the Hispanic community', *International Migration Review* 21:2.

Pascoe, R. (1992) 'Place and community: the construction of Italo-Australian space' in S., Castles, C., Alcorso, G. Rando, and E. Vasta (eds), *Australia's Italians: Culture and Community in a Changing Society* (Sydney: Allen and Unwin).

Péan, L. (1982) 'L'alliance hégémonique insulaire', *Le Monde Diplomatique*, August.

Pelligrino, A. (1984) 'Illegal Immigration from Colombia', *International Migration Review* 18:3.

Perotti, A. and Thepaut, F. (1990) 'Les caractéristiques du débat sur l'immigration dans le contexte italien', *Migrations Société* 2:11.

Perotti, A. and Thepaut, F. (1991) 'Les répercussions de la guerre du golfe sur les arabes et les juifs de France', *Migrations Société* 3:14.

Pfahlmann, H. (1968) *Fremdarbeiter und Kriegsgefangene in der deutschen Kriegswirtschaft 1939–45* (Darmstadt: Wehr und Wissen).

Phizacklea, A. (ed.) (1983) *One Way Ticket? Migration and Female Labour* (London: Routledge and Kegan Paul).

Phizacklea, A. (1990) *Unpacking the Fashion Industry: Gender, Racism and Class in Production* (London: Routledge).

PIC (Population Issues Committee, National Population Council) (1992) *Population Issues and Australia's Future: Final Report* (Canberra: Australian Government Publishing Service).

Picquet, M., Pellegrino, A. and Papail, J. (1986) 'L'immigration au Venezuela', *Revue Européenne des Migrations Internationales* 2:2.

Piore, M.J. (1979) *Birds of Passage: Migrant Labor and Industrial Societies* (Cambridge University Press).

Ponty, J. (1988) 'Les rapatriements des travailleurs polonais dans les années trente' *Hommes et Migrations* 1115.

Portes, A. and Böröcz, J. (1989) 'Contemporary immigration: theoretical perspectives on its determinants and modes of incorporation', *International Migration Review* 23:83.

Portes, A. and Rumbaut, R. G. (1990) *Immigrant America: A Portrait* (Los Angeles: University of California Press).

Potts, L. (1990) *The World Labour Market: A History of Migration* (London: Zed Books).

Price, C. (1963) *Southern Europeans in Australia* (Melbourne: Oxford Univeristy Press).

Pro Asyl (1991) *Fluchtursachen bekämpfen – Flüchtlinge schützen* (pamphlet) (Frankfurt/Main: Pro Asyl).

Prost, A. (1966) 'L'immigration en France depuis cent ans', *Esprit* 34:348.

Rath, J. (1988) 'La participation des immigrés aux élections locales aux Pays-Bas' *Revue Européenne des Migrations Internationales* 4:3.

Ravenstein, E. G. (1885) 'The laws of migration', *Journal of the Statistical Society*, vol. 48.

Ravenstein, E. G. (1889) 'The laws of migration', *Journal of the Statistical Society* vol. 52.

Reed, R. (1977) 'National Front: British threat', *New York Times*, 18 August.

Rex. J. (1986) *Race and Ethnicity* (Milton Keynes: Open University Press).

Rex, J. and Mason, D. (eds), (1986) *Theories of Race and Ethnic Relations* (Cambridge University Press).

Ricca, S. (1990) *Migrations internationales en Afrique* (Paris: L'Harmattan).

Roussillon, A. (1985) 'Migrations de main-d'oeuvre et unité arabe: Les enjeux unitaires du modèle irakien', *Revue Tiers Monde*, 10.

Rutten, T. (1992) 'Why LA burned', *New York Review of Books*, reprinted in *The Independent Monthly*, June.

Salt, J. (1989) 'A comparative overview of international trends and types' *International Migration Review*, Special Silver Anniversary Issue, 23:3.

Sanz, L. C. (1989) 'The Impact of Chilean Migration on Employment in Patagonia' *International Migration*, 27:2.

Sassen, S. (1988) *The Mobility of Labour and Capital* (Cambridge University Press).

Schierup, C.-U. (1991) 'The puzzle of trans-ethnic society' in: A. Ålund, and C.-U. Schierup, *Paradoxes of Multiculturalism* (Aldershot: Avebury).

Schierup, C.-U. and Alund, A. (1987) *Will they still be Dancing? Integration and Ethnic Transformation among Yugoslav Immigrants in Scandinavia* (Stockholm: Almquist & Wiksell International).

Seccombe, I. J. (1986) 'Immigrant Workers in an Emigrant Economy', *International Migration*, 24:2.

Seccombe, I. J. and Lawless, R. I. (1986) 'Foreign Worker Dependence in the Gulf and International Oil Companies', *International Migration Review*, 20:3.

Sekine, M. (1990) *Guest Workers in Japan* (Wollongong: Centre for Multicultural Studies), Occasional Paper no. 21.

Semyonov, M. and Lewin-Epstein, N. (1987) *Hewers of Wood and Drawers of Water* (Ithaca, NY: ILR Press).

Seton-Watson, H. (1977) *Nations and States* (London: Methuen).

Shain, Y. (1989) *Frontier of Loyalty: Political Exiles in the Age of the Nation-State* (Middletown CT: Wesleyan University Press).

Shevstova, L. (1992) 'Soviet Emigration Today and Tomorrow', *International Migration Review*, Special Issue on the New Europe and International Migration, 26:2.

Simon, G. (ed.) (1990) *Les effets des migrations internationales sur les pays d'origine: le cas du Maghreb* (Paris: SEDES).

Simon, J. (1989) *The Economic Consequences of Immigration* (Oxford: Basil Blackwell).

Singaby, T. E. (1985) 'Migrations et capitalisation de la campagne en Egypte: La reconversion de la famille paysanne', *Revue Tiers Monde*, 26:103.

Sivanandan, A. (1982) *A Different Hunger* (London: Pluto Press).

Skeldon, R. (1992) 'International migration within and from the East and Southeast Asian region: a review essay', *Asian and Pacific Migration Journal*, 1:1.

Smith, A. D. (1986) *The Ethnic Origins of Nations* (Oxford: Blackwell).

Smith, S. (1989) *The Politics of 'Race' and Residence* (Cambridge: Polity).

Sole, R. (1990) 'Obsédante immigration', *Le Monde*, 22 May.

Sole, R. (1991) 'Le Front National présente cinquante mesures pour régler le problème de l'immigration', *Le Monde*, 19 November.

Solomos, J. (1988) 'Institutionalised racism: policies of marginalisation in education and training' in P. Cohen and H. S. Bains, (eds), *Multi-Racist Britain* (Basingstoke and London: Macmillan).

Solomos, J. (1993) *Race and Racism in Contemporary Britain* second edition (London: Macmillan).

Solomos, J. and Wrench, J. (1993) *Racism and Migration in Europe* (Oxford and New York: Berg).

Stahl, C. (ed.) *International Migration Today: Emerging Issues* (Paris: UNESCO).

Stahl, C. W. (1990) 'South–North migration in the Asian–Pacific region', paper presented to the *International Organisation for Migration Conference on South–North Migration* Geneva.

Stasiulis, D. K. (1988) 'The symbolic mosaic reaffirmed: multiculturalism policy', in K. A. Graham, (ed.), *How Ottawa Spends, 1988/89* (Ottawa: Carleton University Press).

Steinberg, S. (1981) *The Ethnic Myth: Race, Ethnicity and Class in America* (Boston: Beacon Press).

Stichter, S. (1985) *Migrant Labourers* (Cambridge University Press).

Stirn, H. (1964) *Ausländische Arbeiter im Betrieb* (Frechen/Cologne: Bartmann).

Stola, D. (1992) 'Forced Migrations in Central European History', *International Migration Review*, Special Issue on the New Europe and International Migration, 26:2.

Studlar, D. T. and Layton-Henry, Z. (1990) 'Non-white minority access to the political agenda in Britain', *Policy Studies Review* 9:2 Winter.

Suhrke, A. and Klink, F. (1987) 'Contrasting patterns of Asian refugee movements: the Vietnamese and Afghan syndromes' in J. T. Fawcett, and B. V. Cariño, (eds), *Pacific Bridges: the New Immigration from Asia and the Pacific Islands* (New York: Center for Migration Studies).

Suzuki, H. (1988) 'A new policy for foreign workers in Japan? Current debate and perspective', *Waseda Business and Economic Studies*, no. 24.

Szoke, L. (1992) 'Hungarian Perspectives on Emigration and Immigration in the New European Architecture', *International Migration Review*, Special Issue on the New Europe and International Migration, 26:2.

Taifel, H. (1982) 'The social psychology of minorities' in C. Husband, (ed.) *'Race' in Britain* (London: Hutchinson).

Tichy, R. (1990) *Ausländer rein! Warum es kein 'Ausländerproblem' gibt* (Munich: Piper).

Toth, J. (1992) 'Changing refugee policy in Hungary' *Migration World Magazine*, 20:2.

Tribalat, M. (1992) 'Chronique de l'immigration', *Population*, 47:1.

Trlin, A. D. (1987) 'New Zealand's Admission of Asians and Pacific Islanders' in J. T. Fawcett, and B. V. Cariño, (eds), *Pacific Bridges: the New Immigration from Asia and the Pacific Islands* (New York: Center for Migration Studies).

Tully, S. (1983), 'French Automakers' Lonely Slump', *Fortune*, 28 November 121.

UN (United Nations) (1991) *World Population Monitoring* (draft version) (New York: UN Department of International Economic and Social Affairs, Population Division).

UNHCR (United Nations High Commission for Refugees – Italian Office) (1991) *For Forty Years, UNHCR Alongside Refugees* (Rome: Vita Italiana).

US Department of Labor (1989) *The Effects of Immigration on the US Economy and Labour Market* (Washington, DC: US Government Document).

Vaddamalay, V. (1990) 'Tendances nouvelles dans le commerce étranger en France' *Migrations et Societé*, 2:11.

Vasilena, D. (1992) 'Bulgarian Turkish Emigration and Return', *International Migration Review*, Special Issue on the New Europe and International Migration, 26:2.

Vasta, E. (1990) 'Gender, class and ethnic relations: the domestic and work experiences of Italian migrant women in Australia', *Migration*, no. 7.

Vasta, E. (1991) 'Australia's Post-War Immigration: Power Identity and Resistance' (University of Queeensland, PhD thesis).

Vasta, E. (1992) 'The second generation' in S. Castles, C. Alcorso, G. Rando and E. Vasta (eds), *Australia's Italians: Culture and Community in a Changing Society* (Sydney: Allen and Unwin).

Vasta, E., Rando, G., Castles, S. and Alcorso, C. (1992) 'The Italo-Australian community on the Pacific rim', in S. Castles, A. Alcorso, C. Rando, and E. Vasta (eds), *Australia's Italians: Culture and Community in a Changing Society* (Sydney: Allen and Unwin).

Verbunt, G. (1985) 'France' in T. Hammar (ed.) *European Immigration Policy: a Comparative Study* (Cambridge University Press).

Waldinger, R., Aldrich, H., Ward, R. and Associates (1990) *Ethnic Entrepreneurs – Immigrant Business in Industrial Societies* (Newbury Park, London, New Delhi: Sage).

Wallman, S. (1986) 'Ethnicity and boundary processes', in J. Rex, and D. Mason, (eds), *Theories of Race and Ethnic Relations* (Cambridge University Press).

Weil, P. (1991a) *La France et ses Étrangers* (Paris: Calmann-Levy).

Weil, P. (1991b) 'Immigration and the rise of racism in France: The contradictions of Mitterrand's policies', *French Society and Politics*, 9:3–4.

Weintraub, S. (1990) 'The North American Free Trade Debate', *The Washington Quarterly* 13:4.

Weintraub, S. (1991) 'The Rise of North Americanos: A U.S.-Mexico Union', *The Responsive Community* 1:3, Summer.

Werner, H. (1992) 'Labour market trends and migration from the perspective of the Single European Market', in L. Tomasi (ed.), *In Defense of the Alien* (New York: Center for Migration Studies).

Widgren, J. (1987) 'International Migration: New Challenge to Europe', *Migration News* 2:3–35.

Wieviorka, M. (1991) *L'Espace du Racisme* (Paris: Seuil).

Wieviorka, M. (1992) *La France Raciste* (Paris: Seuil).

Willard, J. C. (1984) 'Conditions d'emploi et salaires de la main d'oeuvre étrangère', *Economie et Statistique* January.

Wilton, J. and Bosworth, R. (1984) *Old Worlds and New Australia* (Ringwood Vic.: Penguin).

Zolberg, A. R. (1983) 'The formation of new states as a refugee generating process', *The Annals of the American Academy of Political and Social Science*, 467.

Zolberg, A. R. (1989) 'The next waves: migration theory for a changing world', *International Migration Review* 23:3.

Zolberg, A. R., Suhrke, A. and Aguayo, S. (1989) *Escape from Violence* (New York: Oxford University Press).

Index

298